The Epicure's Book

OF STEAK
AND BEEF DISHES

The Epicure's Book
OF STEAK
AND BEEF DISHES

by Marguerite Patten

OPTIMUM

Montreal • Toronto

THE EPICURE'S BOOK OF STEAK AND BEEF
DISHES

World copyright © 1979 AB Nordbok,
Gothenburg, Sweden.

First published in Canada in 1979 by
Optimum Publishing Company Limited
245 rue St-Jacques, Montreal,
Quebec, Canada H2Y 1M6

For information, contact:
Michael S. Baxendale, President

ISBN 0-88890-113-5

Typesetting by Ytterlids Sätteri AB,
Falkenberg, Sweden.

Printed in Italy.

THE EPICURE'S BOOK OF STEAK AND BEEF DISHES has been produced by
AB Nordbok, Gothenburg, Sweden.

The author, Marguerite Patten, has worked in close cooperation with the
Nordbok art and editorial departments, under the supervision of
Einar Engelbrektson and Turlough Johnston.

Graphical design: Tommy Berglund.

Colour photography: Holger Edström, Studio Tranan.

Each dish was specially prepared for photography by Åse Graflind.

The line drawings have been made by Ulf Söderqvist.

The chapter vignettes have been drawn by Christian Lefèvre.

Tableware has kindly been provided by the following Stockholm companies:
Afro Art, CFOC, El Indio, Georg Jensen, Hannibal, Indiska Magasinet, Ingrid &
Ingegärd, Möbel-Hansson, NK, Pour Cordon Bleu, Rosenthal Studio-Haus, and
Taurus.

Contents

Canadian Cuts

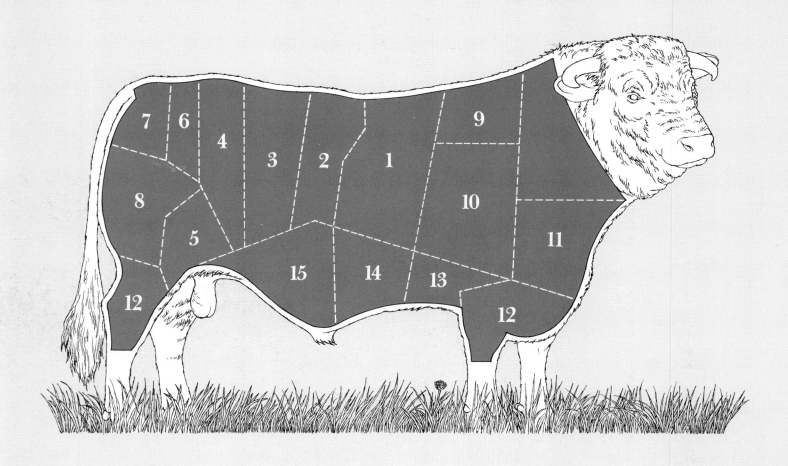

1	Rib	6	Square Rump	11	Shoulder
2	Wing	7	Round Rump	12	Shank
3	Porterhouse or T-Bone	8	Round Steak	13	Brisket Point
4	Sirloin	9	Blade	14	Plate Brisket
5	Sirloin Tip	10	Cross Rib	15	Plank Steak

KNOW YOUR BEEF

I always feel that mine is one of the most interesting of all professions. Throughout my career, it has been my ambition—in the books and articles I write and in the talks and demonstrations I give (often to very large audiences or on television and radio)—to encourage people to learn the art of cooking and to appreciate the pleasures of good food.

David Garrick, the famous eighteenth-century English actor, writes of Doctor Goldsmith's *Characteristical Cookery* that

Heaven sends us good meat,
But the devil sends cooks.

This is less true today than it was years ago, for I believe that our knowledge of food and of the culinary arts as practised in the home has greatly improved; once, we had just talented chefs and professional cooks, but many home cooks of today show a degree of expertise greatly to be admired.

In order to achieve perfection in cooking, it is essential to appreciate the importance of the right technique in handling various foods, the heat and speed at which they should be cooked, and the selection of garnish and accompaniments in the creation of a dish whose appearance will match its flavour. All these points have been covered in the relevant chapters that follow.

Meat, from earliest times, has been one of our most important foods, providing the basis for satisfying and nourishing meals. As more sophisticated tastes developed, it became a food which encouraged creative cooks and chefs to lavish their time, imagination, and skills upon making dishes that were a delight to eat.

Beef has been described as the most important of all meats; it certainly is one that provides infinite variety in the number of ways it can be cut, in the methods of cooking it, and, therefore, in the dishes that can be prepared from it.

Beef is a meat with a long and interesting history of breeding, which has brought it to the high standard of perfection we expect, and should obtain, today. Its value is appreciated around the world, although climatic conditions do not allow every country to produce high-quality meat. Beef justifies our very best efforts in cooking, and I hope you will find the recipes in this book worthy of your skills.

An 'epicure' is defined as 'one who cultivates a refined taste for the table'. It may well be that he or she enjoys simple dishes, perfectly cooked, or those of 'haute cuisine', the more sophisticated dishes created by the great chefs, cooks, and gourmets of all nationalities throughout the ages. One thing is certain, no true epicure will condone imperfections in the cooking or the presentation of food; therein lies our hope of continuing the great traditions of the past.

(*Above*) A butcher's sign, *Aux Deux Frères* ('At the two brothers'), at Colmar, France.

(*Right*) The kitchen of the Royal Pavilion at Brighton, England, was reconstructed by John Nash during the time when the famous French chef, Marie-Antoine Carême, was employed by the Prince Regent.

Serenely full, the epicure would say,
Fate cannot harm me, I have dined today.
I am sure the epicure would add that meals based upon beef demand good wines. Although I have enjoyed learning about wines and would describe myself as having a critical palate and a fair knowledge of the subject, I humbly admit that my knowledge does not match that of Andrew Henderson, the expert I asked to suggest wines to complement my menus at the end of the book. These menus are based upon steak and other beef dishes as the main course of each meal.

Andrew Henderson has established a reputation as one of our modern wine experts. He is a broadcaster, writer, and owner of one of the most delightful wine bars in London.

Some of the wines he suggests may be new to you. If they are not readily obtainable, the brief reasons given for his selection will offer guidance as to the type of wine he feels you might consider.

It has been a pleasure to write this book about beef, a superb meat that challenges my culinary skills and nourishes my epicurean delight.

Shakespeare writes in *The Taming of the Shrew*, 'What say you to a piece of Beefe and Mustard?', a worthy combination of flavours, but only one of the many from the great cuisine based upon beef.

Rearing Beef

It is important to appreciate the planning and expertise needed to produce prime cattle for beef. The modern requirements for this meat demand a good plump carcass with the minimum of fat content, the ideal carcass for today being short and thick at the shoulder and hind legs. It must be appreciated that, with the modern desire for less fat, there is likely to be less flavour in the meat.

The traditional methods of raising beef were fairly leisurely ones. The animals were ready for slaughter at between $2\frac{1}{2}$ and 3 years of age. Due to improved techniques in both rearing and breeding, it is now possible to produce good beef cattle at an earlier age. 'Baby Beef' cattle are between 12 and 15 months and 'Medium Beef' cattle from 20 to 30 months old.

In Britain the favourite animal for beef production is the Hereford, or a cross between the Hereford and the Friesian. It is this cross-breeding which produces the kind of beef demanded by the modern consumer.

Probably the name that suggests high-quality beef more than any other breed of cattle is the Aberden-Angus. This has a worldwide reputation and has been exported to many countries, including China, Russia, and the United States. This breed is found, as the name suggests, more in Scotland than in England. In the Highlands of Scotland you will find the Highland cattle and the newer Luing breed, both of which have been exported to many other countries.

In France and, indeed, in many other countries one of the most popular breeds is the Charolais. The great advantage of this animal is that it produces the greatest weight per age of any breed, at least among those registered in Britain. It could be said that the Charolais have set new standards in weight and the proportion of lean meat in the carcass.

Most American cattle originate from British breeds, but American methods of rearing produce animals that mature at an early age, so giving tender meat with a high percentage of lean.

One of the features of American beef is its good 'marbling', that is the small particles of fat which are distributed throughout the meat.

In Australia the small handful of cattle led ashore in 1788 became the basis for the vast industry of today. Although the familiar Hereford, Angus, and Shorthorn breeds were the original basis for breeding beef cattle in Australia, the farmers now include in their herds Charolais, Simmertal, and even more exotic breeds, such as Brahman (an American-developed strain of the Zebu cattle, native to India) and Santa Gertrudis, based upon a cross between the Brahman and the Shorthorn.

When talking about beef and the animals reared to give this meat, it is not only young bulls, but female animals that are used too. Both males and females are given the name of 'beef cattle'.

The *Hereford*, an old English breed from the county of the same name, is now bred in all the world's major cattle-producing countries.

The *Friesian*, native to the Netherlands, is a widespread dairy cow which also provides beef and veal. It is now bred internationally.

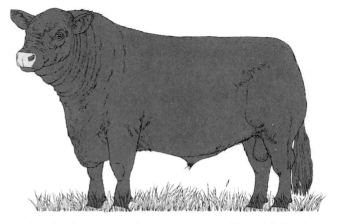

The *Aberdeen-Angus*, the cornerstone of Scottish beef production, has a worldwide reputation for the high quality of its beef and is now found everywhere beef is produced.

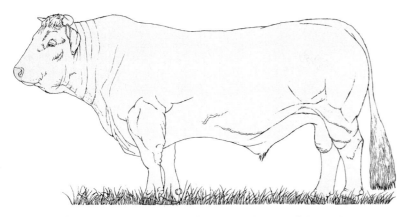

The all-white French-bred *Charolais* is one of the main producers of beef in France and has been exported all over the world.

The *Brahman* was developed in the United states in the nineteenth century from the Zebu breed from India and is widely popular for cross-breeding.

The *Poll Shorthorn* is one of the many derivations from the original English Shorthorn breed (now widespread all over the cattle-producing world).

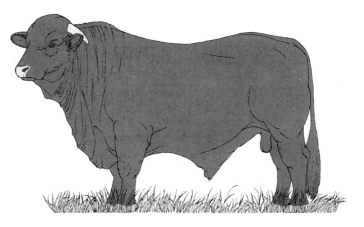

The *Santa Gertrudis* was developed in the United States from the Shorthorn and the Brahman, and is popular there as well as in Australia.

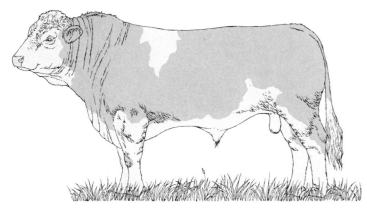

The *Simmenthal*, originally Swiss, is widespread throughout central and southern Europe and is becoming popular in North America, New Zealand, and Australia.

The *Brown Swiss*, developed in the alpine areas of Switzerland, is now bred throughout the mountain ranges of southern Europe as well as in North America.

Cutting Beef

It is surprising to learn the variety of ways in which different countries cut a carcass of beef. It is not just a matter of calling a joint by a different name in each country, but the fact that the division of the meat is made in a slightly different manner.

It may well be that in your particular part of the country the butchers have regional names for the various cuts; they will readily inform you of other names used elsewhere.

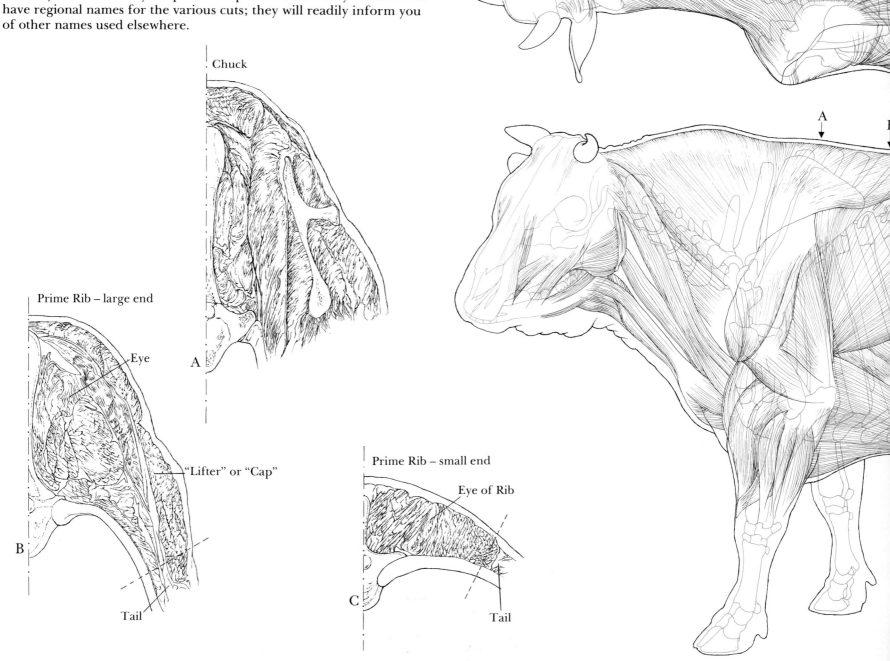

Chuck

A

Prime Rib – large end

Eye

"Lifter" or "Cap"

B

Tail

Prime Rib – small end

Eye of Rib

C

Tail

A

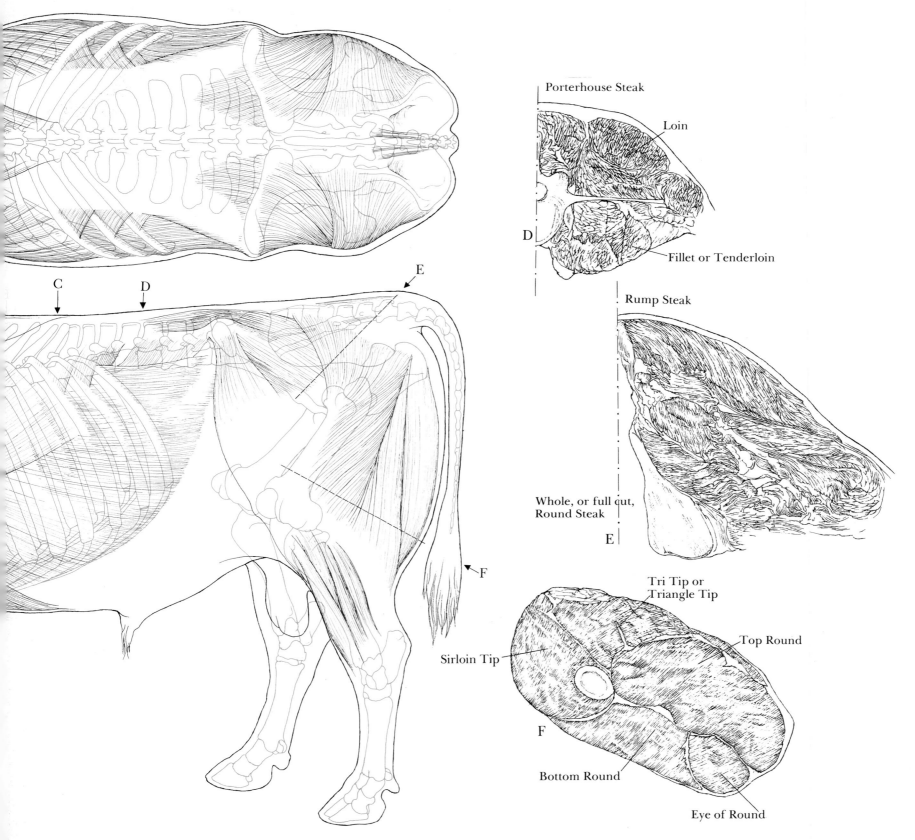

Porterhouse Steak

Loin

D

Fillet or Tenderloin

C   D   E

Rump Steak

Whole, or full cut,
Round Steak

E

F

Tri Tip or
Triangle Tip

Top Round

Sirloin Tip

F

Bottom Round

Eye of Round

15

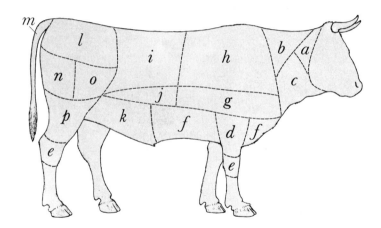

FRENCH CUTS

(a) Jumeaux.
(b) Paleron.
(c) Macreuse.
(d) Gîte de devant.
(e) Crosse.
(f) Poitrine.
(g) Plat de côtes.
(h) Côtes de bœuf.

(i) Aloyau.
(j) Bavette.
(k) Flanchet.
(l) Culotte de bœuf.
(m) Queue de bœuf.
(n) Gîte à la noix.
(o) Tranche grasse.
(p) Gîte de derrière.

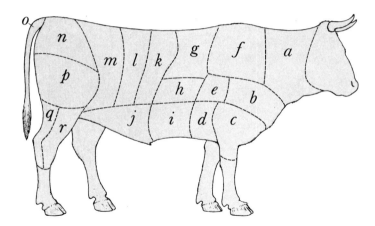

AMERICAN CUTS

(a) Neck.
(b) Arm pot roast, or shoulder.
(c) Fore shank.
(d) Brisket.
(e) English cut.
(f) Chuck.
(g) Rib.
(h) Short ribs.
(i) Short plate.

(j) Flank steak.
(k) Club steaks.
(l) Short loin.
(m) Sirloin.
(n) Rump.
(o) Oxtail.
(p) Round.
(q) Heel of round.
(r) Hind shank.

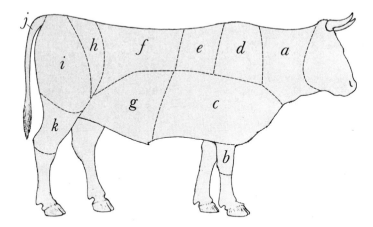

ENGLISH CUTS

(a) Neck.
(b) Shin.
(c) Brisket.
(d) Chuck.
(e) Best rib.
(f) Sirloin.
(g) Flank.

(h) Rumpsteak.
(i) Round, containing rump, aitchbone, topside, and silverside.
(j) Oxtail.
(k) Leg.

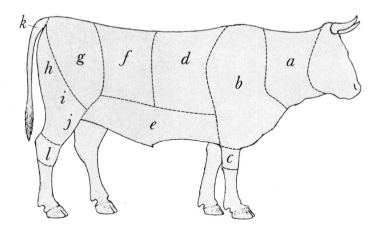

AUSTRALIAN CUTS

(a) Neck.
(b) Chuck and blade.
(c) Shin.
(d) Set of ribs.
(e) Brisket.
(f) Sirloin.
(g) Rump.

(h) Round.
(i) Silverside.
(j) Topside.
(k) Oxtail.
(l) Leg.

Beef Round the World

For centuries, the ox has been respected as an animal of special qualities; according to historical data, it was not originally considered as a source of meat, but rather as an animal to revere, or even to worship.

The Egyptians regarded the ox as 'the emblem of agriculture and all that serves to support existence'. They burned incense on altars in the animal's honour.

Both the Phoenicians and the Phrygians religiously abstained from eating the flesh of the ox; indeed, the Phrygians punished with death anyone who dared to slay a labouring ox.

The Athenians decreed that their coins should show the image of the ox. Homer, the epic poet of Greece, whose birth is estimated at somewhere around 1000 BC (experts differ greatly as to the exact date), mentions beef or oxen on several occasions in his *Iliad*. Even the gods of mythology appeared to have been awed by the great majesty of the bull.

Only a little later in time, Hippocrates, 'Father of Medicine', praises ox flesh as having nutritious qualities but adds that he believes it to be heavy and indigestible. Maybe the methods of cooking the flesh were to blame!

The domesticated ox, a word that has been applied to bulls, cows, or oxen, is believed to have originated in Turkey or Macedonia between 6100 and 5800 BC. As indicated in the previous paragraphs, the ox was originally believed to possess almost legendary powers; but, as people became more dependent upon the animals for agriculture, this belief gradually declined. Today, one finds that only in certain religions in India is the domesticated cow treated with deference, largely from gratitude for the fact that it produces the dairy products considered so essential for life.

Moving on to the third century BC and the glories of Greece, we find that Athenaeus in his *Deiphnosophists* ('The Wise Men at Table') gives an idea of the kind of banquets then served. He gives the ingredients for Beef à l'Iberienne as 'boiled beef, served with pepper, herbs, spice, onions, and vinegar', and includes both 'sweet' and 'sun-made' wines.

Beef was obviously known in the Far East at the same period, and long before, too. As far back as the third century BC, a mention of it was included in a Chinese poem in praise of luxurious foods. This poem, 'The Summons of the Soul', lists such delicacies as 'turtle, kid, braised chicken, goose, casseroled duck, fried flesh of great crane' — so the 'ribs of fatted ox' it also mentions are in good company.

Some of the early recipes for cooking beef are associated with the Romans. We are fortunate that we still have on record the works of the gourmet and culinary expert Apicius, who lived in the first century AD. In his beef recipes the meat is highly flavoured with pepper and spices, probably to disguise the fact that often the meat was far from fresh. It was served with various sauces. In fact, the dishes of this time formed part of a very sophisticated cuisine.

In the Arab world sheep were, and still are, a major source of meat. There was some mention of 'red meat', which could have been beef, being used for kebabs in the thirteenth century; although the elaborate menus and superb cooking of the Arab world at that period does not mention this meat. The feasts and imaginative dishes of this time far surpassed any other cuisine.

Moving nearer the medieval period in Europe, it is true to say that, while the French ate mainly pork, the British were developing a liking for beef. This, and most other meat, was the prerogative of the middle and upper classes only; the poor scarcely tasted meat of any kind.

It is interesting to learn that the castration of male oxen, carried out by the Romans and Greeks, many centuries before, to subdue the animals and accustom them to the yoke, was prevalent in Britain. To quote the description of rearing beef at that time, 'It was carried out upon beeves bred on the hill pastures, to produce a strong constitution and firm bone in order to make them good 'doers' and put on flesh rapidly, when brought down to the richer pastures.'

Although the French did not enjoy a plentiful supply of beef until after the British, they show a very real appreciation of its value. Every Shrove Tuesday, the French celebrate Bœuf Gras. A fatted ox, often a prize-winning beast, is adorned with flowers and ribbons and led through the streets of towns and cities in company with troops of friendly and gaily dressed butchers. They are accompanied by musicians; it is a tribute indeed to the important part beef now plays in the French menu.

Some beef must have been available in France during the late fourteenth century, for in a somewhat haphazard menu, as was the custom at that time, is listed 'beef marrow fritters'—an indication that the French appreciated beef marrow then, as they do today.

In Britain, as in most countries, meat had to be salted or dried to preserve it. In the late eighteenth century, a traveller in South America wrote a description of 'charqui'. This method of drying, originally used for game, treated the meat by first cutting it into slices, then dipping these in strong brine or rubbing them with salt. The next stage was to wrap the meat in the animal's hide for 10–12 hours to absorb the salt and release some of the juices. Finally, the meat was hung in the sun to dry. The method of cooking seems to have been to pound the charqui between stones and then cook it in hot water. The term 'jerked beef' can well have come from this word 'charqui'.

By the end of that century, good cooking had developed in many countries, and a great number of interesting methods of serving and garnishing beef were invented. The eighteenth and nineteenth centuries, and even the beginning of the twentieth, were the era of the gargantuan meal.

Henry Fielding, a well-known English novelist and playwright of the eighteenth century, exclaims, in praise of the meat,

Oh! the roast beef of England,
And old England's roast beef!

A Swedish visitor to England at about the same period also praised beef, but in a very different way. He stated, 'Englishmen understand almost better than any other people the art of properly roasting a large cut of meat', then continues, 'not to be wondered at, since the art of cooking as practised by most Englishmen does not extend much beyond beef and plum pudding'.

In the year 1850, the Royal Agricultural Society held a special banquet in the city of Exeter in Devon for 1,050 members. For this feast, the first ever attempt was made to roast a whole ox by gas. The menu included thirty-three dishes of rib of beef, sixty-six dishes of pressed beef, together with many other meat joints!

I have often been asked if 'beefeaters', the warders of the Tower of London, are so called because they eat, or ate in the past, huge amounts of British beef. While one explanation is that the word is based on the French *beaufaitier*, ('one who attends a buffet'), a more pleasing reason may well be that the name became used to describe 'The Yeomen of Guard' (their correct title) after 1669, when Count Cosimo, grand duke of Tuscany, was in England. Writing on the size and stature of the magnificent men who formed the Guard, he said: 'They are great eaters of beef, of which a very large ration is given them daily at the court, and they might be called "Beefeaters".'

If we leave the history of the past and come to the facts of the present, we find that in the last quarter of the twentieth century, as the recipes in this book will show, beef plays an important part in menus throughout the world.

What is so fascinating is the fact that each country has developed different ways of serving this important food, adding vegetables, herbs, spices, and wines, each according to its particular traditions.

This gives enthusiastic cooks the opportunity to develop their skills and to learn how to cook a variety of beef dishes from different countries throughout the world.

Nowadays, the United States is the largest importer of beef and has the greatest consumption of this meat per head of the population. It exports very little beef; imports come from Australia, Canada, Mexico, and New Zealand. Of course, the United States also produces great quantities of beef for home consumption.

The Soviet Union has become the second largest producer of beef and is followed by the Argentine, which was once the world's largest exporter of beef, until Australia increased so much in importance as a beef-producing country. The Argentine, of course, still exports beef.

In Australia the increased beef production means that they now export to Japan as well as to the United States. Its traditional exports of meat to Britain have been affected by the EEC's virtual ban on imports from non-member countries.

In all European countries beef is a popular meat, France now having the largest consumption. The French beef recipes are, of course, famous and show great imagination in the clever blending of flavours.

In this book I have gathered together those recipes that have given me great pleasure to cook and to eat. I hope they will extend your knowledge of, and delight in, the splendours of beef.

PREPARATION

In order to achieve the best results when cooking beef, the meat should be carefully selected and prepared.

In this chapter you will find information on the preparation of different cuts, roasts and such special steaks as tournedos and the famous Chateaubriand.

Before preparing the beef, however, it is essential that you know that you have purchased the best-quality beef available. How do you ensure that the beef you buy is of good quality?

Firstly, by shopping where scrupulous hygiene is observed and where the meat is carefully stored. Beef, like all meats, is a highly perishable food and can spoil very easily. If handled without care and meticulous cleanliness, meat can be a source of harmful bacteria

Secondly, you can check the beef in the following three ways:

a) By examining the colour of the meat. In the case of beef, it has always been considered that the meat should be bright red and lean, with firm, pale-cream coloured fat. This is correct, but beef of a darker red can also be good, as the colour is due to the fact that the beef has been matured for a slightly longer period. This does not adversely affect the flavour and texture of the meat. A bright-red colour generally indicates that the meat has been cut recently. Nowadays, the use of refrigerated show cases for storing cut beef makes colour less important than it was when the meat was displayed on open counters.

b) By checking that there is a good distribution of fat. Today, there is a tendency to avoid fat, particularly that classed as 'animal fat'. This is wise if you have been advised to follow a low cholesterol diet. There is, however, a need to have some fat on meat to keep it moist during cooking and to add to the flavour. The American method of breeding produces beef cattle with a good distribution of small particles of fat, which is known as 'marbling'.

If you are slimming and/or reducing your intake of fat, it is better to use the natural fat of the animal to give flavour in the cooking and then to cut the fat away after cooking. This generally makes it unnecessary to add extra fat. If your diet does not allow any fat at all, the fat must be removed before cooking and the moist texture preserved by cooking the meat either in foil or in a stew or casserole without the addition of fat.

This is a good point at which to stress that beef is a wise choice if you are on a slimming diet. It is a high-protein food with the least natural fat, compared to most other meats. It lends itself to simple as well as to more elaborate methods of cooking.

c) By ensuring that the meat is tender. While tenderness depends upon good cooking methods and the wise selection of a cut for each cooking process, it is also governed by the correct breeding of the animal, plus the careful handling of the meat after killing.

The animal carcass is chilled after slaughter. The speed of chilling and the maintenance of the desired temperature is a very expert matter. After this, the carcass must be hung and aged to produce the most tender texture. The period of hanging varies with the temperature at which the meat is stored; the higher the temperature the shorter the hanging period. It also varies in different countries; for example, in the United States beef is hung for a longer period than in Britain, as this is considered to produce more tender flavourful meat.

Since handling and hanging of meat is generally out of the average consumer's hands, it is a matter of selecting the butcher's or store which provides meat which has the flavour and tenderness that you want.

Storing Meat

Having purchased meat that has been prepared and stored with great expertise by the butcher, it is essential that you continue this process in your own home.

Advice on freezing meat in the home is given on pages 27 and 28.

Put the meat in the refrigerator as quickly as possible after purchase. It is recommended that you cover the meat during storage. Cooked beef, like all cooked meats, dries easily, so be particularly careful about covering this well; even uncooked beef hardens on the outside if kept uncovered for too long a period. Some experts do not consider that the outer hardening of raw meat matters, since they feel it keeps the inside meat moist. That is really a matter of personal taste. Your particular refrigerator may have special storage containers for cooked and uncooked meats. It must be remembered, though, that the longer the cut surface area is exposed, the greater will be the evaporation and weight loss from the meat.

Individual refrigerator cabinets may vary a little as to the temperature inside the storage compartment (not the freezer), and that may govern the maximum storage time of beef slightly, but I like to cook it within three days if possible, and certainly within a maximum of five days.

If you are storing meat without a refrigerator, choose the coolest place, and if you can, suspend the meat with a hook, so that the air circulates freely around the meat. To prevent flies coming into contact with the meat, wrap it in muslin, and this can be moistened with diluted vinegar to give added protection. Cook the meat as soon as possible.

When defrosting beef, it is advisable to do this slowly in the refrigerator instead of at room temperature. This saves any chance of it spoiling. The following are the approximate times needed for defrosting:

Depending on their size, roasts will take from twelve to twenty-four hours in the refrigerator, and about half that time at room temperature. Steaks and diced stewing beef will take about six hours in a refrigerator and about half that time at room temperature.

There are many occasions upon which beef can be cooked from the frozen state. Advice on this is given in the next chapter under each individual cooking method.

Cutting Beef

The correct cutting of meat makes a great deal of difference to the attractive appearance of a dish, whether it is a simple and economical stew or casserole, or a more luxurious roast or steak.

In order to cut meat correctly and neatly, and to avoid any possibility of cutting your hands, choose the best quality knives you can afford. People often make the mistake of thinking that a sharp knife is a dangerous knife. The fact is that the sharp knife is safer because its action is more efficient. When buying knives, check that they are comfortable to hold.

Place the meat on a proper cutting board or firm surface. Modern laminated surfaces are very strong, but many will mark if you cut or chop on them.

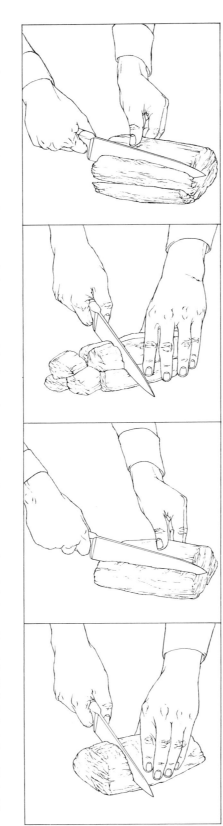

To cut meat for stews and casseroles. Making firm movements with the knife, cut the meat into strips, then divide these into neat dice, as shown in the upper two pictures on this page. Make these of a consistent thickness and size, so that they not only look attractive, but cook evenly. The pictures show the ideal knife, generally called a cook's or chef's knife.

To cut meat for braising. Cut the meat into larger fingers or slices, see the lower two pictures on this page.

Garnishes for Beef

In many recipes the ingredients, such as vegetables, form a pleasing garnish to the beef. In some dishes you may feel that you need extra colour. Tomatoes are one way of giving this. Two methods of cutting tomatoes are shown. The first means the tomato can be served cold, broiled, or baked, but in the second method, you prepare a tomato that can only be served uncooked.

1 To make the familiar waterlily shape (sometimes called a rose), from a tomato, make a diagonal cut downwards in the middle.

2 Make another diagonal cut, this time upwards.

3 Continue in this way, working all round the tomato and feeling the tip of the knife going through to the centre of the tomato.

4 Gently pull the halves apart.

5 To make a more elaborate rose, select fairly small and very firm tomatoes.

6 Cut a 'base' from one end of the tomato; do not sever this from the tomato, though.

7 Insert the tip of the knife under the skin and cut one long strip from the tomato; as you see, this is very thin.

8 Cut a second long strip from the tomato. As you cut these strips, use the knife in an up-and-down movement, to give the uneven edge of a flower petal.

9 Curl the first strip round the base of the tomato.

10 Roll the second strip very tightly indeed and place this in the centre of the shape, to look like the middle of a rose.

11 A simpler method is to follow stage 6, then cut one long strip from the tomato skin; this is not severed at all from the tomato, as happens in stages 7 and 8. You just turn this skin round the flesh of the tomato. It forms a less perfect shape, but a very attractive one.

To make Croûtons

Croûtons of bread are not only a good base for tournedos, but a very attractive garnish also.

1 Cut slices of bread, then decide upon the shape required; if you want a round shape, stamp this out with a pastry cutter.

2 Triangles are easier to cut and waste less bread.

3 Small diced pieces of bread make an interesting garnish on a stew or casserole and give a change of texture too. Cut the bread into narrow fingers, then into small dice.

4 To fry the croûtons, heat a little butter or fat in a frying pan; fry the bread on the one side, then turn and fry until golden on the second side.

5 Drain on absorbent paper. This can be papertowels, tissues, or crumpled tissue paper, but not greaseproof paper, which does not absorb grease.

Garnishes for Beef

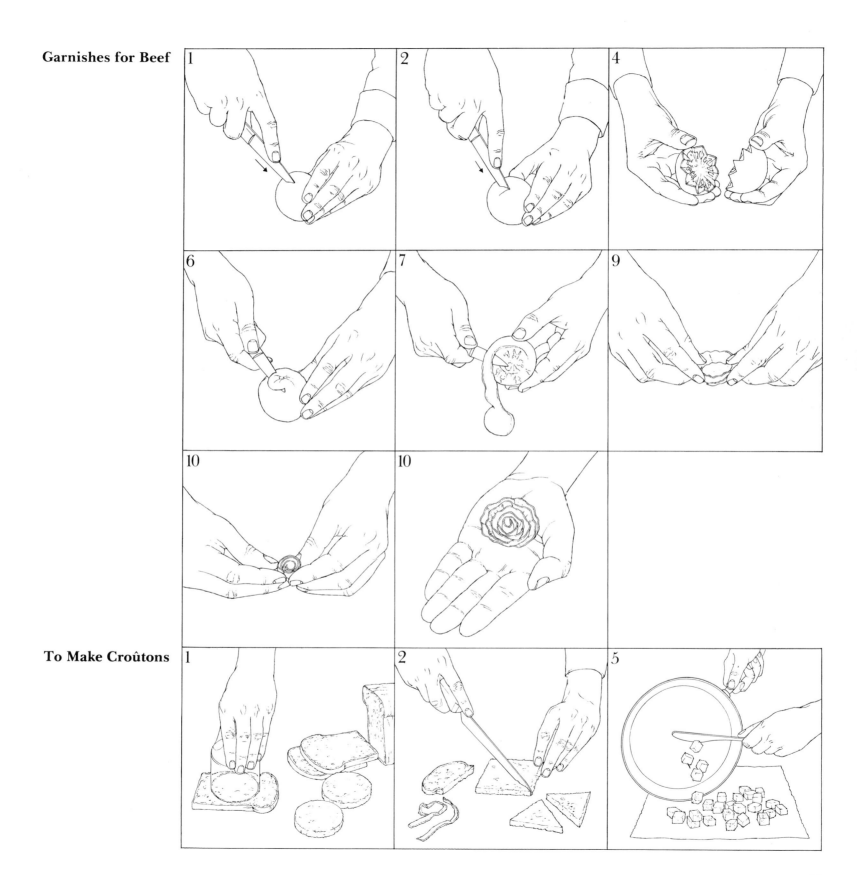

To Make Croûtons

21

To Tenderize Steak

Most steaks are sufficiently tender and need little pre-preparation, but if you are uncertain about the quality of the meat, there are various ways in which it can be tenderized.

The most likely steaks for this treatment are round, rump, chuck, flank steak, full cut sirloin, and top sirloin. Boneless ribsteak (entrecôte), porterhouse, T-bone, and boneless loin (strip, New York, Kansas City) steaks are usually tender enough.

Many authorities on meat have

To Tenderize Steak

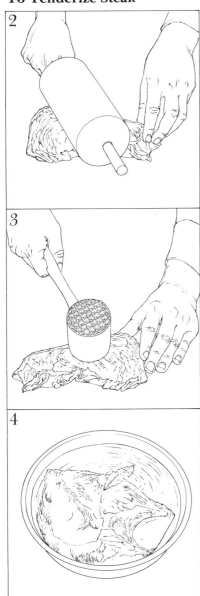

found that beating meat does not tenderize it in the accepted meaning. However, it breaks the fibres, and many consider that this makes the meat easier to chew and, therefore, more tender.

1 Place the steaks on a flat surface; do not use a china plate as it may get broken with the vigorous action in stages 2 and 3.

2 Bang the meat firmly with a rolling pin. This also flattens it somewhat and makes it thinner. You could use the back of a knife or a light weight, as shown under the preparation of a Châteaubriand steak on page 23.

3 We illustrate a small utensil sold for tenderizing steak.

4 Another method of tenderizing steaks is to place them in a marinade. This must contain a certain amount of wine, fruit juice, or vinegar, for it is the acid that softens the meat fibres. More information about marinades will be found on page 34 and in the recipes in the chapter on steaks. The following mixture is excellent for any steaks and is very quickly prepared.

5 Squeeze the juice from a large lemon, and place it into a shallow dish.

6 Add 2 tablespoons olive, or other good-quality, oil with a pinch of salt, a shake of pepper, and 1 teaspoon prepared mustard. This makes enough marinade for 4 steaks.

7 Place the steaks in the marinade and leave for at least an hour; lift from the mixture, and drain by holding the steaks over the dish. Broil, barbecue, or fry in the usual manner.

Cutting a Fillet

The picture on the right shows a whole fillet (tenderloin) of beef and the way in which it could be cut to give:–

a) A Chateaubriand steak.

b) Several tournedos of beef; these generally weigh approximately 4–6 ounces.

c) Filets mignons, or medallions; as these are cut from the smallest part of the fillet, their weight is generally about 3–4 ounces.

To Prepare Tournedos

1 Although fillet (tenderloin) steak should be used for tournedos, you may substitute prime full cut sirloin or top sirloin if fillet is unobtainable. The meat should be a generous 1½ inches thick, for the fillet is small in diameter. Tournedos weigh about 4 ounces when prepared.

2 Many prefer to form the tournedos shape by hand. However, if you press a round pastry or cookie cutter on the meat you will have a better shape; if the meat is very tender and the cutter sharp, you may be able to press it through the meat. If you have no suitable cutter, use a tumbler or cup to help give a perfect round.

3 A knife is used to cut the meat around the shape. Any small pieces of tender steak left may be used for Steak Tartare, see page 59.

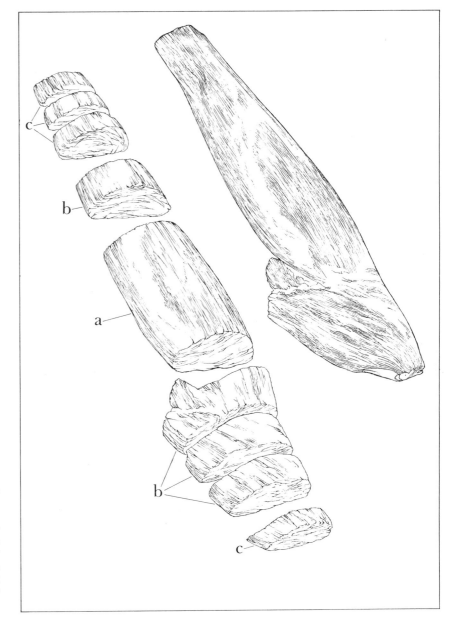

4 When the required number of rounds are ready, either secure with fine string, wooden tooth picks, or fine skewers.

5 Another way to prepare tournedos is to put a long thin strip of pork or bacon around each tournedo and secure it.

6 The meat is then ready to cook, although you will also need to prepare the accompaniment or garnish.

You will find a selection of tournedos on pages 64 – 66.

7 It was traditional to serve a tournedos on a fried croûton of bread, the same size as the round of meat. This practice is used less today, as most people avoid an excess of fried foods or bread. If you decide to follow this method, fry the bread in butter until crisp and golden on both sides, drain on absorbent paper, and keep hot while cooking the tournedos.

To Prepare a Chateaubriand
The part of the fillet used for a Chateaubriand steak is the very thickest portion, although it has only a slightly larger diameter than the ends of the fillet which are cut into tournedos or filets mignons. It has, however, a much greater depth.

In order to make this suitable for broiling, frying, or oven roasting, the steak should be flattened. This also gives the shape for the traditional carving of the steak.

1 Wrap the meat in a cloth.

2 Pound the meat with the back of a large solid knife, a light weight, or a rolling pin until it becomes no more than 1½ inches in thickness.

3 The steak is then ready to cook. The method of cooking and serving is covered on page 78. Details of frying and broiling are given on pages 33 and 34, respectively.

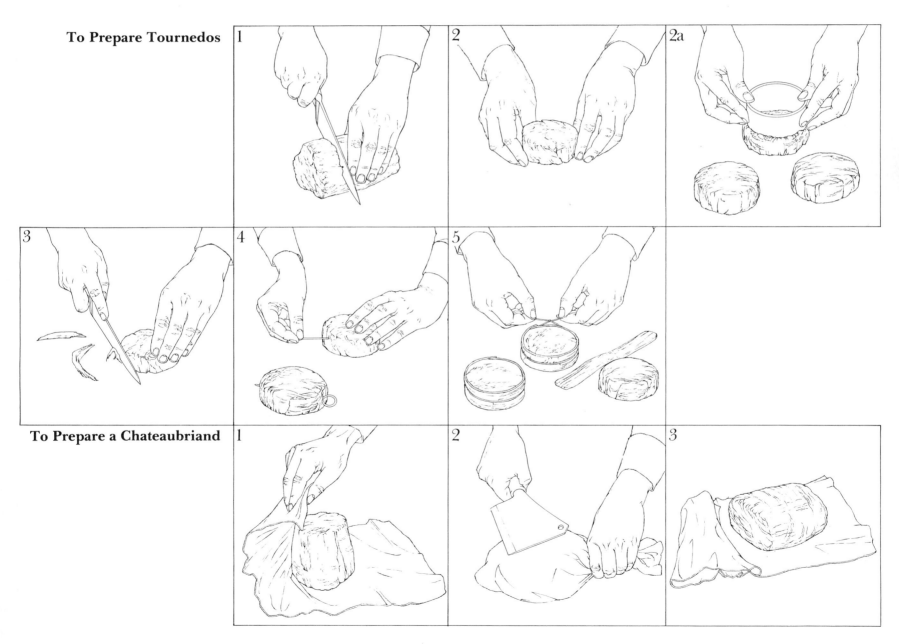

To Prepare Tournedos

1   2   2a

3   4   5

To Prepare a Chateaubriand

1   2   3

To Bone and Roll a Rib Roast of Beef

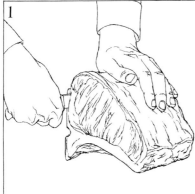

To Bone and Roll a Rib Roast of Beef

The object of boning this or, indeed, any cut is to make it easier to carve. There is, however, always a slightly better flavour when the meat is cooked on the bone.

1 Cut away the end bone, often called the 'chine'.

2 Insert the tip of a sharp pointed knife into the end of the meat, as near the bone as possible, and gradually ease the bone from the meat; do this slowly and carefully.

3 Remove the bone, roll the meat (picture 3a); secure with skewers, then tie in several places with string (picture 3b).

To Bone and Roll a Porterhouse

1 Follow stage 1 in To Bone and Roll a Rib Roast of Beef, then insert the knife on the rib side of the bone; cut away the meat, as in stage 2 of To Bone and Roll a Rib Roast of Beef.

2 Insert the knife into the other side of the bone by the fillet and cut the meat from that side of the bone.

3 Roll and secure as in stage 3 of To Bone and Roll a Rib Roast of Beef.

Sometimes, it is said that learning to carve properly is a waste of time, why not cut the meat as you please?

The traditional way of carving meat is sensible; it simply follows the contours of the bone and, thus, produces more servings.

Loosen bones first, using a short, rather than a carving, knife. A cook's knife is ideal.

Always allow the cooked meat to stand for 4–5 minutes. It will not become cold during this period, but the meat 'sets' and is easier to carve well.

It is easier to carve on a board or the modern stainless steel carving dish with small supports in the centre to hold the meat firmly on the dish.

Good carving plays an important part in the presentation of the cooked meat on the dish or plate. To watch a professional carve can be a

Carving Porterhouse on the Bone

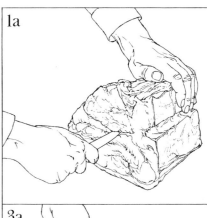

To Carve Boned Porterhouse

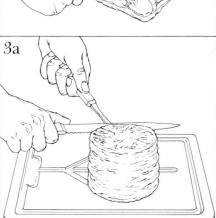

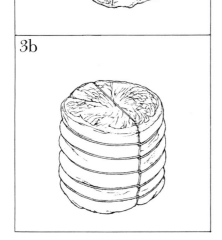
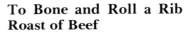
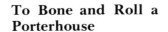

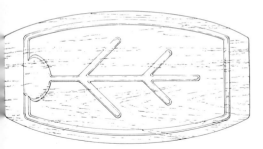

(*Right*) Steel carving dish.

(*Below*) Wood carving board.

(*Above*) French-pattern carving knife.

(*Below*) Serrated-edge carving knife.

(*Above*) Carving knife.

(*Below*) Electric carving knife.

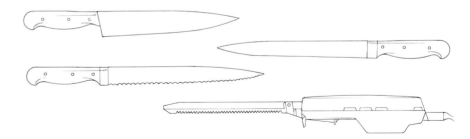

real pleasure. Only practice and experience will produce a good carver.

It is, however, helpful to know the best way to deal with each particular cut of meat.

A good carving knife is an essential tool. A knife with a serrated edge is often easier for a beginner at carving, but the real French-pattern carving knife or the more traditionally shaped knife is better once you are experienced. If you are in the habit of cooking extra large cuts, to serve a good number of portions, then buy two knives. This is not as extravagant as it sounds: the heat of the meat blunts the cutting edge of the knife after quite a short time. If you have to stop and wipe the knife, and then sharpen it on a steel, the meat will begin to get cold.

Treasure your carving knife; keep the blade sharp with a steel, an oilstone, or a knife sharpener. When sharpening, hold the blade of the knife at an angle no greater than 15° to the steel or the oilstone.

Electric carving knives are becoming more popular; they do not necessarily carve better than others, but they do the task quicker.

Always use a proper carving fork, this holds the meat steady, and the thumb-piece acts as a protective guard.

Carving a Porterhouse

You will have cooked the porterhouse either as a boned cut, see page 25, or on the bone.

There is no doubt that the meat has a better flavour if it remains on the bone, but many people fear that it will be too difficult to carve. That is not the case, as the information given on this page will show.

If you or the butcher has boned the meat, always keep the bones to simmer for stock, or to make a good gravy or sauce to serve with the meat.

Carving a Porterhouse on the Bone

1 Cut the end bone from the meat. Do this in the kitchen. Remove the bone, see picture 1a. This end bone may have been cut from the meat before cooking, then tied in position to keep the meat moist, see picture 1b.

2 As the fillet is nicer when hot, use all of this, if possible, since the rest of the sirloin is equally good hot or cold.

3 Carve the meat from the outside to the bone, then carve the fillet (or see stage 6). Each person should have portions of fillet (tenderloin), and then portions of the rest of the meat.

4 Reverse the joint after carving a number of slices and repeat the process on the other side.

5 Arrange the slices on the dish or board, or serve onto each plate.

6 If preferred, you can cut away the whole fillet before starting to carve, and then carve this separately.

To Carve Boned Porterhouse

1 When carving rolled roasts, it is important not to remove the string or the skewers until you have carved down to them, for these hold the meat in position. Remove the skewers only when they impede the progress of the knife.

2 Cut away the top slice; this may be slightly thicker and more uneven than you would wish, but cutting it away makes the top of the roast flat.

3 Continue to carve slices of the desired thickness; use the knife in a gentle sawing action, keeping it quite even with the meat; with an electric carving knife you will just guide the knife and use no energy. Picture 3a shows the way to a perfectly carved boned porterhouse, if the roast is kept upright. If you use this method, always carve away from you. Picture 3b shows the same joint being carved downwards.

This method may be used for all rolled roasts, such as rolled rib of beef.

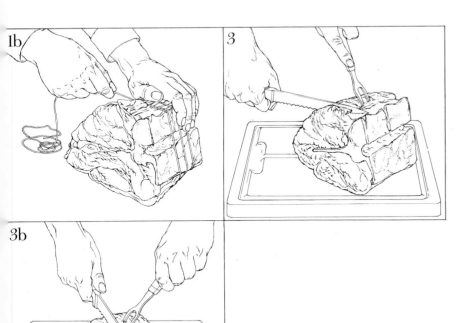

Carving Tongue

1 If the tongue is pressed, see page 52, carve the meat across the round. As the meat is in a jelly, you may turn the round upside down and cut from the bottom part, leaving the smooth glazed top undisturbed and so, keeping the tongue more moist.

2 If the tongue is cooked but not pressed, remove the skin before carving. Cut slices downwards, as shown in Carving Ribs of Beef, stage 2. Work from the thicker to the thinner end of the meat.

Carving a Rib Roast of Beef

1 Cut away the end, or 'chine', bone; this is better done in the kitchen, using a small sharp knife. At the same time, loosen the meat from the bone or bones; this makes carving very much easier.

2 Cut slices from both sides of the meat. Always start from the thick end and carve towards the thinner end.

3 When you reach the first rib bone, loosen the meat from the bone, if not already done at stage 1.

4 Continue carving the rest of the meat in the same way, and arrange on the dish.

Carving Braised Cuts

1 Lift the meat from the top of the 'mirepoix'; this term is explained on page 31. The ingredients are part of the recipes in the braising chapter, beginning on page 39, and generally form a sauce after cooking, although they may be used as a garnish.

2 As the meat is more moist when braised than when roasted, it is advisable to carve on a dish, rather than on a board. The dish shown on page 25 is ideal, as there is a 'trough' into which the moisture provided by the mirepoix can flow.

3 Meats are carved in exactly the same way as if they had been roasted, so follow the directions on pages 24, 25, and this page.

4 When carved, the slices of meat are coated with the sauce or are garnished, as per the recipe.

Carving Bottom Round

Bottom Round is carved downwards, as shown in Carving a Rib Roast of Beef, stage 2, on this page. The meat crumbles easily, particularly if it has been salted and boiled, so carve slowly and firmly. The cooked bottom round may have been glazed, as in the recipe on page 53, in which case carve as boned porterhouse, as on page 25. The same carving procedure is followed for brisket of beef.

Carving a Rump Steak

1 Sometimes a large rump steak is cooked in a long piece, rather than being divided into portions before cooking. This has the advantage that the centre of the meat can be kept very 'rare' (under-done).

2 Carving is really a misnomer, for after being cooked, the meat is simply divided into the desired number of portions.

Carving a Chateaubriand Steak

1 The steak may have been cooked on a board, as suggested under Planked Steak, page 78. If not, lift it onto the board or dish.

2 Allow the complete steak to stand for a few minutes.

3 Calculate the number of even-sized slices you need. Generally, this steak serves two. Carve slightly diagonal slices, so giving larger slices than if the steak was carved in the usual straight manner. Slice the steak completely before serving.

Carving a Rib Roast of Beef

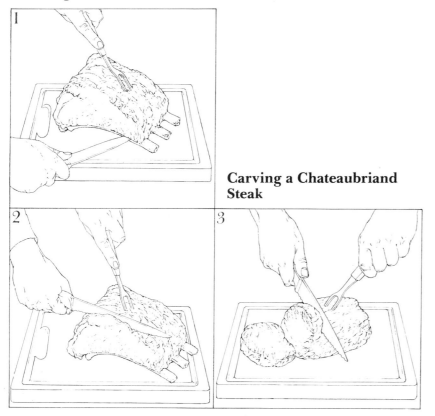

Carving a Chateaubriand Steak

Freezing

The first commercially frozen meat seems to have been cargoes of beef transported from the Argentine to France, and from Australia to Britain, in the 1880s.

It then was accepted that the cool storage of meat was better than those early attempts at freezing, and supplies of chilled beef were sent from South America to Britain from the 1880s to 1910.

Nowadays, the quality of both chilled and frozen meats is high, and facilities for freezing fresh meat at home are available.

A domestic refrigerator has long been accepted as an essential appliance in the home, and now, a high percentage of people find a freezer of equal value. It gives one greater freedom to shop for food when convenient; in fact, you have the facilities of a small supermarket in your freezer, if you fill it wisely.

Many cooked meat dishes freeze well; an excellent time-saver is to cook a larger-than-necessary quantity of a dish, to serve some when it is freshly cooked, and to freeze the remainder for a future occasion. It is important to choose with care the foods and cooked dishes to be frozen, and to accept the fact that they must be used within the given period, if they are to be entirely satisfactory. An indication of the best storage time for frozen beef dishes is given under the recipes, if the dish is suitable for freezing.

A freezer can save you money in that it gives you the opportunity to buy certain foods in bulk, at a slightly more economical price than when purchasing a smaller quantity.

You can either buy a portion of the animal and have this cut up, or a large weight of a particular cut, such as steaks.

These are the questions you ought to ask yourself before you invest money in a bulk purchase:
a) Am I satisfied that the shop from which I buy this meat sells prime or choice quality?
b) If I buy a large portion of the animal and have it divided, shall I make good use of all the various cuts, or am I buying some pieces that do not fit my particular mode of meal planning?

Whether freezing a large amount of meat or just an extra cut, follow the packaging directions given on this and the next page, and follow also the advice given by the maker of your particular freezer.

Here are some of the most important points for the successful freezing of beef, and indeed, of other foods.

1 Select the beef carefully and freeze as soon as possible after purchase.

2 Turn the indicator on your freezer to the coldest position to ensure quick freezing. The position will vary with different makes.

3 Check on the recommended maximum quantity of food that can be frozen in *your* particular cabinet within each twenty-four hour period. Generally, it is a tenth of the freezer's total capacity.

4 Package the food correctly, see this and the next page. It is essential to exclude all air from the food to prevent dehydration. Meat is particularly susceptible to this. Drying out causes spoilage of both texture and flavour. *Close and careful packaging prevents this.*

Wrappings to choose are:
a) Aluminium foil — choose the heavy-duty kind sold for freezers. If not obtainable, use a double thickness of the ordinary quality.
b) Plastic wrap, heavy gauge for freezers; the quality used for wrapping food in a refrigerator is not sufficiently thick.
c) Freezer-quality polythene bags, see comment in **b**) above.
d) Polythene storage boxes; these must be freezer quality.
e) Waxed paper, for separating steaks and hamburgers (and similar small prepared meat cakes).

In addition to the wrappings, you require:—
a) Something with which to close the bags or wrappings, for instance, plastic-coated ties or freezer adhesive tape. The ordinary adhesive tape is unsuitable for a freezer, since the adhesive surface soon becomes damp and inefficient. Nowadays, you can also buy an appliance that closes freezer bags by applying heat. This is simple to use and very efficient.
b) Labels upon which you can write the contents of the package and the date of freezing. It is surprising how difficult it is to identify unlabelled packages of food once they are frozen. Use freezer-type labels and put these on the wrapping, bag, or container before adding the food, so that you have a perfectly flat surface on which to press the label.

If you freeze beef yourself, check that it has been hung *before* freezing.

Information about hanging is given on page 19.

Large cuts of uncooked beef and steaks can be stored for up to eight months, but minced-beef products such as hamburgers for only three months.

'Boil in the Bag' Containers

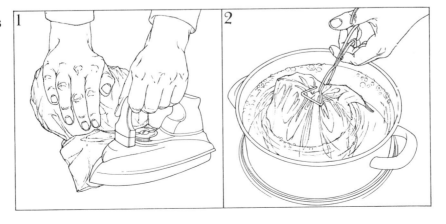

'Boil in the Bag' Containers

These are special-quality bags in which food may be frozen and then reheated. They are suitable for many kinds of dishes and foods, among them beef stews and soups. The bag is supported in a rigid container during the process of filling.

Heat from a warm iron is then used to seal the bag, see picture 1. The bag forms a neat package that is easily stored.

To reheat, place the bag in a saucepan of boiling water, see picture 2, and simmer until the food is ready to serve.

To Freeze Beef

Roasts and Other Large Cuts

1 Prepare the meat in a good shape for cooking; cut away any surplus fat, since this does not keep well during the maximum period of freezing.

2 Cover any sharp bones or skewers with foil, cling wrap, or even a little cotton wool, so that they will not pierce the wrappings.

3 Place into freezer bags or wrap in cling foil. Press the bag or wrap as tightly as possible round the meat.

4 Expel the air in one of the following ways:
a) Slide your hands up the wrap from the bottom or the top;
b) Insert a drinking straw into the package, close the top, and suck out the air;
c) Withdraw any air with a freezer pump.

Pieces of Meat
(such as stewing beef)

5 I find it better to 'open freeze' these on flat trays and then to pack. In this way the small pieces do not stick together. When frozen, pack in bags or containers as stages 3 and 4.

Steaks

6 Separate each steak with a square of waxed paper. Grease-proof paper can be used but is less pliable; the picture shows the steaks with the paper between. Continue as stages 3 and 4. Polythene boxes may be used for steaks, but the steaks must be wrapped first to exclude surplus air, as the boxes may not provide adequate protection.

Hamburgers

7 The process is similar to that given for steaks, or you can 'open freeze' the hamburgers, as in stage 5, wrap completely in waxed paper, then pack a number together.

Casseroles

8 The cooked food must be cooled before freezing. It can then be frozen in a 'boil in the bag' container, as on page 27. The following is another method.

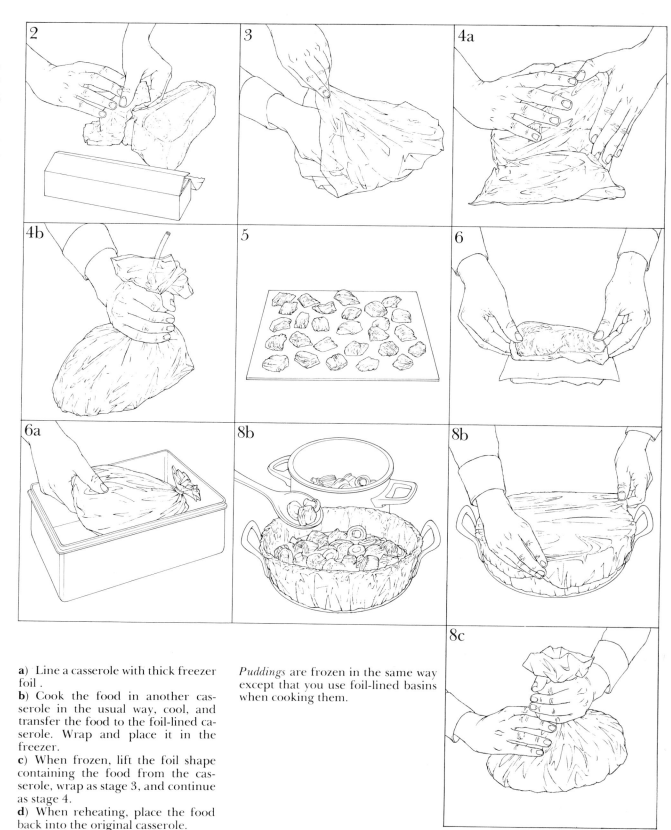

a) Line a casserole with thick freezer foil .
b) Cook the food in another casserole in the usual way, cool, and transfer the food to the foil-lined casserole. Wrap and place it in the freezer.
c) When frozen, lift the foil shape containing the food from the casserole, wrap as stage 3, and continue as stage 4.
d) When reheating, place the food back into the original casserole.

Puddings are frozen in the same way except that you use foil-lined basins when cooking them.

BASIC METHODS

This chapter covers the basic methods of cooking beef, together with advice on the best cuts to buy for each process.

It is essential to use the right temperature for each form of cooking, for an incorrect speed of cooking can ruin a perfect piece of meat.

The choice of utensil is another important factor in successful meat cooking, especially when braising meat.

Although the varying methods of cooking beef and steak need different cuts of meat, they have certain facts in common.

a) The meat is spoiled by over-cooking, so time the cooking period carefully.

b) Meat is improved by subtle flavourings, so make good use of herbs, various seasonings, wine, and good stock.

c) Never waste beef bones — they produce first class stock for soups, stews, and casserole dishes (the method of making stock is given on page 37).

d) Learn how to defrost frozen beef before cooking.

Ways to Cook Beef

Braising
This is a combination of frying the meat to brown the outside and 'seal in' the flavour, and of steady cooking above a small amount of liquid and a mirepoix.
Secrets of success:
The correct choice of utensil, so that the small amount of liquid does not evaporate during cooking.
A good choice of vegetables and other ingredients for the mirepoix — as a garnish or sauce.

Boiling
This is the method in which beef is immersed in liquid which should only simmer steadily throughout the cooking period.
Secrets of success:
Correct cooking temperature; the liquid should not boil.
Imaginative choice of herbs and vegetables to give flavour to the meat.
Adequate soaking of salted beef, if used.

Frying
Frying is an excellent way to cook tender cuts of steak, as the butter, fat, or oil adds moistness to this lean meat.
Secrets of success:
Correct temperature of the frying fat or oil to seal the outside of the meat and so retain the maximum flavour of the steak.
Careful timing so that the steak is not over-cooked.
An interesting choice of garnish or accompaniments.

Broiling
Broiling is one of the simplest and most successful ways of cooking choice steaks.
Secrets of success:
Pre-heating the broiler so that the high heat will seal the outside of the meat very quickly, thus retaining maximum flavour.
Brushing the meat with some kind of fat as it cooks, to make sure that the steak does not dry.
An interesting selection of garnishes and/or accompaniments.

Roasting
This is an excellent way to cook choice cuts of beef.

True roasting is cooking the meat on a turning spit, whereas the method of roasting in a tin in the oven could be said to be baking the meat.
Modern microwave ovens allow one to cook the beef in a relatively short time.
Secrets of success:
Choosing the correct temperature for the particular cut. On pages 36–37 you can find information on roasting fresh as well as frozen or chilled beef.
Adding the correct amount of fat to the meat; too much fat hardens the outside.
Timing the cooking time perfectly to ensure that the beef is cooked to personal taste: rare, medium , or well-done.

Stewing
This is a method of cooking beef in liquid but is unlike boiling, for the meat is generally browned in a little fat before adding any liquid, and the liquid is thickened after being added. If the meat is cooked in a covered container in the oven, it is described as being cooked in a casserole.
Secrets of success:
As the less expensive cuts of beef are generally used for this purpose, slow cooking is essential (unless using a pressure cooker) to produce tender meat.
A beef stew or casserole should be well flavoured with herbs, seasonings, and various vegetables, which are cooked with the meat.

Braising

Do not confuse braising with stewing. When beef or other foods are braised, they are *not* cooked *in* a liquid, as when stewed, but first browned and then cooked *above* a little liquid and a mirepoix. This is described on page 31. There is certainly a similarity between braising and pot-roasting, as you will see when you read page 37, but braising generally gives a more subtle flavour to both meat and sauce.

The ingredients needed for braising are: –

a) The correct cut of beef.
b) The fat in which to brown this, unless there is sufficient fat on the beef.
c) The mirepoix.
d) The liquid, which keeps the mirepoix moist and creates steam in the cooking utensil.

To Braise Beef

Individual recipes will vary somewhat, but these are the basic stages.

1 Choose one of the cuts of beef suggested on page 31, or as in the particular recipe.

2 Prepare the meat. The individual recipe may suggest just tying the meat into a neat shape or cutting it into smaller portions. Often, the recipe has further requirements, such as 'larding' the meat with extra fat, as in the recipe and pictures on page 43, or putting it into a marinade, described on page 41.

3 Select the correct cooking utensil, as advised on page 31, for this is very important.

4 Heat a little fat, or the amount specified in the recipe, in the selected cooking utensil. Add the meat and brown this on all sides, turning with tongs or two spoons.

Do not insert a fork in the meat, as this encourages the meat juices to flow and the purpose of browning the meat is to 'seal in' all these juices.

5 Remove the meat from the pan onto a plate, unless specified otherwise in the recipe.

6 Add any ingredients for the mirepoix that need to be browned (see the notes about this on page 31). Heat these in any fat remaining in the pan, until golden brown or as instructed in the recipe.

7 Check at this point that there is not too much fat left in the bottom of the pan, for the mirepoix should never be over-greasy; if there is a surplus of fat, remove the vegetables and any other ingredients with a perforated spoon and place them on a dish; pour away the surplus fat. Replace the vegetables and any other ingredients used for the mirepoix in the pan (or you may wish to transfer them to an oven-proof casserole).

8 Add the recommended amount of liquid; this may cover the mirepoix in the base of the pan or casserole or may be a rather smaller amount, depending upon the actual recipe. The liquid should *never* be so high in the pan that it covers the meat, the approximate amount is shown in picture 8. Page 31 gives suggestions for the choice of liquid to use.

9 Return the browned meat to the pan together with a little salt and pepper or any other flavouring specified in the recipe.

10 Cover the pan tightly, see suggestions on page 31 for ensuring that the lid *does* fit firmly.

11 *If braising on the top of the stove:* Lower the heat, so that there is just an occasional bubble on the surface of the liquid in the pan, and time the cooking. Recipes will give detailed timing, but generally you will need to allow: –

25 minutes per pound for really prime cuts, like rib of beef, see Paradeisbraten, page 40.

30–35 minutes per pound for slightly less tender cuts such as topside of beef, used in Rinderschmorbraten on page 43.

2–2¼ hours for stewing beef, as used in the recipes on page 42.

12 *If braising in the oven:* Follow the specific recipe or the timing as below. Place the container in the centre of the oven, unless you have a fan (convection) oven.

To Braise Beef 4

Utensils for Braising 1

Use a very moderate oven, 325°F, for the really prime cuts and 25 minutes per pound *plus* 25 minutes. Choose a slightly lower temperature, 300°F, for the less tender pieces of meat, and a longer cooking period, i.e., 30–35 minutes per pound *plus* 30–35 minutes.

Naturally, personal taste will govern the total cooking time, although braised beef is not generally served underdone.

13 At the end of the cooking time, remove the meat onto a hot serving dish.

14 Recipes vary, but it is usual to sieve or liquidize the mirepoix in a blender to form the basis of a sauce.

15 Check the consistency of the purée, as made in stage 14, and, if necessary, add a little extra liquid to produce a coating consistency.

16 The sauce made from the mirepoix can be served separately, or the meat can be carved, arranged on a dish, and then coated with the sauce.

Cuts of Beef for Braising
Prime cuts:
Round (top and bottom); rump; sirloin tip; brisket; flank steak; eye of round.
Cheaper stewing cuts:
chuck steak (round bone and blade bone); short ribs; flank; ox-tails.
The full explanation of cuts, including British, Australian, and French, is given on pages 14–16.

Frozen Beef
Allow this to defrost before braising. Any juices that flow from the beef can be used as part of the liquid.

Fat to Use
The fat used in braising can be butter, oil, beef drippings, or a mixture of fats.

Often, thin strips of fatback or bacon are threaded into lean beef to give a good distribution of fat.

The Mirepoix
Individual recipes will suggest the particular foods to use, but if you are creating your own recipe, choose a selection of seasonal root vegetables, plus a little celery, leek, herbs, and spices to taste. Bacon is often included, and this adds flavour to the mirepoix.

It is usual to sieve the mirepoix or to put this into the blender and make it into a sauce. As you can imagine, the flavour is delicious. No thickening is necessary, for the root vegetables give the bulk desired. If you find the sieved or liquidized purée a trifle thick, add a little stock or other liquid to achieve the desired consistency.

Remember to allow a sufficient depth of mirepoix ingredients to form a good base in the pan.

If you have any of the purée left, use it as a basis for a soup.

Liquids to Choose
The liquid used in braising combines with the mirepoix to form a pleasant accompaniment or sauce; the choice of liquid is, therefore, important.

Select beer or stout to provide a robust sauce; and red or white wine for a more delicate taste. Beef stock is a good choice for economy or when you do not want to detract from the flavour of the mirepoix. The subtle use of a small amount of vinegar in braising gives a 'bite' to the mirepoix.

Utensils for Braising
You may own, or be able to purchase, a traditional braising pan, shown in picture 1. This gives ample space for good-sized cuts and is made of heavy metal, which is ideal for the initial browning of the meat; it also has a very well-fitting lid, and this is *essential*, as it prevents the small quantity of liquid used in braising from evaporating during the cooking process. The braising pan can be used both on top of a cooker or in the oven.

A heavy saucepan should be used to braise the beef on top of the cooker; light pans are more likely to allow the mirepoix to burn.

It is essential to control the heat of the electric plate or gas ring carefully, so that the liquid does not boil too rapidly and so evaporate during cooking. If you are doubtful on this point, then braise the food in the oven instead.

Check that the saucepan lid fits tightly, so that no liquid escapes during the cooking process. If the lid is a poor fit, then remedy this by using aluminium foil.

Picture 2 shows a large piece of foil being laid over the top of a saucepan before putting on the lid. Picture 3 shows the surplus foil being tucked round the place where the lid and pan come together to give a good seal.

A deep frying pan may be used in place of a saucepan when braising portions of meat, such as the meat rolls in the recipe on page 106. Naturally, you need a frying pan with a lid.

A deep casserole can also be used for braising meat. Remember that an oven-proof casserole cannot be used on the burners, but that a flame-proof casserole is equally suitable on either the burners or in the oven. This means that you can brown the meat and vegetables in hot fat on top of the stove, and then transfer the casserole to the oven.

Boiling

The term 'boiling' is really a misnomer when applied to cooking beef. If the liquid in which the meat is cooked *is* allowed to boil rather than simmer, it can toughen the beef and at the same time over-cook the outside of the meat to such an extent that the beef breaks into dry flakes. This means the meat loses flavour, texture, and is impossible to carve.

The ingredients used in boiling beef are:

a) The cured or fresh cut of beef.
b) The liquid in which it is cooked.
c) Any vegetables and herbs added to give extra flavour to the meat and liquid.
d) Accompaniments, such as dumplings, see pages 55–56.

To Boil Beef

1 If boiling heavily salted corned beef, soak this in cold water to cover for twelve hours (seldom necessary in the United States). Pour the water away before cooking the beef. This stage is not followed when cooking fresh beef.

2 Put the beef into a large pan and add sufficient liquid to cover the meat; this is very important, as the beef must be immersed in liquid at all times.

3 Add the prepared vegetables and herbs; in some recipes a proportion of vegetables is added at this stage to flavour the meat and liquid, and more are put in later. The latter vegetables retain both colour and texture and are served as an accompaniment to the meat.

4 Season the liquid; use only pepper if cooking corned meat.

5 Bring the liquid just to boiling point.

6 At this stage you may find the surface of the liquid covered with a grey 'scum'; remove this with a spoon, so that the liquid is kept clear.

7 Cover the pan, lower the heat, and allow the liquid to simmer steadily. This means that the temperature should not drop below 200°F or rise above 205°F, and that you will see a gentle bubbling on the surface.

8 Time the cooking period from the end of stage 7, i.e., when the liquid is bubbling. This will vary in individual recipes, but on an average, allow 40 minutes per pound.

9 Add any extra vegetables or dumplings, etc., to the liquid as given in the special recipes, pages 49–56.

10 *If serving the meat hot*, lift from the liquid onto a heated dish.

You may need to glaze or press the meat, but if this procedure is not being followed, garnish it with the cooked vegetables and/or dumplings.

If serving the meat cold, without extra preparations, allow to cool in the cooking liquid. This makes an appreciable improvement to the moist texture of the beef. When the meat is quite cold, remove from the pan, drain well, then serve.

Cuts of Beef for Boiling

Prime cuts:
fresh or corned brisket; rump; rib 'flanken'; chuck; flank. In the United States, top or bottom round is not generally used for boiling.

Cheaper stewing cuts:
neck meat; shank meat; plate; heel of round; ox-tongue.

The full explanation of cuts, including British, Australian, and French, is on pages 14–16.

Frozen Beef
This should be defrosted before boiling.

Liquids to Choose
Diluted wine vinegar, cider, beer, stock, water, wine.

Utensils for Boiling
Choose solid saucepans with well-fitting lids; the comments on page 31 are applicable to boiling.

To Cook Dumplings

Although a dumpling mixture, to serve with boiled beef, is described as 'cuisine Anglaise' by Escoffier, other countries also enjoy these light balls.

The British use suet with flour, salt, and water; the Americans use equal quantities of cornmeal and flour in a similar recipe, instead of all flour; other European recipes are based on potatoes, liver, and other interesting ingredients, see pages 55 and 56.

The basic principle of cooking any dumplings, though, is the same.

1 Make quite sure the liquid is boiling before you attempt to cook the mixture.

2 Check that there is enough liquid in the pan; the dumpling mixture absorbs a considerable amount in cooking.

3 Make the dumpling mixture; do not make it too stiff.

4 Roll into small balls with lightly floured hands; remember many dumpling mixtures rise during cooking, so do not make the balls too large.

5 Drop into the boiling liquid, keep the liquid boiling during the first few minutes of cooking.

6 When the dumplings are cooked, remove them from the liquid with a perforated spoon.

To Cook Dumplings

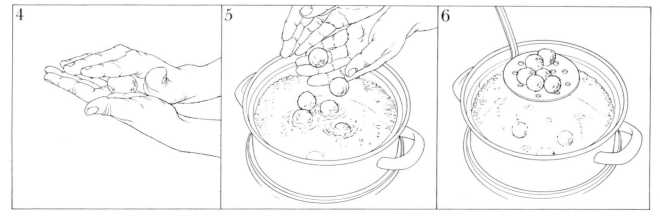

Frying

This method of cooking beef steaks enables one to prepare an almost unbelievable variety of dishes, ranging from a simple but perfectly cooked fried steak to the great classic dishes, in which frying, or to give the French term, 'sautéing', is just the initial stage.

The ingredients for this method of cooking are:

a) Choice beef that will be tender when cooked in this speedy manner.
b) The fat in which to sauté the lean meat; this also adds additional flavour.
c) Flavourings, which range from simple seasonings—herbs—to exotic mixtures of vegetables, wine, sauces, and cream.

To Fry Steak

1 Select the correct cut of meat, as given on this page.

2 It may be necessary to cut and tie this into tournedos, but that will depend upon the particular recipe. The method of preparing tournedos is given on pages 22–23.

3 If you desire a thinner steak than that purchased or cut, then pound this with a rolling pin or steak tenderizer before cooking.

This will also help to tenderize the meat, as it breaks down the fibres, but this procedure is not necessary with good-quality meat, unless you are making the portions larger in size and thinner.

It is possible to marinate steak before frying. Follow the suggestions given on page 34 for broiled steak.

4 Take a good-sized frying pan, hints on choosing these are given on the right.

5 Season the steak with a little salt and pepper, and add any herbs or other flavourings suggested or required.

6 Put butter, butter and oil, all oil, or other fat into the frying pan. If you are creating your own recipe, then use just enough fat or oil to give a thin coating to the base of the pan.

7 Heat this; the temperature of the oil should be high enough to start the meat cooking steadily as soon as it goes into the pan.

If the fat or oil is too cool, it will not seal in the juices of the meat. If, on the other hand, the frying fat or oil is too hot, it will harden and crisp the outside of the steak; this may appeal to some people, but it is not the way to fry steaks for most recipes.

8 Cook the meat for 1–2 minutes, then turn with a tongs or a palette knife; either of these are better than a fork, which punctures the steak and allows juices to run out.

9 If you are just frying the steak and will not be adding liquid, you should cook on the second side for the same time, then, if necessary, lower the heat to cook the steak to your personal taste.

As an approximate guide, allow a *total* cooking time as follows for a steak approximately 1 inch thick:

    Rare .... 6 minutes
    Medium .... 8 minutes
    Well done .... 10 minutes

(The cooking time will vary depending upon the thickness of the meat.) If you are frying a 'minute' steak, then allow a *total* of 1½–2 minutes cooking time for moderately rare meat.

10 If you are adding a sauce or other liquid to the meat in the pan, check that the time given to the initial frying is not too long. Remember it will take several minutes to heat the liquid in the pan and, during that time, the steak continues cooking. It is important that choice steaks are not over-cooked.

11 Lift the cooked steak onto the hot serving dish and garnish according to the suggestions given in the particular recipe.

12 Serve the fried steak as soon as possible after cooking.

Cuts of Beef for Frying

Fillet or tenderloin—the most tender steak, from which is served fillet itself; the fillet is also used for Chateaubriand, mignon or medallion steaks, and tournedos. It is not as flavourous as other cuts from short loin or hip-sirloin.

Some markets and restaurants sell *boneless loin steak* cut from the short loin (also called *shell steak, strip steak, New York cut, Kansas City cut, Omaha steak, contre-filet,* or *faux filet* and in England, *sirloin*) as an *entrecôte*. By definition, *entrecôte* literally means *between the ribs*. A proper *entrecôte* should be a boneless rib steak cut from between the ribs. Boneless steak cut from solid center eye meat of "first cut" ribs closer to the hind is often called *Spencer steak* in the United States.
Minute steak—generally from rump or rib (boneless), very thin.
Porterhouse—very large thick steak similar to T-bone, but with larger fillet.

Planked—often whole fillet or tenderloin, so called because cooked, or partially cooked, on plank.
Rump—firmer texture than many, but excellent flavour. Should be prime quality meat.
Sirloin—from centre of sirloin, excellent flavour, good lean and fat distribution. Some U.S. meat counters sell thick, boneless, *top sirloin steak* cut from the hip-sirloin section close to the rump, as *chateaubriand*.
T-bone—end of sirloin near bone, forming T shape.
Sirloin or *hip steak* - first 6–8 full cut steaks taken from the large hind end of the hip-sirloin section adjoining the rump and round. A good choice for feeding 4 or more people. Makes an excellent barbecue steak cut 2 inches thick. With bone and bottom section removed it is often called *top sirloin*. Somewhat leaner and often slightly chewier than (short loin cuts) *boneless loin, T-bone,* or *porterhouse* steaks, but with excellent flavour.
Delmonico or *club steak* – a boneless *loin* steak, ideally a first cut from the small end (toward the head) of the short loin closest to the rib. *Rib steaks, top sirloins* from the hip-sirloin, and cuts of rump are often represented as *Delmonico* or *club steaks*.

The full explanation of cuts, including British, Australian, and French, is on pages 14–16.

Frozen Steaks
Frozen steaks can often be cooked without defrosting, unless they are to be coated or marinated.

Fats to Use
Butter, top-quality frying oil, fat, drippings, a marinade.

Utensils for Frying
It is a wise expenditure of money to choose a really good-quality frying pan. Thin, poor-quality pans buckle with heat and give an unsatisfactory result.

Electric frying pans for use at table are available, and as these are thermostatically controlled, they enable you to keep a very rigid control on the heat.

Table cookers enable you to cook steak dishes in the dining room, rather than the kitchen. If buying a table cooker, check that it will produce sufficient heat for quick cooking.

To Fry Steak

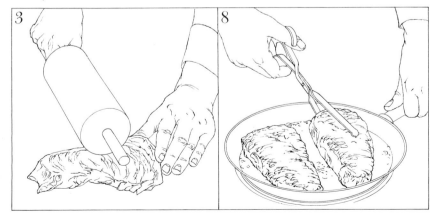

Grilling

Broiling is one of the best ways to cook good-quality steak. It has the advantage of being exceptionally quick, like frying, but the meat tends to be more easily digested, and the cooked dish can be lower in calories, since one can broil steak quite successfully with a very little butter, oil, or other fat or even without any, if the doctor says so.

Broiling is also a basic method of cooking steaks which form the foundation of many famous recipes, see pages 58–86.

The ingredients required for broiling are:
a) Choice beef that lends itself to this rapid method of cooking;
b) Optional. Fat or oil with which to brush the meat before and during the cooking process; this is sometimes replaced by a marinade in which the steaks are kept for a period *before* cooking; however, a well-marbled choice steak with good fat needs no added oil, fat, or an oily marinade;
c) Flavourings, which range, as in frying, from simple seasonings and herbs to elaborate sauces and garnishes.

To Grill Steak

1 Select the correct cut of meat as given on this page, cutting or tying it if required. The method of preparing tournedos is given on pages 22–23.

2 Optional. Prepare the marinade and place the steak in this, see suggestion on the right, or add seasoning and/or flavourings to the meat. If the meat has not been marinated, brush it with melted butter, oil, or other fat.

3 PREHEAT THE BROILER. This is an essential part of this method of cooking, whatever kind of broiler you are using. This means that, if you have a charcoal broiler, which is of course an excellent way of imparting extra flavour to the meat, the charcoal must be glowing red before the steak is subjected to the heat. Gas or electric broilers must be really hot, too. Information about infra-red broilers is on this page, and hints on cooking over a barbecue fire, which is a type of broiling, are on page 118.

4 Put the steak on the pan; place under the broiler and cook quickly for 1½–2 minutes to seal in the juices on one side. Turn with a tongs or two knives, rather than a fork.

5 Optional. Brush the meat on the second side with the melted butter, oil, or other fat, and cook rapidly for the same time.

If you like a rare steak, then this cooking time is nearly sufficient, and there is no need to adjust the heat of the broiler or the position of the pan under the broiler. If you like the meat moderately cooked, or well done, it may well be advisable to lower the heat slightly or move the pan with the steak slightly lower, so that the outside does not become too brown before the inside is adequately cooked.

As an approximate guide, allow a *total* cooking time as follows for a steak approximately 1 inch in thickness:

Rare	6 minutes
Medium	8 minutes
Well done	10 minutes

If you are broiling a 'minute' steak, then allow a *total* of 1½–2 minutes cooking time for moderately rare meat. The cooking time will vary depending upon the thickness of the meat.

6 During the process of cooking a medium or well-done steak, you may find it advisable to brush the meat with a little more melted butter, oil, or fat, to keep the meat moist. It is at this time that one often adds additional ingredients for extra flavour, as you will find in many of the recipes for cooking steaks on pages 58–86.

7 Lift the cooked steak on a hot serving dish and garnish or top with the sauce or savoury butter or other foods suggested in the recipe.

8 Serve as soon as possible after broiling to keep the freshly cooked flavour.

Cuts of Beef for Broiling
These are the same as those given on page 33, and so are the recommendations about defrosting steaks and about fats to use.

Marinade for Steaks
The purpose of a marinade is to tenderize the meat and to give a certain moist texture. too.

If you marinate steaks, there will be little need to use butter or oil in cooking; instead the steaks can be brushed with the marinade.

A simple marinade for 4 average steaks is made by blending 4 tablespoons oil with an equal amount of red or white wine, salt and pepper to taste, 1–2 crushed cloves of garlic (optional), and/or a small amount of chopped herbs. Leave the steaks in this mixture for at least an hour and turn once or twice.

Utensils for Broiling
When broiling steak, you will probably use the pan supplied with your particular stove.

The broiler may be eye-level or lower down on the stove or situated in the oven.

Nowadays, infra-red broilers are available. With this neat type of electric broiler, infra-red rays are used to cook steaks rapidly. There is no need to turn steaks, as the broiler cooks the steak on both sides at once.

To Grill Steak 6

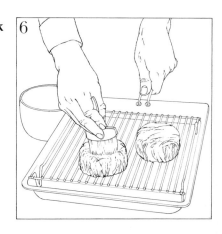

Roasting

As explained on page 29, the method of roasting meat is often described as baking, since it is cooked in the closed heat of the oven.

If you use a spit or rôtisserie, the timings will be similar to those given for the methods on page 36.

Choose the beef for roasting carefully. Do not try to roast meat that is better used for stewing or in a casserole, for you will only be disappointed. The reasons for selecting either the quicker or slower methods of roasting are given under the two headings on page 36.

The ingredients used for roasting beef are:

a) The piece of beef.
b) A little fat.
c) Any vegetables or flavourings added to give flavour to the meat.
d) Accompaniments such as those given in the chapter on Classic Roasts beginning on page 87.

To Roast Beef

1 Have your butcher give you the exact weight of the beef; many American supermarkets have computer-like scales that give precise weight in pounds and hundredths of a pound. The cuts are given on this page. As timing is very important for roasting beef, the total cooking time needs to be more carefully calculated than when using the slower heat of boiling, braising, and stewing. If you are roasting a large cut, loose or inaccurate weight could make a great deal of difference to the total cooking time and, thus, to the result.

2 Wipe the meat and put into the roasting pan; add a little fat.

Our attitude to fat in roasting has changed during recent years, and many people are now anxious to avoid using too much fat in cooking, due to weight and medical problems.

There is another good reason for not adding too much fat: this becomes very hot in cooking and tends to harden the outside of the meat.

If roasting sirloin or rib of beef which already has a reasonable amount of fat, you could manage without any extra. If the meat is very lean, use just about 1 ounce. If you intend roasting potatoes round the beef, then you will need at least 2 ounces, see page 86.

When cooking the meat in foil, a covered roasting pan, or polythene roaster bag, you can omit the fat, unless roasting fillet, when a little fat is essential; otherwise, very lean meat can be larded, as illustrated in pictures on page 43; this is ideal, since it gives an even distribution of fat throughout the joint. In the United States, a tenderloin (fillet) is often roasted without added fat to give a dark crusty exterior and a red or pink interior.

3 Select the heat of the oven and the timings for quick or slow roasting as detailed on page 36.

Basting Meat in Roasting

This means spooning any drippings from the meat collected in the pan over the meat several times during the cooking process. It is not necessary if you use foil, a covered roasting pan, or roaster bag, but it helps to keep lean beef moist and is important in spit roasting.

Cuts of Beef for Roasting

The following cuts are those selected for roasting.

Baron of Beef – a very large ceremonial cut used for banquets. It is the whole sirloin saddle of beef cut from the hip, including the backbone with both short loins from each side of the animal attached, extending forward to the second rib.

Bottom sirloin, triangle or *tri tip roast* – small (1–3 pound average) triangular piece trimmed from bottom of a (top) sirloin cut from the hip-sirloin section.

Fillet or *tenderloin* – the most tender cut, usually with far less flavour than other choice cuts from the hip-sirloin, short loin, or rib.

Loin or *short loin roast* – called *sirloin* in England, this section extends from the smaller (head) end of hip-sirloin to the rib. It contains *T-bone*, *porterhouse*, and *fillet*. American butchers remove the fillet and usually the bone, leaving *boneless loin* (whole shell strip) for roasting or cutting off steaks. British butchers sell this cut with bone and fillet attached, like a super porterhouse, as *sirloin roast*.

Prime rib or *rib roast* – excellent roast similiar to loin roast sans fillet. The first 2–3 ribs closer to the hind, with smaller eye, adjoining the short loin, are generally considered the most choice "first ribs" or "first cut". The round of rib eye meat from these ribs, trimmed and boneless, is also known as "first cut" or *Spencer*.

Rump roast – not as tender or juicy as some cuts, but can be excellent if meat is prime or aged. Lesser grades should be pot roasted.

Round or *top round* – lean and less tender cut similar to rump. *Eye of round* is most tender roasting section. Treat it like rump.

Shoulder clod or arm chuck (blade roast), and *brisket* – all are economy cuts less tender than choice cuts, but quite acceptable for roasting if meat is prime or well aged.

The full explanation of cuts, including British, Australian, and French, is given on pages 14–16.

Frozen Beef

Frozen beef can be cooked from the frozen state, without defrosting but follow the advice about roasting frozen beef, see page 36.

Fats to Use

Butter, drippings, fat.

Beef Drippings

In a number of recipes in this book, drippings are used as an alternative to fat. Really nothing can surpass the taste of perfect beef drippings. These come from the roasting pan after cooking; pour the residue from the pan and allow to set. There will be the hard drippings on top and underneath a layer of jelly, which should be treasured, for, if added to many beef dishes, such as stews, it can give so much additional flavour. In order to store the drippings, they must be clarified (cleaned). To do this, heat them with water to cover, cool again, and lift from the water. The residue will be at the bottom of the drippings and can be cut away, leaving the clarified, or cleaned, drippings.

Spit Roasting

The position of the spit varies with individual stoves; sometimes it is in the oven and sometimes under a broiler. The latter gives open roasting, whereas the former is similar in many ways to roasting in a pan, except that the entire roast becomes evenly brown and crisp on the outside, whereas in a pan it is only the exposed parts which do.

1 Dry the meat well to absorb any moisture and to reduce splashing.

2 Put on the spit, see the picture; if the beef is very lean, such as fillet, brush with fat or drippings. Very lean meat could also be larded, as shown in the pictures on page 43, or barded, which means tying fat bacon all over the roast, the drawback to this being that it gives too definite a flavour to the beef.

3 Preheat the broiler or oven, set the spit to turn and cook according to the temperatures and timings given below.

4 You can baste the meat several times with the melted fat or drippings during the cooking process.

Note: You must have a drip pan under the meat to catch the fat.

Utensils and Aids for Roasting

Most stoves are supplied with a roasting pan, and extra equipment is, therefore, not necessary. You may, however, care to consider the following utensils and aids to roasting, although the traditional methods in which the meat is uncovered, i.e., cooking in an open pan or on a spit, produce the most attractive-looking roast.

A covered roasting pan keeps your oven clean and the beef moist during cooking. It also enables you to use less fat. The meat does not crisp on the outside, unless you remove the lid before the end of the cooking period. Always add about 15 minutes to the total cooking time to compensate for the fact that the heat has to penetrate the lid of the covered roasting pan. When buying such a pan, select one that is really deep, so that the lid does not press down on the roast. If you do this, there is sufficient room for the fat to splash up inside the lid, drop back

onto the roast and, so, automatically baste the meat and give it a pleasant brown colour. The meat has a softer exterior if cooked in this manner, but the appearance and flavour are good. You cannot crisp potatoes when roasting them round the meat in a covered roasting pan.

Foil is extremely popular for wrapping meat and keeping it moist during cooking. Grease the foil if the beef is very lean. Always allow an extra 15 minutes cooking time, or use a slightly higher cooking temperature. To produce an appetizing brown outside to the meat, unwrap the foil for the last 15–30 minutes of the cooking time. The criticism of foil roasting is that the meat tends to have a less pleasing appearance and tastes slightly as though braised, rather than roasted.

Modern roaster bags are made of a special polythene which is heat-resistant up to a temperature of 400°F, which means that the initial heating in Quick Roasting should not be used. If the meat has a fair proportion of fat, simply shake a little flour inside the bag, insert the

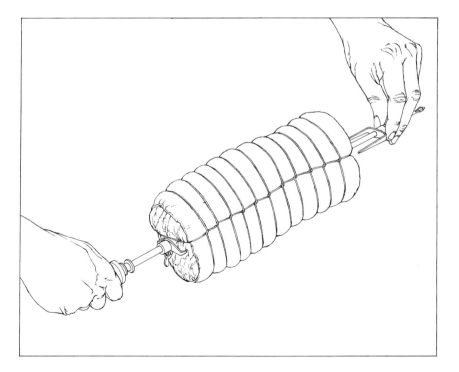

beef, and close the bag loosely with the special tag supplied. Follow the instructions for Slow Roasting. It is important to make slits in the bag to allow for air expansion. There is no need to allow extra cooking time with these bags. The beef browns quite well but does not become at all crisp on the outside.

Quick Roasting

This method is ideal for the prime cuts of beef, such as loin, rib, and fillet, or for beef that has not been frozen or chilled.

There was a belief that slower roasting produces less shrinkage, but this has been tested and found untrue; the quicker method is better.

1 Preheat the oven at hot, 425°F. Cook the beef on this setting for 15 minutes.

2 Reset the oven to moderately hot, which can vary between 375–400°F, and continue cooking.

3 Allow 15 minutes per pound plus 15 minutes to produce rare beef, and 20 minutes per pound plus 20

minutes for medium-cooked beef. It really is a sin to over-cook prime beef, but if you do want it very well cooked then allow nearly 25 minutes per pound plus 25 minutes.

If roasting a very large piece, over 6 lb, it is advisable to reduce the heat slightly after the first 1¾ hours to ensure that the beef is underdone.

Slow Roasting

Undoubtedly, this is better for the less choice cuts, such as rump, round or shoulder. I would also use this when cooking a defrosted roast or chilled meat, or when cooking from the frozen state, se below.

1 Set the oven to moderate, this is 350°F.

2 Allow 25 minutes per pound with 25 minutes over for rare beef. Allow 30 minutes per pound plus 30 minutes for medium-cooked, and up to 35 minutes per pound plus 35 minutes if you like it well cooked.

Note: Meat will become more crisp if put on a rack in the roasting tin.

Roasting Frozen Beef

There has always been much disagreement upon whether one has a better result if meat is allowed to defrost before roasting. The ease with which one can defrost in a microwave cooker makes this less troublesome, for if you own one, no longer is it necessary to remember to take the meat from the freezer a day before it is required.

My own personal opinion, with which many other people seem to agree, is that you cannot generalize on this matter. I always defrost lamb, mutton, and pork, and one must defrost poultry and game for safety reasons. However, I find beef is a meat which can be cooked from the frozen state, but the only foolproof way to do this is to use a meat thermometer, see below. If you have no meat thermometer, then follow the slow roasting method, but put the meat into a cold oven, set the heat to 350°F, bring up to this setting (allow about 15 minutes for this), then follow the timings, but add an extra 5 minutes per pound.

Using a Meat Thermometer

A thermometer which is inserted in the joint when raw and remains in place throughout the cooking process is the only completely accurate way to check that the meat is cooked exactly as *you* require it.

If cooking a roast from the frozen state, you cannot insert the thermometer until the meat begins to soften.

These readings on the thermometer indicate when the meat is:

rare . . . . . . .140°F; little change in colour
medium . . .150–160°F; pink interior
well done . .165–175°F; grey/brown colour

Pot Roasting

1 Wipe the beef well to absorb surface moisture and minimize splashing.

2 Select a really strong saucepan or flame-proof casserole with a well-fitting lid, or one which can be made secure, as illustrated on page 31.

3 Heat 2–4 tbsp fat or drippings in the saucepan.

4 Brown the meat on all sides; this can be floured as suggested in stage 1 under Pressure Cooking, see page 38; remove the meat from the pan.

5 Brown a selection of vegetables such as onions, carrots, and potatoes; these must be sufficiently large to retain a good shape during cooking, to keep the meat *above* the liquid.

6 If any fat remains after this stage, pour it away. Add enough water, stock, or wine to *almost* cover the vegetables, with salt, pepper, and herbs to taste.

7 Put the meat on the vegetables in the pan; cover.

8 You can pot roast in the oven or on top of the stove; follow the timings and temperatures given on page 30 under Braising, stages 11 and 12.

9 Lift the meat and vegetables from the saucepan onto a heated serving dish and use the liquid as a basis for a sauce or gravy.

Stewing

Stew and casserole recipes enable one to cook less expensive cuts of beef and still enjoy delicious, and often luxurious, dishes.

The various cuts of beef, often collectively known just as 'stewing beef', are given on this page. Although these are quite unsuitable for the faster methods of cooking, such as frying, grilling, or roasting, they have the great advantage of being rich in flavour and, therefore, are ideal for creating a good sauce or stock in the stew or casserole and an appetizing meat dish at the same time.

It is not easy to list the ingredients needed for stews or casseroles, since they vary so much, but the following are the most usual:
a) The selected cuts of beef; although we tend to use the cuts given on this page, other pieces, such as rib, can be used for this purpose.
b) Thickening for the stew; often this is added as an initial coating round the beef or at the end of the cooking period as a beurre manie (see below).
c) Fat in which to brown the beef and vegetables before adding liquid and other ingredients, see stage 3.
d) Liquid, which can vary from water to stock or wine. The importance of good beef stock cannot be sufficiently stressed.
To make beef stock: Cover beef bones with water, add salt, pepper, herbs, and vegetables to flavour (however, stock will not keep as well when vegetables are added). Simmer gently for several hours, strain and cool the liquid. Store carefully in the refrigerator or freezer.
e) Various flavourings.

How to Prepare a Stew

1 Prepare and cut all the ingredients to the desired size.

2 *Method A* – thickening at the beginning of the cooking period:
Coat the meat with flour blended with salt and pepper (often called 'seasoned flour'). Allow scant 3 tbsp

to each 2 ½ cups (2oz) liquid. If using cornstarch, allow half the amount.

3 Fry the meat in fat or drippings, together with the onions, or other vegetables. Use approximately ¼ cup (2oz) fat for each 1½ lb meat.

4 Blend in the liquid, stir until slightly thickened; do not have the stew too thick at this stage, since the liquid is also thickened by slow, steady evaporation.

5 Add the other ingredients to make the mixture interesting: herbs, spices, and a selection of vegetables.

6 Simmer gently until tender, this takes approximately 2½ hours with most cuts of stewing beef.

Method B – thickening at the end of the cooking period:

1 Simply put the meat, vegetables, and any other ingredients, see stage 5, into the saucepan, with salt and pepper to taste, and simmer until tender, timing as stage 6.

2 When the meat is tender, thicken the liquid with a **beurre manie**. Blend equal quantities, 4 tbsp (¼ cup) each, of butter and flour. Drop a small amount, the size of a small walnut, into the simmering liquid of the stew, whisk vigorously until incorporated into the mixture. Continue like this until the desired thickness is achieved.

Cuts of Beef for Stews and Casseroles
Prime cuts:
As listed under braising and roasting.
Cheaper stewing cuts: brisket – rarely used; rump; round including sirloin tip; clod; chuck; flank; short ribs; plate, including flanken and skirt – this is lean steak from inside the animal, e.g. the diaphragm; neck; shin; tongue; heart; oxtail.

The full explanation of cuts, in-

cluding British, Australian, and French, is given on pages 14–16

Frozen Beef
Frozen beef is generally better defrosted before being used.

Liquids to Choose
Beer, cider, water, wine, stock.

How to Prepare a Casserole
The method of preparing a casserole dish is similar to that of preparing a stew (both method A and B).

There is, however, one difference. Liquid tends to evaporate more in a saucepan over the heat on a burner than in a *well-covered* casserole in the oven, so when adapting a stew recipe to be cooked in a casserole, reduce the liquid by one-third.

Conversely, you would increase it if you decide to cook a casserole dish in a saucepan instead.

The cooking time for most beef casseroles is similar to stage 6, i.e., 2½ hours in a slow to very moderate oven, 300–325°F.

Utensils to Use
There is an almost bewildering variety of saucepans and casseroles on the market today. Some of the types mentioned under Braising, page 31, are used for stews and casseroles too.

If investing in new equipment, consider the advantages of flame-proof ware. This differs from oven-proof and ordinary cooking equipment in that it can be used both on the burners and in the oven, whereas oven-proof casseroles, useful as they may be, are limited to oven use, while ordinary saucepans often have handles and knobs which are harmed by exposure to oven heat.

A flame-proof casserole can, therefore, be used for the whole cooking process, i.e., as a saucepan when browning the meat and vegetables on a burner, and as a casserole when cooking in the oven. They are obtainable in ceramic, enamel, and cast iron, and generally look most attractive.

It is advisable to use heavy pans for stews, since the food tends to burn in a light utensil. Follow the advice on page 31 if the lid is not a good fit, otherwise, too much liquid will evaporate.

Using a Pressure Cooker

It is important to appreciate just why a pressure cooker tenderizes food so quickly. Until pressure is built up, you have an ordinary saucepan. When the pressure weight is placed in position, the steam, which normally escapes into the atmosphere, is controlled and only allowed to escape under pressure. This produces a boiling point above the normal 212°F, ranging from approximately 228°F–252°F, depending upon the weight used.

To Roast Meat by Pressure

1 Choose a suitable cut, see page 35; wipe the meat to absorb surface moisture and minimize splashing in the cooker. Dust very lightly with flour blended with salt and pepper to give a firmer outside to the meat. Never exceed the maximum weight of meat for your particular cooker.

2 Heat 2–4 tbsp fat in the base of the cooker, the quantity depending on the amount of fat already on the beef.

3 Brown the meat on all sides, remove from the heat, pour out any surplus fat.

4 Put the cooking rack into the cooker, add 2½ cups (20 oz) water, wine, or stock. Replace the beef in the cooker, standing on the rack.

5 Fix the lid, bring to pressure – if using 15lb pressure you will cook as follows:

loin, rib,   8–10 minutes
or fillet . . . . .per pound
cheaper cuts, e.g.,   11–15 minutes
round . . . . .per pound

These times are average; the times for different makes of cookers may vary slightly according to the pressure weight, and you may vary them yourself, depending on whether you like the beef rare, medium, or well done. Every minute in a pressure cooker is important.

6 Reduce pressure rapidly under cold water, or as advised by the manufacturer.

7 If you want to cook vegetables with the meat, calculate their pressure-cooking time, reduce the pressure at the appropriate time, add the vegetables, bring to pressure once more, and complete the cooking.

8 The liquid in the pressure cooker makes a delicious gravy or sauce.

To Braise Meat by Pressure

Brown the meat, as explained in stage 3, To Roast Meat by Pressure, then follow the actual braising recipe. The pressure-cooking technique is as for To Roast Meat by Pressure. There is one very important point: you must use sufficient liquid in the cooker, so you may have to increase the quantity given in the recipe. Use a minimum of 1 cup where the dish is cooked for 15 minutes. The timing for diced braised beef is as for a stew, see stage 4 on this page. Use up to 2 cups when braising roasts or large cuts and follow the timing given in stage 5, To Roast Meat by Pressure, on this page.

To Boil Meat by Pressure

1 Follow the directions for soaking corned (salted) beef given on page 32, or check instructions from cooker manufacturer or butcher. Prepackaged corned beef sealed in plastic wrap usually carries full instructions on the package.

2 Put the beef into the pressure cooker with water or other liquid to cover, and add any ingredients suggested in the recipes, which begin on page 50.

3 Fix the lid, bring to pressure. If using 15 lb pressure, allow:

corned beef . . 12–15 minutes* per pound

*see stage 5 in To Roast Meat by Pressure. Other cuts need similar timing, but check the instructions given by the cooker manufacturer; cut up portions of beef require a similar timing to stage 4 in Stews, see below.

4 Reduce the pressure under cold water or as recommended.

Stews and Casseroles by Pressure

The basic information on page 37 is just as important when using a pressure cooker as when cooking in a casserole or saucepan. A variety of beef stews and casseroles that can be adapted to pressure cooking are given on pages 96–110.

The method of using pressure cooking for a stew is as follows:

1 Prepare the ingredients.

2 If the recipe begins by frying the food, heat the fat in the base of the cooker and fry the ingredients as instructed in the recipe. It is very important that the meat is not coated with flour, since this will cause burning on the base of the cooker; one thickens at the end of the cooking period. The light dusting of flour used in To Roast Meat by Pressure is sufficient here.

3 Add the liquid and flavourings, as per the recipe, but use only half the normal amount of liquid, as the cooking period is much shorter than usual. The smaller amount of liquid means that you should be sparing with any salt and pepper added.

4 Fix the lid, bring up to the recommended pressure. If using 15 lb pressure, the time for an average beef stew would be 12–14 minutes at sea level (2–3 minutes longer if the meat is rolled), as for Beef Olives, page 106.

5 Reduce the pressure under cold water, remove the lid.

6 Thicken the liquid, with a beurre manie, explained on page 37, and serve.

Using a Microwave Oven

As users of these appliances know, the method of cooking is different from conventional means. Energy is produced by high-frequency radio waves, circulated throughout the oven. As they come into contact with food, they are converted into heat energy, which is absorbed by the food and results in faster cooking. Not all food is suitable for microwave cooking, but meat is.

Microwave ovens are made with different wattage and workload capacities so timings vary; always check with the manufacturer's recommendations. An average time for roasting beef is:

loin, rib, fillet . . . . .6–8 minutes
per pound
less tender cuts . . . .8–10 minutes
per pound

The only satisfactory way to cook less tender cuts is at low power or simmer setting for a longer period.

You will find that the cooked meat is tender, may have less shrinkage than when cooked by the usual method, but looks pale. It is advisable to brown the meat under the broiler after cooking.

Steaks are cooked within 2–4 minutes but may need browning under the broiler before putting into the microwave oven; you may well feel they are better broiled.

Casseroles and stews take approximately half the time than when cooked by conventional means. Brown the meat in a saucepan before transferring to a dish in the microwave oven.

Always defrost frozen meat before cooking in a microwave oven. However, many ovens have settings for defrosting food.

BRAISING

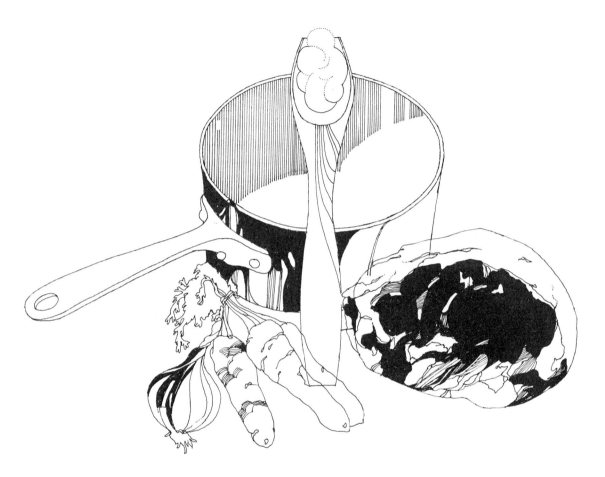

The method of cooking known as 'braising' comes from the French *braise,* which means 'live coals or embers'. If you look at the picture of the true braising pan on page 31, you will see that it has an absolutely flat top; other types have concave lids. The idea was to cover the lid with glowing charcoal, so that the braising pan, or *daubière,* was heated from above as well as from below. Braising today more closely resembles the classic French method of cooking, if the container is placed in the oven, rather than on top of the stove.

Personally, I find braised dishes, when prepared properly, absolutely delicious. One of my favourite culinary experts, Monsieur Henri Pellaprat, who taught at the Cordon Bleu in Paris and spent fifty-seven years of his life in the catering profession before writing his *Great Book of the French Cuisine,* says with emphasis:

> Braising is one of the most frequently used methods of cooking but is only rarely done properly. All too often one is offered a piece of brown meat with all the goodness boiled out of it, instead of a piece of braised meat.

How very true. Braising is not stewing, although like stewing, it can produce a luxurious meal from relatively inexpensive meat. It is a mode of cooking which gives moist and tender beef, which, at the same time, has much of the flavour of roasting.

Many readers will have read Michel Guérard's book, *Cuisine Minceur,* which represents what almost amounts to a revolution in *haute cuisine.* Although his recipes are based on the best traditions of classic French cooking, Guérard takes into account the fact that many people today are anxious to avoid an excess of fat or carbohydrates and, therefore, approves of braising, with its use of natural ingredients to make a sauce. However, he suggests that any excess fat be removed before serving the dish. I cannot but agree with Guérard when he describes the results obtained by this method of cooking as *par excellence.* How true this is.

Paradeisbraten

Austrian Braised Beef and Tomatoes
Serves 6–8
Cooking Time: 1½ hours

INGREDIENTS

boneless rib of beef – weight when boned: 3 lb
salt and pepper: to taste
paprika: 1 teaspoon
butter: ¼ cup (½ stick)
onions: 2 small
tomatoes: 1½ lb or 3–4 medium
red wine: ¼ cup, generous (2½ oz)
lemon: 1
bouquet garni:
parsley: sprig
lemon thyme: sprig

1 Tie the meat firmly.

2 Dry the meat well, then sprinkle with salt, pepper, and paprika.

3 Heat the butter in the bottom of a heavy saucepan, casserole, Dutch oven, or braising pan and brown the meat on either side until golden coloured.

4 Lift out of the pan.

5 Peel and slice the onions thinly. Skin the tomatoes and halve them.

6 Put the onions in the pan and cook gently for a few minutes until just golden; add the tomatoes and wine.

7 Cut one or two strips of peel from the lemon; use just the top yellow zest and none of the bitter white pith from the fruit.

8 Add the peel to the ingredients in the pan, along with 1 tbsp lemon juice and a little salt and pepper to taste, together with the bouquet garni.

9 Place the browned beef on top of the tomato mixture.

10 Cover the pan; read the hints about making lids fit well on page 31.

11 Put the saucepan over low heat, and allow the mixture to simmer steadily for 1¼ hours or until the beef is tender.

12 Remove the beef from the pan onto a hot serving dish.

13 Sieve or liquidize the tomato mixture in a blender to a smooth purée. If too thick, add a little extra wine or stock to give a coating consistency.

To serve: Carve the meat, and serve with the wine and tomato purée as a sauce.

To freeze: This dish is better freshly cooked.

To vary:
(i) Use eye of round, sirloin tip, or rump instead of the boned rib.
(ii) *Braised Venison with Tomatoes:* The method above is an excellent way to cook venison.

Tokány

Hungarian Braised Beef with Paprika and Sour Cream
Serves 6–8
Cooking Time: 2 hours 25 minutes

INGREDIENTS

top round, thick cut: 3 lb
celery: 4 stalks
onions: 2 medium
carrots: 2 medium
bacon: 2 strips
lemon juice: 1 tbsp
white wine vinegar: 1 tbsp
beef stock: 1 cup (8 oz)
salt and pepper: to taste
butter: 2 tbsp (¼ stick)
bay leaves: 2
paprika: 3 teaspoons
sour cream: 1 cup

1 Have your butcher tie the beef neatly, so that it keeps a good shape throughout cooking. Put it into a dish with a marinade of the lemon juice, vinegar, stock, salt, and pepper. Keep the dish in a refrigerator for 2–6 hours.

2 Lift the meat from the marinade, allow to drain well, then dry it on absorbent paper, so that it will brown more readily.

3 Cut the vegetables into neat pieces, dice the bacon, and line the bottom of the casserole with these. Add enough marinade to just cover.

4 Put the meat into the casserole. Make sure that it is above the vegetables and bacon.

5 Melt the butter and brush over the meat. Do not cover the casserole at this stage.

6 Cook the meat for 20–25 minutes in the centre of a hot oven, 425°F, until it becomes golden brown.

7 Add the bay leaves, then cover the casserole; lower the heat to 300°F, and continue cooking for 2 hours, or until tender enough to slice without crumbling.

8 Lift the meat from the casserole onto a serving dish.

9 Rub all the vegetables with the bacon and liquid through a sieve or liquidize them in a blender or food processor, to a smooth purée; it is better to remove the bay leaves, as they tend to give too strong a taste to the purée.

10 Pour the vegetable and bacon mixture into a saucepan.

11 Blend the paprika with the sour cream, add to the purée in the saucepan, stir over a low heat until just at boiling point.

To serve: Carve the meat and coat with the sauce.

To freeze: The meat and vegetables freeze well, but the sour cream mixture should be added when reheating this dish.

Bœuf à la Mode

French Braised Beef
Serves 6–8
Cooking Time: 2½ hours

This famous French dish is, in many ways, similar to the Belgian braised-beef dish on page 45, which is not surprising, as the countries adjoin and some of their recipes 'overlap'.

The differences are, however, important, since they give you a splendid dish with a subtle change of flavour. There are many ways of preparing this dish; the following is one of the simplest.

1 Make slits in the beef as in picture 1 on page 43.

2 Cut half the fatty pork into narrow strips and insert into the beef, see picture 3, also on page 43.

3 Peel and thinly slice the onion, garlic, and carrot; put into a suitable container for a marinade; add the Burgundy or wine selected, and salt and pepper to taste.

4 Put in the prepared beef and leave for 24 hours in the refrigerator or for 5–6 hours at room temperature; turn once or twice.

5 Remove the meat from the marinade, allow it to drain well, then pat dry on absorbent paper.

6 Heat the butter or fat in a large heavy sauté pan or skillet and put in the beef. Cook with sufficient heat to brown well on both sides. Add the brandy (if using this); heat for 20–30 seconds, then ignite and flame till the spirits are burned out. Page 71 explains the process of igniting meat dishes.

7 Lift the meat out of the sauté pan into a casserole.

8 Peel the small onions and carrots but leave these whole; split the calf's

INGREDIENTS

top round or eye of round: 3 lb
fatty pork (fresh side pork): ½ lb
for the marinade:
onion: 1 medium
garlic clove: 1
carrot: 1 medium
red Burgundy: 1¼ cups (10 oz)
salt and pepper: to taste

butter or fat: 1 oz (¼ stick) or 2 tbsp
brandy (optional): 2 tbsp
small pickling onions: 1 lb
young baby carrots: 12 oz
calf's foot split lengthwise: 1
bouquet garni:
parsley: 2 sprigs
thyme: 2 sprigs
bay leaf: 1

foot lengthwise, if the butcher has not done this; dice the remaining fat pork.

9 Heat the pork in the sauté pan for 2–3 minutes until there is sufficient melted fat in the pan to give a thin film; add the onions and carrots and turn in the fat until golden coloured.

10 Remove the vegetables and pork from the pan; arrange the pork only round the meat; add the calf's foot and the bouquet garni with a little salt and pepper to taste.

11 Strain the marinade liquid into the pan; stir well to absorb any meat juices, then pour round the meat in the casserole.

12 Cover the dish with a lid and cook for 1 hour in the centre of a slow oven (200°F).

13 Add the small onions and carrots to the casserole and continue cooking for another 1¼ hours, or until tender.

To serve: Lift the beef and vegetables onto a hot serving dish; strain the liquid into a sauce boat; dice the meat from the cow heel and arrange it round the beef.

To freeze: This loses some flavour in freezing.

To vary:
The meat is delicious if served cold.
(i) Use white wine instead of red.
(ii) To give more sauce, blend some beef stock with the wine left from cooking the beef in the casserole. This could be thickened with a beurre manie, see page 37.

Irish Braised Beef in Stout

Serves 4–6
Cooking Time: 2½ hours

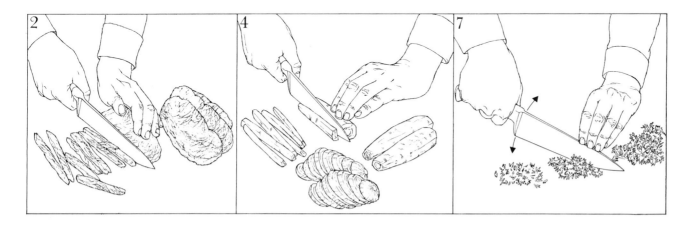

1 Put the prunes into a basin to soak overnight; add the stout and water.

2 Place the meat on a cutting board, cut into thin diagonal strips.

3 Blend the salt, pepper, and mustard with the flour; turn the strips of meat in this.

4 Peel the onions; cut into fairly thick slices; peel the carrots and cut into long narrow strips. Keep them separated.

5 Heat the fat in a skillet and fry the onions until golden. Lift them into a casserole; do not add fat from skillet; add the carrots, then the prunes and liquid in which they have been soaking.

6 Fry the meat in the skillet until golden brown on both sides. Put it on top of the prune and vegetable layer, making sure that it is above the vegetables.

7 Chop the parsley finely. The picture shows the easiest way to do this.

INGREDIENTS

prunes: ¾ cup
stout: 1 cup (8 oz)
water: ½ cup (4 oz)
stewing beef
choose cuts given on page 31: 2 lb
salt and pepper: to taste
dry mustard: pinch
flour: 2 tbsp
onions: 2 large
carrots: 4–5 medium (12 oz)
fat: ¼ cup
parsley: few sprigs

8 Sprinkle half the parsley over the beef.

9 Cover the casserole and cook in the centre of a very moderate oven, 325°F, for 2¼ hours or until tender, but firm enough to slice.

To serve: Arrange the meat in a border of vegetables and prunes. Top with the rest of the parsley. Serve any liquid separately.

To freeze: This dish freezes well. Use within 3 months.

Braised Steak and Vegetables
This traditional British method of braising beef is somewhat similar to the Irish one on the left, but the prunes are omitted and a more interesting selection of vegetables is used instead.

1 Prepare the meat as in stage 2 on the left. Add a little salt, pepper, and mustard to season, but omit the flour.

2 Prepare and slice 2 medium onions, 2 carrots, 1 small turnip, and 2–3 stalks celery; and chop 2–3 slices of fairly fat bacon.

3 Heat the fat in a pan and brown the meat. Remove the meat to a plate and fry the bacon and vegetables together in any fat left in the pan.

4 Add a little pepper and very little salt to the vegetable mixture.

5 Add 1–2 bay leaves and a sprinkling of parsley, together with ½ cup liquid; this can be stock, water, white or red wine, or cider.

6 Place the meat on top of the mirepoix. Cover the pan tightly and simmer over low heat for approximately 2 hours or till tender but firm enough to slice. Check carefully that the liquid does not evaporate too much during cooking. If preferred, transfer the vegetable mirepoix to a casserole, top with the beef, cover the casserole, and cook as the Irish dish, stage 9.

To serve: Sieve, or liquidize the vegetable and bacon mixture in a blender or food processor, and serve as a sauce over the meat.

To freeze: This dish freezes well; use within 3 months.

Rinderschmorbraten

German Spiced Beef
Serves 4–6
Cooking Time: 1½ hours

1 Dry the beef thoroughly, then make several slits in it.

2 Cut the fatty bacon or saltpork into very thin narrow strips.

3 Put the strips into a large larding needle, thread through the beef, giving an even distribution of fat.

4 Blend the salt, pepper, and cinnamon.

5 Sprinkle over the beef.

6 Heat the drippings in a large heavy pan and brown the beef on both sides, then remove from the pan.

7 Peel the onions or shallots, keep whole, and brown these in any drippings left in the pan.

8 Replace the beef, add the capers and the beer or water.

9 Put on the lid, turn the heat very low, and allow the beef to cook very gently for 1¼ hours, or until tender.

10 It is wise to check once or twice to make sure that there is sufficient liquid in the pan.

To serve: Carve the meat, spoon the onions and capers over the slices, and serve the unthickened liquid as a sauce.

To freeze: Do not freeze.

To vary:
Use a piece of veal instead of the beef, and substitute white wine for the beer or water. When the meat is removed from the pan with the onions and capers, stir 2–3 tbsp heavy whipping cream into the liquid, heat gently, and serve as a sauce.

INGREDIENTS

top round: 2 lb
fatty bacon or saltpork: 2 oz
salt and pepper: to taste
ground cinnamon: 1 teaspoon
drippings: 2 tbsp
small onions or shallots: 12
capers: 2 teaspoons
beer or water: ½ cup (8 oz)

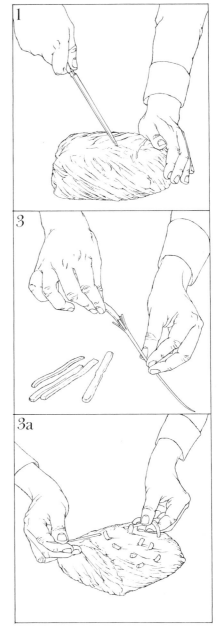

Esterhazy Rostélyos

Braised Beef Esterhazy
Serves 4–6
Cooking Time: 1 hour

INGREDIENTS

top round steak, thick cut: 2 lb
salt and pepper: to taste
paprika: 1 teaspoon
tomatoes: 3
onions: 2 medium
carrots: 1–2 medium
button mushrooms: ¼ cup fresh or 4 oz can
fat: 6 tbsp
stock or water (see method): 3–4 tbsp

1 Cut the round steak into 4 thick slices, sprinkle with a little salt and pepper and the paprika.

2 Skin the tomatoes and quarter them; then peel and slice the onions, carrot(s), and mushrooms.

3 Heat the fat in a heavy frying pan or saucepan, and fry the meat for 2–3 minutes on either side, then remove from the pan.

4 Fry the sliced onions and carrot(s) for several minutes, then add the tomatoes with the stock or water; add a very little salt and pepper.

5 Place the meat on top of the vegetables, cover the pan; read the hints about making lids fit well, page 31.

6 Cook over a steady low to medium heat for 30 minutes; check once or twice that the pan is in no danger of boiling dry, add stock or water if necessary; add the mushrooms and continue cooking for a further 20 minutes or until tender.

To serve: Lift the slices of meat onto a hot dish, and spoon the vegetable mixture round them.

To freeze: This dish is better freshly cooked.

To vary:
Fillets of veal are excellent cooked in this manner and so are *lean* lamb chops or slices of lamb taken from the leg.

Luxury Esterhazy Rostélyos
This recipe gives a family version of the famous Hungarian dish.

1 Prepare the beef as in the recipe; fry in the hot fat, then remove from the pan.

2 Prepare the vegetables, but add 2–3 diced strips of bacon, and fry these with the onions and carrots.

3 Continue as in the basic recipe.

4 When the meat is cooked, remove from the pan onto a hot dish; sieve or liquidize the vegetables in a blender or food processor, to make a smooth purée.

5 Return the purée to the pan, add ½ cup (4 oz) heavy whipping cream and a very little white wine vinegar or lemon juice to taste.

6 Heat gently, *without boiling*, then spoon over the meat.

To serve: Garnish with fans of small pickled cucumbers or gherkins, and slices of lemon. Serve in a border of diced root vegetables.

Bœuf Braisé

Belgian Braised Beef
Serves 6–8
Cooking Time: 2¼ hours

1 Put the beef into a dish, sprinkle with a very little salt and pepper; halve the calf's foot, unless the butcher has done this for you, add to the beef with the vinegar and beer.

2 Leave the meats to marinate for 24 hours in the refrigerator, turning once or twice.

3 Lift the beef and cow heel from the liquid, drain well, and dry on absorbent paper; save all the marinade.

4 Put the beef into a casserole, but do not cover the dish, and cook in the centre of a hot oven, 425°F, for 15 minutes until the fat begins to flow.

5 Meanwhile, peel the onions and carrots, and chop the celery; place the vegetables and calf's foot round the beef, turn in any fat in the pan and continue cooking for a further 10 minutes to enable the vegetables to become slightly browned. If, by chance, there is insufficient fat from the meat, you will need to add a small amount to keep the vegetables moist as they begin to brown.

6 Pour just enough liquid from the marinade to half cover the vegetables; save the remainder of the liquid for making the sauce; add a little more salt and pepper and the bouquet garni.

7 Cover the casserole, lower the heat to 300°F. Continue cooking for a further 1¾ hours, but add the whole mushrooms and the halved or quartered heads of white chicory for the last 15 minutes. When these are added, spoon some of the liquid from the casserole over them to keep them moist.

INGREDIENTS

top round, thick cut, or eye of round: 3 lb
salt and pepper: to taste
calf's foot split lengthwise: 1
onions: 6–8 medium
carrots: 6–8 medium
celery: 1–2 stalks
for the marinade:
red wine vinegar *or* brown malt vinegar: ¼ cup plus 1 tbs (2½ oz)
beer: 2 cups (16 oz)
bouquet garni:
parsley: sprig
bay leaves: 2
mace: 1 blade
or ground mace: pinch
button mushrooms: ½ cup fresh or 4 oz can
heads of chicory: 2–4
for the sauce:
butter or drippings: 1½ oz
flour: 3 tbsp

8 Use a perforated spoon or spatula turner to lift the well-drained beef, calf's foot, and vegetables onto a hot dish.

9 Blend the butter or drippings and flour together to make a beurre manie, this is explained on page 37.

10 Strain the liquid from the casserole, together with the remaining liquid from the marinade, into a saucepan.

11 Gradually, add the beurre manie and whisk until you have a smooth and thickened sauce.

To serve: Carve the beef; dice the meat from the calf's foot and arrange on a serving dish with the vegetables. Coat the meat with the sauce.

To freeze: This loses some flavour in freezing.

To vary:
The meat is delicious served cold.
(If you would rather have this as a classic casserole dish rather than a braised-beef dish, add all the liquid at stage 6.)

Braciola di Manzo Farcita

Beef Braciola
Serves 6–8
Cooking Time: 1¾ hours

INGREDIENTS

rib of beef with bone: 3 lb
for the stuffing:
veal or lean pork: ½ lb
cooked ham: 2 oz
salami: 2 oz
Parmesan cheese, grated: ¼ cup
butter, melted: 2 tbsp
soft breadcrumbs: ¼ cup
egg: 1
a little milk: as required
salt and pepper: to taste

butter or fat: ¼ cup (½ stick) or 4 tbsp
onion: 1 medium
carrot: 1 medium
tomatoes: 4 medium or about 1 lb
garlic clove: 1
white wine: 1 cup (8 oz)
dried oregano: pinch

Have your butcher cut, flatten, and grind meats to requirements given in steps 1–4, or carry out directions in steps 1–4.

1 Lay the beef on a cutting board and cut away the bone.

2 Cut the piece of meat horizontally through the middle to give two thinner portions.

3 Take a heavy rolling pin and gently but firmly roll the meat until very thin; be careful not to break it.

4 Put the veal or pork, and the ham and salami through a grinder or food processor.

5 To the ground meat add the cheese, melted butter, breadcrumbs, egg, just enough milk to bind, and salt and pepper to taste.

6 Spread this mixture over the two pieces of meat.

7 Roll carefully.

8 Tie securely with string into neat rolls.

9 Heat the butter or fat in a heavy sauté pan or saucepan, put in the meat rolls, and cook for several minutes until brown.

10 Remove them from the pan and turn off the heat.

11 Peel and chop the onion and carrot. Skin the tomatoes by making incisions in the skins (11a), then plunging them into boiling water for a few seconds (11b) and then into cold water; this makes the skin easy to peel off (11c).

12 Crush the clove of garlic. Put it on a little salt on the chopping board and press the tip of a firm-bladed knife against it.

13 Heat the pan again and fry the onion, garlic, and carrot for a few minutes in any fat left in the pan, then add the wine and the oregano.

14 Place the meat rolls on top of the mixture.

15 Cover the pan very tightly.

16 Cook over a very low heat for 1 hour.

17 Add the tomatoes to the pan, with a little salt and pepper to taste; turn the beef rolls with two spoons.

18 Continue cooking for another 35 minutes.

To serve: Lift the meat rolls onto a serving dish, remove the string, and arrange the tomatoes round them. Strain the liquid into a sauceboat. Serve with gnocchi, see below.

To freeze: This dish freezes well. Use within 2 months.

To vary:
Braciola alla Napoletana
Prepare the meat as the basic recipe. Omit the ham, salami, and cheese from the stuffing and substitute 3 oz seedless raisins, 3 oz chopped almonds, and 2–3 tbsp chopped parsley.

To make Gnocchi

1 Put 3 cups (24 oz) milk into a saucepan, with a good pinch of salt and pepper.

2 Bring the milk to the boil, then pour in ¾ cup semolina *steadily*.

3 Add ¼ cup (½ stick) butter to the mixture; cook gently and slowly, stirring most of the time, until a thick consistency is reached; this takes 15–20 minutes.

4 Remove from the heat, beat in ¼ cup grated Parmesan cheese and an egg yolk.

5 Spread the semolina over a damp large dish and leave in a cool place for 1–2 hours until firm.

6 Turn onto a lightly floured board and cut into small rounds.

7 Arrange the rounds in a shallow, greased baking dish, top with a little grated cheese and melted butter, and cook for 15 minutes in a moderately hot oven, 400°F.

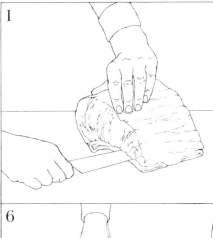

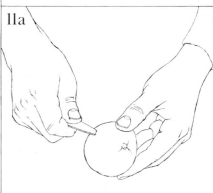

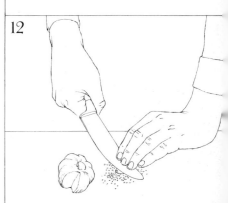

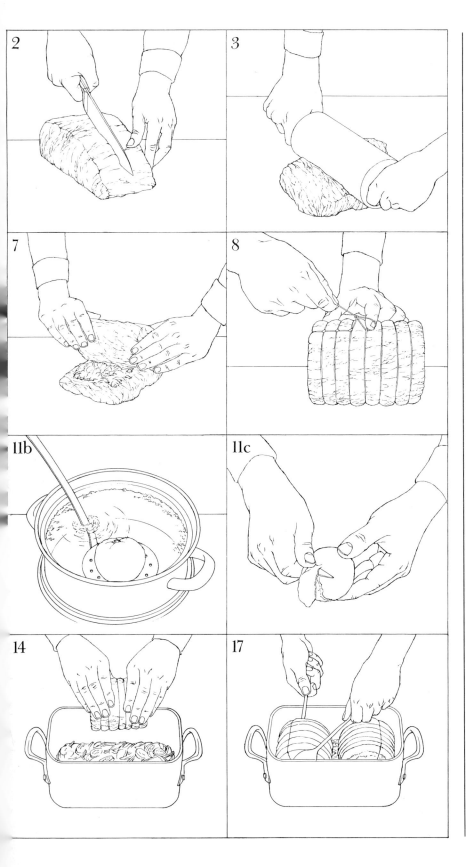

Stifatho

Greek Braised Beef in Tomato Sauce
Serves 4–6
Cooking Time: 2½ hours

INGREDIENTS

small onions (shallots could be used): 1½ lb
garlic cloves: 2–3
tomatoes: 1 lb or 3–4 medium
water: ½ cup
stewing beef, choose cuts given on page 31: 2 lb
olive oil: 3 tbsp
bay leaves: 2
rosemary: small sprig
salt and pepper: to taste
red wine vinegar: 3 tbsp

1 Peel the onions or shallots, and leave whole.

2 Skin the garlic cloves and crush.

3 Skin the tomatoes.

4 Rub the tomatoes through a sieve to give a smooth purée; a blender could be used, but this does not get rid of all the pips.

5 Dilute the tomato purée with the water.

6 Cut the steak into neat cubes.

7 Heat the oil in a large heavy saucepan or frying pan with a lid.

8 Fry the onions or shallots and the crushed garlic until golden coloured; do not allow these to become too dark in colour.

9 Remove from the pan, then fry the meat for a few minutes.

10 Add the tomato liquid, onions, bay leaves, rosemary, and vinegar, with salt and pepper to taste.

11 Cover the pan tightly for the first hour of the cooking time. For suggestions on making the lid fit for this method of cooking consult page 31, but see the next stage.

12 Cook over a very low heat for 2 hours. Although this is not quite the usual method of braising, the principle does apply, for the meat is not covered in liquid when it is served. In this particular recipe, the liquid should be allowed to evaporate towards the end of the cooking time, leaving just tomato-coated onions and meat. This may well mean you need to remove the lid for the last 20 minutes.

To serve: There is such a generous amount of onions in this dish that another vegetable is not necessary. Serve with a crisp green salad.

To freeze: This dish is better freshly cooked.

To vary:
Use veal instead of beef.

47

Cadera de Toro

Braised Beef in Wine and Vinegar Sauce
Serves 6–8
Cooking Time: 1¾ hours

INGREDIENTS

for the marinade:
onions: 2 large
garlic cloves: 2
red wine: 1 cup (8 oz)
red wine vinegar: 5 tbsp
bay leaf: 1
salt and pepper: to taste

eye of round or thick round steak: 3 lb
olive oil: 2 tbsp
sweet green peppers: 2
sweet red peppers: 2
tomatoes: 8 medium
to garnish:
olives, black and green: to taste

1 First prepare the marinade: peel the onions and garlic; chop the onions coarsely.

2 Put into a deep dish and add the wine, vinegar, bay leaf, and a little salt and pepper.

3 Place the beef in this mixture, and leave for 24 hours in the refrigerator. Turn the meat several times.

4 Lift the beef from the marinade, drain well, and pat dry with absorbent paper; keep all the marinade.

5 Heat the oil in a large heavy saucepan, put in the meat, brown carefully, and turn once or twice.

6 Remove the meat from the pan and pour away any surplus oil.

7 Cut the peppers into quarters, discard the cores and seeds.

8 Skin the tomatoes as described on page 46, leave whole; place into the pan with the peppers and the whole marinade.

9 Put the meat on top of these ingredients; sprinkle with a very little salt and pepper.

10 Cover the pan, making sure the lid fits firmly, see page 31.

11 Cook slowly for 1½ hours or until the meat is tender.

To serve: Place the meat on a hot serving dish and carve into thin slices. Using a perforated spoon, lift the vegetables out of the liquid remaining in the pan and arrange round the meat. Garnish with the olives. Serve the wine and vinegar from the pan as an unthickened sauce; if more sauce is required, add a little extra wine.

To freeze: This dish freezes well. The best method of freezing is to slice any meat left and put it with the vegetables and sauce.

To vary:
(i) The wine and vinegar sauce can be given a subtle and interesting flavour if it is blended with 1 tbsp of unsweetened cocoa powder and then heated gently until smooth in texture and dark-brown in colour.
(ii) *Braised Leg of Lamb.* This is an excellent way of cooking a boned and rolled leg of lamb.

BOILING

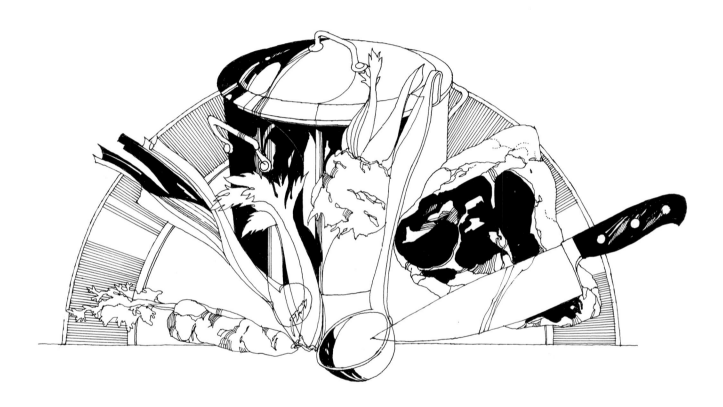

It is, of course, a misnomer to use the term 'boiling' for this method of cooking; 'simmering' is more correct. Boiled beef sounds dull, but this, too, is incorrect, for with this method a wide range of excellent dishes with interesting accompaniments may be cooked.

Among the dishes which are considered representative of a country's best traditions in cookery, you will almost always find some which are based on boiling.

Think of the fame of Sauerbraten, in which the beef is marinated in a savoury mixture before being cooked with a variety of ingredients; no wonder this dish is esteemed not only in Germany, but internationally.

Pot-au-Feu is a traditional weekend family meal, much loved by the French. And it really is a whole meal, as it provides both a soup and a main dish.

I have no doubt that, if presented with a choice of dishes, many Americans would pick their cherished New England Boiled Dinner, which recalls the early settlers and the need to 'corn' beef to keep it from spoiling. In many other countries where meat had to be preserved for cooking at a later stage, corning was the accepted procedure.

There has always been a tendency to underestimate simple dishes and to try and make them sound more elaborate than they really are. This is illustrated by an episode that occurred during Grover Cleveland's first term as the president of the United States, when there was a move to 'dress up' the menus by giving French names to American dishes. One day, when President Cleveland was being served some 'refined' dishes, he smelled corned beef and cabbage, the basic ingredients of the traditional dinner, from the servants' quarters and asked to trade his dinner for that of the servants. He was given the appetizing New England Boiled Dinner and commented afterwards that it was 'the best dinner I have had for months … this bœuf corné au cabeau'.

This is one of the traditional dishes of the United States. It is based upon 'corned beef', which, strangely enough, has no connection with corn or cornmeal. It appears that this particular name was given to the dish in Anglo-Saxon times in Britain. The meat is cured in a mixture of boiling water, salt, and sugar. The salt of Anglo-Saxon days was so large-grained and coarse that it looked like corn, hence the name.

Today, this method of preparing the meat is still used in the United States, usually by injecting the curing solution, but you can, of course, buy the meat ready-prepared for cooking.

To Prepare Corned Beef

Use fresh brisket, flank, or plate. These are American cuts, and in Britain one would ask for either brisket or flank; see the diagrams on pages 14–16 of cuts in various countries.

1 Weigh the beef, since the amount of solution depends upon the quantity of meat. As this dish is equally good hot or cold, it is worthwhile 'corning' a good-sized piece of meat. The following amount would give 8 generous portions.

2 To a scant 4 lb of meat allow:
1 gallon plus a generous quart water, 1½ lb salt, and 1 generous cup sugar.

3 Heat the water, add the salt and sugar, and allow to dissolve.

4 Put the meat into a large earthenware or enamel container; pour the solution over the meat.

5 Cover the meat with a plate so that the meat is pushed under the solution; leave for 48 hours before cooking.

To Make New England Boiled Dinner

1 Lift the corned beef from the solution and rinse under cold water to remove the surplus salt. There is no necessity to soak the meat overnight.

2 Put the meat into a saucepan with cold water to cover.

3 Bring the water just to boiling point, remove any grey scum from the liquid, lower the heat, and sim-

New England Boiled Beef

mer gently, as explained on page 32. Allow 40 minutes per pound for brisket, but almost an hour per pound for the slightly less tender flank or plate.

4 Add the vegetables 30–45 minutes before the meat is cooked. The time depends upon the size and cooking time necessary for each vegetable. Choose whole carrots, parsnips, potatoes, turnips, diced rutabagas, zucchini, and quartered cabbage.

5 Lift the meat and vegetables onto a hot dish. Add small cooked hot beets to the selection of vegetables; serve with Horseradish Sauce, page 56.

1 Ask the butcher to cut the bones into small pieces; this enables more flavour to be extracted.

2 Wash the marrow bone and tie in muslin; this is added towards the end of the cooking time.

3 Put the bones, chicken giblets, and beef into a pot or pan.

4 Add most of the water, bring slowly to boiling point, and remove the scum.

5 Add the rest of the cold water, bring again to boiling point, and then skim the liquid again; it is essential to do this at the beginning of the cooking period and, ideally, once or twice during cooking, so that the soup liquid is very clear.

6 Peel the onions and garlic, press the cloves into the onions, and put into the liquid.

7 Peel the carrots, celery root, parsnip, and turnips; cut into narrow strips. Cut away the green part of the leeks and leave the white part whole; clean thoroughly.

8 Dice the celery, then put all the vegetables with the herbs and salt and pepper into the liquid.

9 Cover the container and simmer very gently until the meat is tender.

10 Add the marrow bone for the last 40 minutes of the cooking time.

To serve: Lift the meat and vegetables onto a dish and keep hot while serving the soup; but take a small amount of the vegetables and chop these finely. Strain the liquid into a soup tureen, top with the chopped vegetables. The marrow can be removed from the bone, spread on small pieces of toasted bread, and served with the soup.

To freeze: The clear soup liquid can be frozen for 3 months. The meat is better eaten when freshly cooked.

To vary:
(i) *Consommé Nana:* This gives more body to the soup from the Pot-au-Feu. Cut and toast slices of French bread.

Blend a little tomato purée with the liquid from the Pot-au-Feu.

Put the toast into a soup tureen

Pot-au-Feu

French Boiled Beef and Vegetables
Serves 4–6
Cooking Time: 3 hours

INGREDIENTS

beef bones: 1 lb
marrow bone: 1
chicken giblets (exclude liver): from 1–2 chickens
fresh eye of round: 2 lb
water: 9 cups
onions: 2 large
garlic cloves: 2
cloves: 2–3
carrots: 8 small
celery root: 1 small
parsnip: 1 medium
turnips: 2 small
leeks: 4 small
celery stalks: 2
bay leaf: 1–2
chervil: small bunch or use dried
salt and pepper: to taste

with a generous amount of grated Gruyère cheese (or use a mixture of Gruyère and Parmesan cheeses).

Top with a poached egg for each person, then pour the hot liquid over the eggs, cheese, and toast, and serve at once.

(ii) *Pot-au-Feu Languedoc Style:* Omit the chicken giblets and add about ½ lb diced salt pork.

Poule-au-Pot

This dish is a combination of beef and chicken, and the two flavours produce both a first-class soup and an interesting main dish.

1 Blend ½ lb sausage meat, a chopped or minced small onion, ¼ lb finely chopped ham, and the chopped uncooked liver from the chicken.

2 Spoon this mixture into the chicken, tie the bird firmly, so that the stuffing cannot come out during cooking.

3 Follow the directions for Pot-au-Feu, adding the chicken to the beef. Naturally, the stage at which you do this will depend upon the size and tenderness of the chicken.

To serve: As Pot-au-Feu.

Dutch Boiled Beef

This is really the Dutch equivalent of Pot-au-Feu. There are, however, sufficient differences to make it into a dish with a new flavour.

The Dutch cook sometimes mixes two different cuts of beef, such as brisket and a little sirloin, and omits marrow bone and chicken giblets.

1 Cook the meat and vegetables as for Pot-au-Feu to the end of stage 9.

2 At the same time, cook and mash enough potatoes to give 2 cups (1 lb).

3 Strain the liquid, serve as a soup, and keep the meat hot on a serving dish.

4 Mash or sieve all the vegetables, blend with the mashed potato, and heat together for a few minutes. Spoon this delicious purée round the edge of a serving dish, carve the meats, and arrange in the centre of the dish.

Boiled Ox-tongue

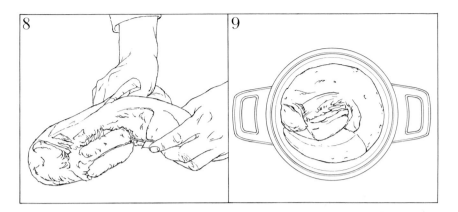

A cooked and pressed ox-tongue is an ideal dish to serve cold for a buffet. Although fresh tongue is used in many dishes, it is advisable in the following recipe to purchase the tongue pickled for this process gives additional flavour and produces the pinkish colour which makes the cooked meat so much more appetizing in appearance.

To Cook and Press a Tongue

1 Remove any excess fat from the tongue, then place the pickled meat to soak for 12 hours in cold water to cover, if necessary. Consult your butcher or the directions on the package.

2 Remove the tongue from this water and put into a large pan, and cover with fresh cold water or other liquid.

3 Add 1 or 2 peeled and sliced onions and carrots, the finely pared yellow peel from half a lemon (avoid using any bitter pith), a bay leaf, and 8 peppercorns or a shake of black pepper.

4 Bring the water to the boil, remove any scum, lower the heat, and simmer gently, as described on page 32. Allow 40 minutes per pound.

5 When the tongue is cooked, lift it from the liquid, drain well, and allow it to cool sufficiently to handle.

6 Meanwhile, boil the liquid steadily in an uncovered pan until it is reduced to 1 cup liquid.

7 Use a small sharp knife and cut away the tiny bones at the root end of the tongue; discard these.

8 Slit the tough skin on the tongue, being careful not to cut the meat; gently ease the skin off the meat.

9 Roll the meat to form a good shape. Place in a saucepan, in a round cake tin without a loose base, or in a deep soufflé dish. The meat should fit fairly tightly, but there must be space around it to include the glaze, see the next stage.

10 Soften a teaspoon of gelatine in 1 tbsp of cold water or dry sherry, and blend with the hot liquid, reduced as in stage 6.

11 Strain over the tongue; on top of the meat place a flat plate under a light weight; leave until quite cold.

To serve: Put a tea towel in hot water, wring it out, and wrap it round the container for a few seconds to soften the gelatine glaze; invert over a serving dish. Garnish with salad.

To freeze: The tongue freezes well, but as the meat is pickled, it should be used within 6 weeks.

To vary:
(i) Cook the tongue in a mixture of cider or light white wine and water.
(ii) Allow stock to be reduced to ½ cup at stage 6, then add the same amount of dry sherry.
(iii) Fresh ox-tongue is cooked in the same way but does not need soaking as stage 1.
(iv) An ox-tongue is fairly large for a small family; you can use lamb or calf tongue instead of ox-tongue in recipes on this or the next page.

Polish Ox-tongue

1 Cook the ox-tongue as per the directions on this page. It is usual to choose a fresh tongue for this particular dish, as it blends better with the interesting sauce. If you are using pickled tongue, however, omit the salt in the sauce below and add *slightly* more sugar.

2 First make the quantity of Brown Sauce given on page 85.

3 When the sauce has thickened, blend in 1¼ cup red wine, the finely grated peel and juice of half a lemon.

4 Add scant ½ cup seedless raisins and 4 tbsp sugar, simmer gently for 3–4 minutes, stirring well to dissolve the sugar. It is a good idea to allow the mixture to stand in the pan for 20–30 minutes, so that the raisins can become plump in the sauce. Do not heat the mixture during this period, for this makes it too thick.

5 Reheat and gradually add 2–3 tbsp red wine or brown malt vinegar and a little salt and pepper. Taste the sauce critically, as you stir in the vinegar, for it should not be too sharp.

6 Finally, add ½–1 cup blanched almonds.

To serve: Slice the hot tongue, arrange on a dish, and top with the sauce. This dish is generally served with small dumplings – there are recipes on pages 55 and 56. If you are reheating slices of tongue, transfer the sauce to a large frying pan or shallow saucepan. Add a few extra spoons of beef stock or wine to the sauce to allow for evaporation as you heat the tongue. Place the sliced tongue in the sauce and reheat for 5–6 minutes only.

The ingredients in the sauce serve 6–8 portions.

To freeze: This sauce, or the tongue and sauce, can be prepared and frozen together, although the dish loses a little flavour when defrosted.

Interesting Ways to Serve Ox-tongue

We have given here directions on preparing and cooking a pickled tongue and a Polish method of serving tongue. Below are other suggestions. Each gives 4 portions.

Langue de Bœuf à la Flamande

1 Heat 3 tbsp butter in a pan.

2 Fry 2 peeled and thinly sliced onions in the butter.

3 Add 2 tbsp flour and cook for 2–3 minutes, stirring well.

4 Blend in 1¼ cup good beef stock, with ⅔ cup red wine or light ale.

5 Bring to the boil and cook until a smooth, fairly thin, sauce.

6 Put 8 medium-sized slices of cooked, pickled or fresh, tongue in the sauce, together with salt and pepper to taste.

7 Heat gently for 5–6 minutes.

To serve: In a border of diced carrots, peas, and green beans, and with mashed turnips.

To freeze: Freezes well for 6 weeks.

Lingua di Bue Gratinata

1 Heat 4 tbsp (½ stick) butter in a pan.

2 Peel and chop 2 medium onions, fry in the butter for 5 minutes or until nearly cooked, then add 1 cup or a 4-oz can sliced button mushrooms and ⅔ cup red wine.

3 Heat gently for 3–4 minutes, add a little chopped parsley, and salt and pepper to taste.

4 Arrange 8 thin slices of cooked, pickled or fresh, tongue in a shallow oven-proof dish. Top with the onion mixture.

5 Melt 2 tbsp (¼ stick) butter, blend with scant ½ cup soft breadcrumbs, and sprinkle over the tongue and onion mixture.

6 Heat and brown the topping, allowing about 20 minutes towards the top of a moderately hot oven, 400°F.

To serve: Hot with a green salad.

To freeze: This dish is better freshly prepared.

To vary:
Use Brown, Madeira, or Espagnole Sauces, see page 85, in place of the wine, for a thicker mixture.

Lengua con Almendras
An Argentinian recipe which combines tongue with a very interesting sauce.

1 Peel and chop 1 or 2 cloves of garlic and a small onion, fry in 1 tbsp oil for a few minutes, then add a skinned and chopped tomato with 1¼ cup stock from cooking the tongue; or use chicken stock, but not beef stock, which is too strong.

2 Add 2 teaspoons chopped parsley and 2 bay leaves, and simmer for 10 minutes.

3 Remove the bay leaves and add generous ¼ cup ground almonds and 2 generous tbsp soft breadcrumbs.

4 Stir into the sauce.

5 Cut about 1 lb cooked ox-tongue into neat slices or thin fingers, put into a hot dish, and top with the sauce.

Glazed Brisket and Eye of Round

These two cuts of meat are extremely popular in Britain, either as a hot dish with vegetables and dumplings, which you will find on page 56, or as a cold roast to serve with salad.

Brisket and eye of round are both sold already salted or pickled by the butcher, and this treatment gives the meat an attractive pink colour when it is cooked.

Since the pickling brine is fairly strong, it is advisable, however, to soak the meat for 12 hours in cold water to cover before it is cooked; this removes the excess salt, but leaves enough to give the meat an extra flavour.

1 Put the meat into a pan and cover with cold water, or you may like to use a mixture of water and cider, which gives a pleasant taste to the meat, particularly when the beef is served as a cold cut.

2 Add one or two onions and carrots to give flavour to the meat, together with pepper, or about 6 peppercorns, but no salt.

3 Make a bouquet garni, tied in muslin, of a bay leaf, a sprig of parsley (keep the stalk, it gives a lot of flavour), and a small sprig of thyme. The muslin makes it easy to remove.

4 In order to set the meat liquid for glazing, you will need either to add gelatine, as in the tongue recipe, stage 10 on page 52, or to put a calf's foot in with the meat; the latter gives a very good flavour but produces quite a lot of fat which will need removing. If you decide on the calf's foot, cut it in two, lengthwise, before adding it to the pan.

5 Bring the liquid to boiling point, remove any scum, lower the heat and simmer gently, as described on page 32. Allow 40 minutes per pound for eye of round, but just a few minutes longer for the brisket, which may be a little less tender.

6 When the meat is cooked, remove from the pan and place in a suitable container. If using gelatine,

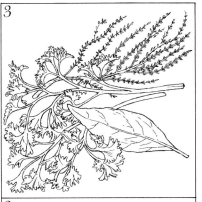

follow the directions given for tongue on page 52, stages 6 (to reduce the liquid), 10 and 11. If using the calf's foot, then simply boil the stock vigorously as stage 6, pour over the meat, and leave to set in a cool place.

7 After some hours, remove any fat from the top of the meat and jelly.

To serve: Cold with salads and mustard or Cumberland Sauce.

To freeze: As this is salted meat, it should be used from the freezer within 6 weeks.

To vary:
I was delighted to find this recipe in a book, *Recipes of Old England – Three Centuries of English Cooking*, modernized by Bernard N. Bessunger. It gives a recipe published in 1715 by Mary Kittelby, and in it she describes:

> *A Very Pretty Way to Eat Cold Boiled Beef:* Slice it (the beef) as thin as 'tis possible. Slice also an onion, or a shallot, and squeeze on it the juice of a lemon or two, then beat it between two plates, as you do cucumbers; when 'tis very well beaten and tastes sharp of the lemon, put into a deep china dish, pick out the onion, and pour on oil, shake in also some shred parsley, and garnish with sliced lemon; 'tis very savoury and delicious.

This book went through seven editions (the last in 1759). The authoress recommends her book to the clergy 'especially to those whose Parishes are remote from other Help'.

Svíčková na Smetaně

Czechoslovakian Boiled Beef and Sour Cream Sauce
Serves 4–6
Cooking Time: from 1½ hours

INGREDIENTS

1 If using corned brisket, put to soak for about 12 hours in cold water to cover, if necessary. Consult your butcher or the directions on the package.

2 Place the meat in a large saucepan with water to cover.

3 Peel and cut the vegetables into fairly large dice or slices, add to the meat with the parsley, bay leaf, a shake of pepper, and the vinegar. Use the given amount of vinegar first, then taste the stock towards the end of cooking and add more if desired.

corned brisket or fresh brisket: 2 lb
onions: 2 medium
celery root: 1 small
carrots: 3–4 medium
turnips: 2 small
parsley: sprig
bay leaf: 1
pepper: to taste
white malt or wine vinegar: 1 tbsp
for the sauce:
beef stock, see method: 1¼ cup
flour: 3 tbsp
sour cream: 1¼ cup
grated horseradish: 1–2 tbsp
salt and pepper: to taste

4 Bring the liquid just to boiling point, remove any scum, lower the heat, cover the pan, and simmer as on page 32.

5 Allow it to simmer for about 1 hour 20 minutes or slightly more.

6 At the end of the cooking time, spoon out 1¼ cup of stock, and put this into another saucepan.

Sauerbraten

German Marinated Boiled Beef
Serves 8–10
Cooking Time: 3¼ hours

INGREDIENTS

top round or eye of round: generous 4 lb
fatty bacon or pork: 4 oz
onions: 4 medium
celeriac: 1 medium
butter: 2 oz
white wine: 1¼ cup
sugar: 2–3 teaspoons
for the marinade:
onion: 1 medium
carrot: 1 medium
beef stock: 2½ cups
red wine vinegar: 2½ cups
peppercorns: 4–6
salt and pepper: to taste
bay leaf: 1
juniper berries: 3–4
for the sauce:
sour cream: 1¼ cup
seedless raisins: 4 oz
blanched chopped almonds: 2 oz
butter: 2 tbsp

7 Blend the flour with the sour cream, making sure that this is evenly blended, so that there is no possibility of the sauce becoming lumpy.

8 Gradually whisk the flour and sour cream mixture into the hot stock, then continue whisking or stirring as the sauce comes just to boiling point.

9 Lower the heat, simmer gently, stirring all the time, until the sauce thickens, and add the horseradish, and salt and pepper to taste.

To serve: Carve the meat and top with some of the sauce; serve the rest separately. Strain the vegetables from the stock and arrange round the meat.

To freeze: The sauce does not freeze well, but the cooked meat in the stock freezes well for 6 weeks.

1 Peel and chop the onion and the carrot, then mix with all the other ingredients for the marinade.

2 Pour into a saucepan (enamel if possible), and boil steadily for 10 minutes. Allow to cool.

3 Dry the meat well, cut the bacon or pork into narrow strips, thread through a larding needle and insert into the meat, then place this in a glass or china dish.

4 Pour the marinade over the meat and leave in a cool place for 2–3 days, turning several times.

5 Peel the onions and the celery root and dice neatly.

6 Lift the meat from the marinade, drain, then dry on absorbent paper.

7 Strain and keep ¼ cup of the marinade.

8 Heat the butter in a large saucepan, fry the meat on both sides until golden, add the diced vegetables, strained marinade liquid, white wine, a little salt and pepper, and the sugar.

9 Cover the pan and simmer gently for about 3 hours.

10 Lift the meat and vegetables from the liquid onto a hot serving dish.

11 Blend the sour cream with an equal amount of the strained liquid from cooking the beef.

12 Pour into a small saucepan, add the raisins and almonds, and heat, without boiling, for several minutes.

13 Stir in the butter just before serving.

To serve: Carve the beef and top with the sauce. Serve with noodles or, better still, with Kartoffelklösse, see below.

To freeze: This dish is better freshly cooked.

Kartoffelklösse
These potato dumplings are as light as a feather and, while they form the perfect accompaniment to any form of hot boiled beef, they are the classic accompaniment to Sauerbraten.

1 Peel enough old potatoes to give ½ lb.

2 Grate into a basin of cold water.

3 Lift out and drain, then blend with generous ⅓ cup plain flour sieved with ¾ teaspoon baking powder, 1 teaspoon grated raw onion, generous ¼ cup or 2 oz soft breadcrumbs, a little salt and pepper, and 1 egg.

4 Drop spoonfuls of the mixture into boiling salted water and cook for about 15 minutes or until they float to the top of the liquid.

5 Drain well and serve.

Boiled Beef with Dumplings

One of the pleasures of cooking is the fact that one can create new dishes by combining the best recipes and accompaniments from many parts of the world. Boiled beef is prepared in many countries, and so are dumplings, but the two are rarely served together except in Britain, or in places where British food is served.

This is a pity, for some of the interesting dumplings from other countries can turn boiled beef into a very excellent meal.

If cooking corned beef or other brine-pickled meat, soak the meat, as described on page 54, to extract any excess salt, then proceed according to the basic instructions on boiling, see page 32.

In most countries an interesting selection of vegetables is usually added to the meat and the liquid in which it is to be cooked. It is advisable to put a small quantity of vegetables into the pan when cooking commences, and then to add others later in the cooking period; these will retain colour, texture, and flavour and will look inviting when served with the beef.

Here, briefly, are some ideas for dumplings and sauces that can be served with boiled beef.

In Austria fresh, not pickled, meat is used for boiling. Sometimes, a more tender cut of meat, such as rib, is preferred to brisket, round or eye of round, so you may need to shorten the cooking time slightly.

A selection of vegetables is added, together with beef bones, so that you have an excellent stock as well as a tender piece of meat.

Although Austrian cooks make dumplings from an almost unbelievable selection of ingredients, they are not a traditional accompaniment to boiled beef. I have, however, experimented and find that Kartoffelknödel, the Austrian word for the potato dumplings given on page 55, are an excellent accompaniment.

In Britain dumplings are made from suet crust pastry, see page 126. The quantities given would produce rather too many dumplings for a family of 4, so halve all the ingredients and make the mixture very slightly more moist. With floured hands, roll the mixture into about 8 small balls, and put into the saucepan with the beef about 20 minutes before this is cooked. Make sure the liquid is boiling before the dumplings are added and allow it to boil, rather than simmer, during the 15–20 minutes' cooking period; page 32 describes this process.

Chopped parsley, crushed garlic, or other herbs, added to the flour, make the dumplings less bland.

In Czechoslovakia, as in Austria, liver dumplings are served in beef soup; these are equally good with boiled beef and vegetables. This recipe may well please those who might not like liver alone.

1 Mince enough liver to give $\frac{1}{4}$ lb.

2 Chop or mince 1–2 garlic cloves.

3 Blend with 1 cup soft breadcrumbs, 1–2 teaspoons chopped parsley, a little salt and pepper, 1 tbsp melted butter, and a small egg.

4 Form the mixture into small rounds.

5 Either cook the dumplings in the pan containing the beef and vegetables or in some of the beef stock in a separate pan. Allow just about 6–7 minutes' cooking time.

To serve: Place the dumplings round the meat and vegetables.

Horseradish Sauces
The generally accepted sauce to serve with boiled beef is horseradish sauce, but it is interesting how this varies in the way it is made in different countries. The quantities given make enough sauce for 4. None of these sauces are good when frozen.

Several Austrian recipes use horseradish, but in one of the most unusual, you have a combination of the hot flavouring and applesauce.

1 Blend grated fresh horseradish with a thick applesauce.

2 Add a little lemon juice or vinegar to sharpen the flavour, plus a few chopped blanched almonds.

The proportions are a matter of personal taste.

A sauce from Norway combines milk and beef stock.

1 Heat 2 tbsp ($\frac{1}{4}$ stick) butter in a pan.

2 Stir in scant 3 tbsp flour.

3 Add $\frac{2}{3}$ cup milk and $\frac{2}{3}$ cup stock, made from cooking the beef.

4 Stir over a low heat until thickened, then add a little salt, pepper, and 2–3 tbsp grated horseradish.

A particularly pleasant sauce, of the type enjoyed in Germany, is made as follows:

1 Blend 1–2 tbsp finely grated horseradish with the same amount of very fine soft breadcrumbs.

2 Add $\frac{2}{3}$ cup heavy whipping cream.

3 Stir together, then add 1–2 tbsp lemon juice or vinegar; the amount depends upon personal taste.

4 Finally, add a little salt, pepper, and sugar.

The type of horseradish sauce or cream served in Britain with roast beef blends equally well with boiled beef.

1 Heat 2 tbsp ($\frac{1}{4}$ stick) butter in a saucepan.

2 Stir in scant 3 tbsp flour, cook gently, stirring well.

3 Gradually blend in $1\frac{1}{4}$ cup milk.

4 Bring to the boil, stirring well, and cook until thickened.

5 Add 1–2 tbsp finely grated fresh horseradish, or as desired.

6 Remove from the heat, and whisk in a little heavy whipping cream.

7 Add salt and pepper and a pinch sugar to taste, together with a few drops of vinegar or lemon juice. Heat without boiling.

Horseradish Cream

1 Mix together $\frac{2}{3}$ cup heavy whipping cream, 1–2 tbsp finely grated horseradish.

2 Add a little salt, pepper, and sugar to taste, and stir briskly until thickened.

3 Add lemon juice or vinegar to taste.

To freeze: This freezes well for 2–3 weeks.

STEAK

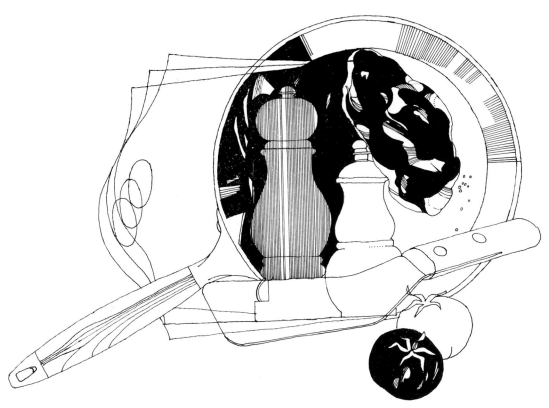

In modern times, there has been a distinct move towards simpler foods, and broiled or fried steaks have gained popularity with people in all beef-eating countries; so much so that, in Australia and parts of the United States, you can still find steak as part of a 'proper' breakfast menu.

Certainly, the texture and taste of prime beef steaks do not necessarily need adornment. If the meat is well chosen and perfectly cooked, it possesses infinite flavour. Simplicity, however, can become tedious, and it is a pity to confine oneself to a restricted method of serving a meat that is capable of endless variety. Indeed, it was a problem to limit my choice of steak dishes to the space available, but I have given a selection for all occasions.

There is a golden rule about cooking steak that one should always remember: speed of cooking and serving is the essence of success. A steak that is over-cooked or kept waiting before being served is easily spoiled.

The following is a clear indication that this point has always been appreciated.

Many London clubs were famous for their food. One of these was the Sublime Society of Beefsteaks (The Beefsteak Club), of which rule 4 was:

> That beefsteaks shall be the only meat for dinner, and the broiling begins at two of the clock on each day of meeting, and the table cloth be removed at half an hour after three.

Their motto was: 'When 'tis done, 'twere well it were done quickly!'.

Beefsteaks were not only served in London at exclusive clubs; a record given us by Boswell in his London Journal recommends 'Dolly's Chop House in St. Paul's Churchyard for chops, steaks and a "cut direct" from the joint'. He continues, 'Anyone like a young guardsman could rough it on beefsteaks and port', then goes on, 'A beef-steak house is a most excellent place to dine at. ... My dinner (beef, bread and beer, and waiter) was only a shilling'. Oh for those days!!

Entrecôte au Ratatouille

Ratatouille
Provençal Vegetable Stew
Serves 6–8
Cooking Time: 1–1¼ hours

INGREDIENTS

eggplant: 1 lb
zucchini: 1 lb
tomatoes: 1½–2 lb
onions: 2–3 medium
garlic cloves: 2–3
sweet red pepper: 1
sweet green pepper: 1
sweet yellow pepper (optional): 1
olive oil: ¼ cup
chopped parsley: 2 tbsp
salt and pepper: to taste
to garnish:
chopped parsley: to taste

Although any steak can be served with Ratatouille, a sirloin or entrecôte combines better with this highly flavoured mixture of vegetables.

Broil, rather than fry, the steak and arrange on the dish with a border of the mixed vegetables.

Ratatouille, the vegetable stew from Provence, is one of the most adaptable as well as delicious of dishes.

It can be served hot or cold as an hors d'œuvre or as a vegetable with main dishes, and steaks blend particularly well with it.

1 Wipe the eggplants; if you dislike the slightly bitter taste, score the skin, sprinkle with a little salt and leave for about 30 minutes; you then will find that the vegetable no longer has this bitter flavour.

2 Cut the eggplants into small dice; wipe and slice or dice the zucchini, discard just the rather tough ends.

3 Skin, halve, and de-seed the tomatoes; peel and chop the onions and garlic.

4 Dice the flesh from the peppers; discard the core and seeds.

5 Heat the oil in a heavy saucepan and gently fry the onions and garlic, then add the tomatoes and heat for a few minutes, so that the juice begins to flow.

6 Add the rest of the vegetables and the parsley; season well.

7 Cover the pan, lower the heat, and allow the vegetables to cook until they are tender and have produced a thick pulp. It will be necessary to stir once or twice during the cooking period.
To serve: Hot or cold, topped with chopped parsley.

To freeze: This vegetable dish freezes perfectly for up to six months. The garlic tends to lose some of its potency, so be generous with this before freezing or, better still, add a little crushed garlic when reheating.

To vary:
(i) Add 1 or 2 bay leaves and 1–2 sprigs of fresh thyme; remove these before serving the dish.
(ii) To give a more pronounced flavour, add a little tomato purée to the cooked vegetables, and taste as you do so, for no flavour should be completely dominating.
(iii) Use rather less oil in cooking; this would be particularly appropriate when serving the dish with very rich foods.
(iv) Adjust the proportions of vegetables to your own taste.
(v) Although variation (iii) suggests using less oil than in the recipe, many classic recipes use two to three times the amount given.

Steak Tartare

Serves 4
No Cooking

To freeze: One cannot freeze this dish, as the steak must be eaten as soon as it is blended with the other ingredients.

To vary:
The recipe above is the classic method of preparing the uncooked meat, but I have enjoyed this dish with varying additions, such as a dash of brandy, Worcestershire sauce, soy sauce, and even a little concentrated tomato purée. Cayenne pepper may be used sparingly for those people who enjoy a rather hot taste. Another way of introducing additional flavour to the steak is to add several finely chopped canned anchovy fillets. This means you will need less salt. Serve finely chopped cooked beets with the prepared mixture.

INGREDIENTS

fillet steak: 1–2 lb
salt and pepper: to taste
capers: to taste
small onions or shallots: 2–4
gherkins: 6–10
parsley: to taste
eggs: 4

The presentation of this dish is important, but the freshness of the beef is essential. It is advisable to grind the meat just before serving. The rather large differences in quantities listed in the ingredients is not only because people's appetites vary, and this dish is very 'easy to eat', but also because it is an acceptable hors d'œuvre and, as such, a smaller portion could be served.

1 Grind the beef; at this stage a little salt and pepper could be added, but it is better to use these sparingly, so that each Steak Tartare conforms to personal taste.

2 Form the meat into four neat rounds on a platter.

3 Put capers into one small dish; finely chop the onions or shallots, and put into a second dish. Drain and dice the gherkins neatly and spoon into a third dish.

4 Chop enough parsley to give about 4 tbsp and place in a fourth dish.

5 If you have no suitable dishes, then arrange these ingredients round the steaks.

6 Break the eggs carefully, pour away the egg whites (to use in another dish), tip the yolks into 4 halved egg shells and place on the steak rounds.

7 To prepare the completed dish, put each portion of meat into a bowl, add an egg yolk, salt, pepper, and some of the capers, onions or shallots, gherkins, and parsley, adjusting the quantities as desired.

To serve: Form each portion into a neat round on the serving plate. It is traditional to prepare this dish at the table. Steak Tartare can be served with a green salad if desired.

Churrasco Rebosado

Spanish-style Fried Fillet Steak in Batter
Serves 6
Cooking Time: 7–12 minutes

INGREDIENTS

fillet steak: $1\frac{1}{2}$ lb
salt and pepper: to taste
for the batter:
flour: $\frac{1}{2}$ cup
eggs: 3
milk: $\frac{1}{2}$–$\frac{2}{3}$ cup
onion: 1 small
chopped chives: 1 teaspoon
for frying:
oil: generous $\frac{1}{2}$ cup
to garnish:
watercress: to taste
tomatoes: 4–5

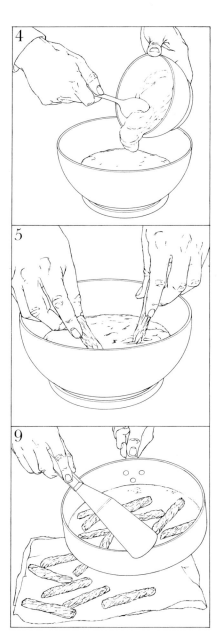

1 Cut the beef into narrow strips; these should be no more than $\frac{1}{2}$ inch in thickness. Sprinkle with a little salt and pepper; cover and leave in the refrigerator for an hour.

2 Sieve the flour into a large mixing bowl, separate the eggs, and beat the egg yolks and the milk into the flour until you have a smooth batter.

3 Peel and grate the onion, add to the batter together with the chives and a little salt and pepper.

4 Whisk the egg whites until stiff, fold into the batter; this should not be done until just before the steak is about to be cooked.

5 Drop the steak into the batter and turn gently, so that it is evenly coated.

6 Heat the oil in a large, heavy frying pan; to test if this is the right heat, put in a cube of day-old bread and it should turn golden within 30 seconds.

7 Spoon the steak into the hot oil, fry quickly until golden brown; this takes about 2 minutes. Turn and cook on the second side for the same time.

8 Lower the heat and continue cooking for another 3–8 minutes, depending upon how well done you like the meat.

9 Lift the batter-coated steak onto absorbent paper to drain.

To serve: Garnish with the watercress and thinly sliced tomatoes.

To freeze: This dish should be eaten freshly cooked.

To vary:
The food could be fried in a deep pan of hot oil or fat if preferred, but care must be taken that the coating does not become too brown before the meat is cooked.

Carucho

Steak with Peanut Sauce
Serves 4
Cooking Time: 30 minutes

INGREDIENTS

for the peanut sauce:
roasted peanuts: ¼ lb
onions: 2 medium
tomatoes: 3 medium
sweet green pepper: 1 small
olive oil: 2 tbsp
chicken stock: 1¼ cup
salt and pepper: to taste
cayenne pepper: pinch
and/or Tabasco sauce: 2–3 drops
heavy whipping cream: 3 tbsp
T-bone or top sirloin steaks: 4
butter or oil: to taste
to garnish:
lettuce: to taste
green olives: 8

1 Put the peanuts through a grinder or food processor until quite smooth.

2 Peel and chop the onions, skin and slice the tomatoes, and dice the sweet green pepper, discarding the core and seeds.

3 Heat the oil in a saucepan and fry the onions in this for several minutes, then add the rest of the ingredients for the sauce, except the cream.

4 Cover the pan and simmer gently for 15–20 minutes, remove the lid towards the end of the cooking time to allow the sauce to become a thicker mixture, and stir once or twice.

5 Meanwhile, add a little salt and pepper to the steaks, brush with a little melted butter or oil, and broil, see page 34.

6 Blend the cream into the sauce, heat for 2–3 minutes, but do not boil the mixture.

To serve: Arrange the steaks on a dish, garnish with lettuce, and top with the sauce and olives.

To freeze: The sauce freezes well for up to 6 months, but do not add the cream until reheating it.

Filet Cordon Bleu

This is a very pleasant adaptation of the well-known veal dish.

1 Broil or fry 4 fillet steaks to personal taste.

2 Put the steaks on a flameproof dish or in the broiler pan.

3 Place a slice of lean ham on each steak.

4 Top the ham with canned or cooked fresh asparagus tips. This is not essential but adds interest to the dish.

5 Cover the asparagus, ham, and steaks with a large thin slice of Gruyère or other good cooking cheese.

6 Place the dish or pan under the flame and cook only until the cheese has melted and the ingredients are thoroughly heated.

To serve: With new potatoes and a green salad or vegetable.

To freeze: Do not freeze.

Filetes Rellenos con Jamon

Fillet Steak with Ham
Serves 4
Cooking Time: 5–10 minutes

INGREDIENTS

fillet steaks: 4
gammon, or sliced bacon, or cooked ham slices: 4
for the coating:
garlic clove: 1
egg: 1
salt and pepper: to taste
chopped parsley: 2 tbsp
chopped thyme: $\frac{1}{4}$ teaspoon
crisp or toasted breadcrumbs: $\frac{1}{2}$ cup
for frying:
oil: 3 tbsp

This simple Spanish dish gives lean steak a very pleasant moist texture.

Although one can use cooked ham as the filling, I prefer to take a thin slice of uncooked bacon or ham; a gammon slice is ideal, but any lean bacon could be used.

You need to fry or broil the bacon for about 1–2 minutes only, then put it, still hot, onto the steak.

In this way it will be cooked, and the flavour penetrates the steak better.

1 Take the fillets of beef and roll and/or pound the meat until very thin.

2 Place a slice of cooked ham or the bacon, see above, on each fillet; you may need to cut a long slice of bacon to make it fit.

3 Roll the steaks and tie with cotton string or secure with wooden cocktail sticks.

4 Peel and crush the garlic, as illustrated on page 46, blend with the egg and a very little salt and pepper.

5 Add the chopped parsley and thyme to the breadcrumbs.

6 Brush the steak rolls with the beaten egg and garlic; then roll in the breadcrumbs until evenly coated; one of the easiest ways to do this is to put the breadcrumb mixture into a polythene bag, add the rolls, and shake the bag gently but continually, so that the crumbs stick to the rolls.

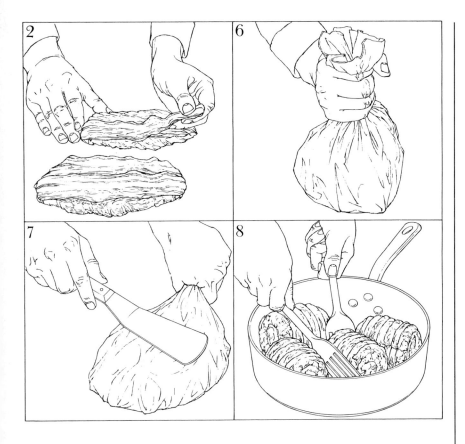

Steak Diane

Steak Diane
Serves 4
Cooking Time: 5–6 minutes

INGREDIENTS

shallot or small onion: 1
parsley: 2–3 sprigs
salt and pepper: to taste
minute steaks, cut from sirloin, rib, or even rump: 4
butter: generous $\frac{1}{3}$ cup ($\frac{3}{4}$ stick)
Worcestershire sauce: to taste
brandy: 2 tbsp

7 When the steak is coated, press the crumb mixture against the meat with the back of a palette knife or spatula to make quite certain it will not fall off during cooking.

8 Heat the oil in a large frying pan and fry the rolls for 3–4 minutes fairly briskly, turning them with tongs or knives so that they brown evenly, then lower the heat and continue cooking for a further 2–6 minutes, depending upon personal taste.

9 Drain the rolls on absorbent paper.

To serve: As soon as cooked. The golden brown rolls look most attractive on a large dish surrounded with a selection of cooked vegetables. Tomato Sauce, as per page 96, is an excellent accompaniment.

To freeze: The prepared rolls may be frozen on a flat tray, then wrapped and stored for up to 6 weeks. Unwrap the meat while still frozen, then allow the rolls to defrost before cooking.

To vary:
Fillets of veal may be used instead of steak.

1 Peel and chop the shallot or onion very finely, then chop enough parsley to give about 2 tbsp; this should be chopped very finely.

2 Sprinkle a little salt and pepper over the steaks.

3 Heat the butter in a large frying pan over a table heater, in an electric table frying pan, or on an ordinary burner. Fry the shallot or onion with a little of the parsley in the butter for just about 2 minutes, add the steaks, and fry for just one minute on either side.

4 Sprinkle with a little Worcestershire sauce, but sparingly, for tastes for it vary greatly.

5 Lift the steaks onto a hot dish.

6 Pour the brandy into the pan, stir to absorb any butter and meat juices, and flambé if desired.

7 Add the rest of the parsley, then spoon the liquid over the steaks.

To serve: With vegetables or a salad.

The Epicure's Tournedos

A tournedos prepared from tender steak is the basis for an almost endless variety of dishes. The French alone produce well over fifty recipes for this dish.

Some are difficult to prepare in a domestic kitchen, as they require a blending of several sauces which a chef has readily available; but many are comparatively simple, as we show on the following pages.

Most butchers will prepare tournedos, but this is not a difficult task, as pages 22 and 23 indicate.

1 Peel and finely chop the shallot, chop the tarragon to give 1 tbsp and enough thyme to produce ½ teaspoon.

2 Put the shallot, half the tarragon, all the thyme, and the bay leaf into a saucepan with the vinegar; simmer until this is reduced to about three-quarters of the original volume, cool slightly.

3 Meanwhile, soften, but do not melt, the butter; this makes it easier to incorporate into the egg mixture.

4 Put the egg yolks into the top of a double boiler or metal mixing bowl, strain the vinegar on top of these, and blend.

5 Stand over a pan of hot, *but not boiling*, water and whisk briskly until the mixture is thick and creamy.

6 Gradually add the butter; it is essential to do this slowly and carefully, as the mixture will curdle if the butter is added too quickly; continue whisking all this time. A small electric whisk is ideal for this purpose.

7 Finally, add salt and pepper to taste. Since the sauce requires continual attention, it is really advisable to prepare this before cooking the tournedos, for it need not be very hot when it is served; it should, however, be pleasantly warm.

8 Season the tournedos with a little salt and pepper, and fry in the butter, as indicated on page 33, or, if preferred, brush with melted butter and broil as page 34. The cooking time depends upon personal taste.

To serve: Lift the tournedos onto a

Tournedos Béarnaise
Tournedos with Béarnaise Sauce
Serves 4
Cooking Time: 18–25 minutes

INGREDIENTS

for the sauce:
shallot: 1 small
tarragon: 1–2 sprigs
thyme: 1–2 sprigs
bay leaf: 1
white wine vinegar: ¼ cup
butter: ½ lb (2 sticks)
egg yolks: 4–5
salt and pepper: to taste
tournedos, prepared as pages 22 and 23: 4
butter: ¼ cup (½ stick)
fried croûtons: optional
to garnish:
chopped chervil: to taste

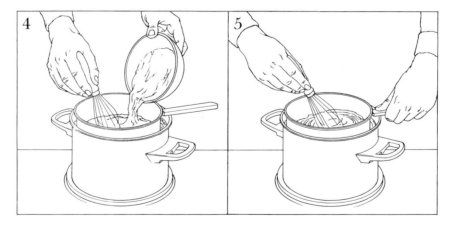

hot serving dish. These can be placed on fried croûtons, but as the sauce is so rich it may be better to omit these. Spoon a little sauce on each tournedos and top with the remainder of the chopped tarragon and the chervil. Put the remainder of the sauce into a hot sauce boat.

To freeze: Béarnaise Sauce can be frozen for 2–3 weeks; when defrosted, it should be placed in a metal mixing bowl and beaten over hot water for a few minutes to restore any light texture that may have been lost.

To vary:
(i) The recipe on this page gives a generous amount of sauce and can serve up to 8 portions.
(ii) For a richer dish, coat the tournedos with Chateaubriand Sauce, page 79, then add the Béarnaise Sauce; the two sauces blend well.

Béarnaise Sauce is part of the following well-known dishes.
(iii) *Tournedos Rubens:* Make both the Béarnaise Sauce, as on this page, and the Tomato Sauce, as on page 96. If using the full quantities, these will be sufficient for at least 8 tournedos. Top half the cooked steaks with the Tomato Sauce and half with the Béarnaise Sauce. This gives a two-toned effect on the serving dish. Extra sauce should be served individually in sauce boats, so each person may taste both flavours.
(iv) *Tournedos Baronne:* Top each steak with small fried or broiled button mushrooms, then with the sauce. For a more elaborate dish, garnish with thick, fresh tomato purée and sliced truffles.
(v) *Tournedos Chéron:* Top each steak with cooked artichoke bottoms, a little macedoine of vegetables, cream, and then the sauce.
(vi) Top each steak with cooked asparagus and the sauce.

More Classic Tournedos

Although the following recipes are based upon using the tender round of steak known as a tournedos, you may substitute other cuts of beef steak, if preferred. All the accompaniments given for the tournedos blend well with fried or broiled veal, lean pork, lamb, and young chicken, too.

In the particular recipes that follow, the steaks may be either fried or broiled, and detailed advice on both these methods of cooking beef are to be found on pages 33 and 34.

To make a more substantial meal and an impressive-looking tournedos, place the cooked meat on a fried croûton of bread. Slices of bread are cut into neat rounds or other shapes, such as a heart, of about the same size as the tournedos. They are fried until crisp and golden brown on either side. It is usual to fry the bread in butter or oil, or in a combination of butter and oil, but well clarified beef dripping can be used instead.

Always cook the croûtons before, or while, you fry or broil the meat, so that there is no unnecessary waiting before the steaks are served. The same advice applies to the garnishes and accompaniments for the steaks.

No specific information regarding freezing is given under the individual recipes on this page; in several cases the garnishes and accompaniments are better freshly prepared, and in other cases the necessary information is given elsewhere. Frozen steaks may be used, if desired. All the dishes on this page are for 4 people.

Tournedos Africaine

1 Prepare one of the Horseradish Sauces or the Horseradish Cream, see page 56.

2 Broil or fry 4 tournedos.

3 Towards the end of the cooking time, halve 4 bananas and fry in a little butter. The bananas may be fried in the same pan as the steaks, if space permits and the meat is being cooked by this method.

To serve: Place two halved bananas on each tournedos and top with a little of the sauce or cream.

Tournedos Arlésienne

1 Peel and chop a medium-sized onion and a clove of garlic; slice a medium eggplant; skin, halve, and de-seed 3–4 medium tomatoes, then cut into slices.

2 Heat a little butter or oil in a pan and fry the vegetables slowly for about 20 minutes or until a soft purée.

3 Add salt, pepper, and chopped parsley to taste, and spoon into a hot serving dish.

4 Fry or broil 4 tournedos. If frying the steaks, add 2–3 tbsp good beef stock to the frying pan (after cooking and removing the meat); stir well to absorb the meat juices, then spoon over the meat.

To serve: Place the meat on the purée.

Tournedos Dumas

1 Prepare Onion Sauce: Finely chop 2 onions and simmer in a little salted water until tender, then drain. Meanwhile, heat 2 tbsp (¼ stick) butter in a pan, stir in 2 tbsp flour, then add 1¼ cup milk. Bring the sauce to the boil, cook until thickened, then add a little salt and pepper and the chopped onions.

2 Cut 4 slices of ham into rounds the same size as the tournedos.

3 Grate enough Gruyère or other good cooking cheese to give ½ cup (2 oz).

4 Broil or fry 4 tournedos. Put on a flame-proof dish.

To serve: Top with the onion sauce, the ham slices, and the grated cheese, in that order. Put under a hot grill for about 2 minutes until the cheese has melted. Garnish with watercress.

Tournedos Genève

1 Prepare Espagnole Sauce, see page 85. When cooked, sieve until quite smooth, then return to the pan.

Tournedos Rubens

2 Allow the sauce to simmer, without a lid on the pan, for about 15 minutes, until it becomes thicker in consistency.

3 Slice about 6 fairly large mushrooms and 2 truffles (when obtainable); fry in 2 tbsp (¼ stick) butter, add to the sauce, together with a generous pinch of allspice and 2–3 tbsp red wine.

4 Allow the sauce to simmer while preparing the steaks.

5 Broil or fry 4 tournedos.

To serve: Top each tournedos with a generous amount of the sauce.

Tournedos Helder

1 Skin, halve, and de-seed 4 large tomatoes; dice the pulp neatly.

2 Skin and crush 1–2 cloves of garlic.

3 Fry the tomatoes and garlic for a few minutes until tender but still with an interesting texture. Add salt, pepper, and chopped parsley to taste.

4 Broil or fry 4 tournedos.

To serve: Top with the tomato mixture.

Tournedos Niçoise

This dish is capable of several variations. I have been given all the recipes on this page, and each one has been sworn to be the only true version. All are very pleasant, so you can try them and decide for yourself which is your "true" version.

The garnishes and accompaniments are suitable for other steaks, and the very impressive T-bone steak would be a good choice.

Version 1

1 Broil or fry the tournedos or other steaks and cook small tomatoes at the same time.

2 Top the broiled or fried steaks with a lattice design of anchovy fillets and black olives, and serve with the tomatoes.

Version 2

1 Peel and chop 2 medium onions; skin and chop a clove of garlic and 3 medium tomatoes.

2 Heat 2 tbsp oil in a pan and fry the vegetables for several minutes.

3 Add ½–⅔ cup red or white wine, a little salt and pepper, and simmer for about 10 minutes, or until the vegetables are tender.

4 Broil or fry the tournedos.

5 Add 2–3 chopped anchovy fillets, 2 tbsp chopped black olives, and the same amount of chopped parsley to the vegetable mixture.

To serve: Top the steaks with the sauce and garnish with whole black or green olives.

Version 3

1 Make Brown Sauce, see page 85, and add 3 tbsp tomato purée.

2 Broil or fry the steaks.

To serve: Arrange the steaks on a dish with cooked French beans and cooked tomatoes. Top with the sauce.

Tournedos Rossini

Tournedos with Pâté
Serves 4
Cooking Time: 10–15 minutes
plus time to make pâté

INGREDIENTS

pâté de foie de veau: as recipe on
salt and pepper: to taste
tournedos, prepared as pages 22 and 23: 4
butter or oil for cooking: to taste

The pâté must be made some time beforehand, to cool and set. The quantity in the recipe below will top 4 tournedos and leave enough for a small hors d'œuvre for 4 people.

1 Put 1 lb calves' liver and ¼ lb fatback (fresh pork fat) or bacon through a fine meat grinder once or even twice.

2 Blend with 2 eggs, scant ⅔ cup heavy whipping cream, 2 tbsp brandy or dry sherry, 2½ tbsp good beef stock, and a little salt and pepper.

3 Add a pinch of chopped or dried thyme and grated nutmeg.

4 Spoon the mixture into a well buttered dish, cover with buttered foil, stand in a 'bain-marie' (or pan of cold water); bake for 1¼ hours in the centre of a very moderate oven, 325°F. Allow to cool and set.

5 If storing the pâté, top with a layer of melted butter.

To freeze: This particular pâté freezes well for just a month.

1 Add a little salt and pepper to the tournedos; do not over-season, as the pâté has plenty of flavour.

2 Fry or broil the steaks, see pages 33 and 34, using butter or oil to personal taste, but since the pâté is rich, it is better not to be over-generous with the fat.

3 Cut some of the pâté into small neat rounds or squares.

To serve: Lift the steaks onto a hot serving dish, top with the pâté, and serve at once. It is important that the pâté is not put on the steaks until the last minute, lest it melt and look un-attractive before presentation.

To vary:
(i) *Veal Rossini:* Top cooked fillet of veal with the pâté.
(ii) *Chicken Rossini:* Split breast portions of young frying chicken, insert some of the pâté inside these pockets. Coat the chicken in beaten egg and fine breadcrumbs, then fry for about 15 minutes in hot butter.

Paprika Steak

Serves 4
Cooking Time: 25–30 minutes

INGREDIENTS

onions: 2 medium
flour: 2 tbsp
salt and pepper: to taste
rump steaks: 4
oil: 3 tbsp
paprika: 1–2 tbsp
beef stock: scant ⅔ cup
white wine: scant ⅔ cup
sour cream: ¼ pint
capers: 1–2 tbsp
chopped parsley: 2 tbsp

1 Peel and slice the onions.

2 Blend the flour with a fairly generous amount of salt and pepper; coat the steaks evenly with the seasoned flour.

3 Heat the oil in a large frying pan and fry the steaks on either side for 2 minutes, then remove from the pan.

4 Add the onions to the pan and fry steadily until golden brown.

5 Blend the paprika with the stock and wine, pour into the pan, and simmer gently for 10 minutes until the liquid is reduced to about half the original volume.

6 Replace the steaks in the pan and cook for a further 5–10 minutes, depending upon personal taste.

7 Finally, stir in the sour cream, capers, and parsley; heat gently for 2–3 minutes.

To serve: This dish is excellent with rice, a green salad, and a tomato salad.

To freeze: This dish is better freshly made.

Boeuf Provençale
The method of cooking this dish is similar to that used for Paprika Steaks, that is, the steaks are first fried for a short time in oil, and then cooked in the sauce. The ingredients in the sauce are different and typical of the Provence region of France.

1 Peel the onions, as in stage 1, but chop, rather than slice, them.

2 Skin and chop 1 clove of garlic and 3 medium tomatoes, and slice 4–6 large mushrooms.

3 Heat the oil, as in stage 3, and fry the steaks; these are not coated with flour in this recipe. Remove the meat from the pan after cooking for 1 minute on either side.

4 Add all the vegetables to the pan, fry for several minutes, as in stage 4. Continue as in stages 5 and 6, but omit the paprika.

5 Add 1–2 tbsp chopped black olives and the same amount of chopped parsley.
Note: This method of cooking is suitable for any type of steak but is especially good with a T-bone steak.

Filetti di Bue Capriccioso

Fillet Steak with Lemon and Anchovies
Serves 4
Cooking Time: 7–12 minutes

INGREDIENTS

for the marinade:
olive oil: 2 tbsp
lemon juice: 1 tbsp
grated lemon peel: 1 teaspoon
chopped sage: 2 teaspoons
chopped rosemary: 2 teaspoons
salt and pepper: to taste
fillet steaks: 4
for the coating:
breadcrumbs: 2 oz
for frying and the topping:
anchovy fillet: 3
unsalted butter: $\frac{1}{2}$ cup (1 stick)
to garnish:
lettuce: to taste
lemon: 1

1 Blend together all the ingredients for the marinade.

2 Pour these into a shallow dish and place the beef steaks in it.

3 Leave for an hour, turning over at least 3 times.

4 Lift the steaks from the marinade, hold over the dish for any surplus moisture to drain off; keep any marinade left and use at stage 7, if desired.

5 Spread the crumbs on a flat sheet of greaseproof paper and press the steaks into the crumbs, coating them on either side. If time permits, chill for about 30 minutes in the refrigerator.

6 Make Anchovy Butter with half the amount of butter (see the recipe on the right).

7 Heat the remaining butter in a large frying pan and fry the steaks until crisp and golden on either side, then lower the heat and continue cooking for a further time, if well done steaks are desired, see page 33, stage 9. Any marinade left can be added to the pan when the steaks are removed, heated and poured round the meat.

To serve: Lift the steaks onto the hot serving dish, arrange crisp lettuce round the meat. Cut the lemon into slices, put onto the steaks, then top with the anchovy butter. This dish is delicious served with anchovy fillets.

To vary:
This method of cooking steaks is equally good with thin slices of veal, lean pork, or with boned and rolled lamb cutlets.

Entrecotas con Acciughe e Olive

Entrecôtes with Anchovies and Olives
Serves 4
Cooking Time: 8–10 minutes

INGREDIENTS

for the topping:
anchovy fillets: 11
unsalted butter: $\frac{1}{4}$ cup ($\frac{1}{2}$ stick)
green olives, pitted: 3 oz
boneless rib or boneless loin steaks: 4
pepper: to taste
butter: $\frac{1}{4}$ cup ($\frac{1}{2}$ stick)

1 *Anchovy Butter:* Take 3 anchovy fillets and chop them finely. Blend with the butter. It is important to use unsalted butter to make this garnish, so that the mixture is not too salty. If the anchovies are very salty, e.g., the type you buy in jars, then rinse away the surplus salt and pat dry on absorbent paper. Form the mixture into 4 neat pats and chill.

2 Use the other fillets for garnish; rinse these, too, if necessary.

3 Soften the olives by simmering them for about 5 minutes in a little water.

4 Meanwhile, season the steaks with pepper only.

5 Heat the butter in a frying pan, fry the steaks to personal taste, as per the directions on page 33.

To serve: Drain the olives and arrange round the steaks. Top with the anchovy butter and anchovy fillets.

To freeze: Does not freeze well.

To vary:
(i) This garnish is suitable for serving with hamburgers, other steaks, or dishes prepared with minced beef or even with lean lamb or veal chops.
(ii) Beurre d'ail: This garlic butter is a good alternative to the anchovy butter in the recipe on this page. Add 1–2 skinned and crushed garlic cloves to the butter together with a little salt and pepper to taste.
(iii) *Maître d'hôtel butter:* Cream $\frac{1}{4}$ cup ($\frac{1}{2}$ stick) butter with 1 tbsp finely chopped parsley, a little salt and pepper, and a generous squeeze of lemon juice.
(iv) *Mustard butter:* Cream $\frac{1}{4}$ cup ($\frac{1}{2}$ stick) butter with prepared English, French, or other mustard; the amount is a matter of personal taste. Add salt and pepper to taste.
(v) *Speedy Anchovy Butter:* If no anchovy fillets are available, add anchovy essence to taste to the butter.

To serve: Chill savoury butters, form into neat pats and put on the steak just before serving.

To freeze: These butters freeze for up to 2 months.

Cooking at the Table

Many steak dishes are cooked at the table in a restaurant, and there is no reason why you cannot emulate this in your home.

You can begin the cooking process in the kitchen, then bring the pan into the dining room, and complete the cooking over a table heater; or you can use an electric frying pan for the whole of the cooking and serve the food from it.

For table cookery, choose a dish that has a certain drama about it – by that I mean that it has to be flambéed at some stage, or that its essence lies in the fact that it has to be cooked by the family and guests, as in the case of a fondue.

Making Fondues

One of the most pleasing dishes for an informal party is Fondue Bourguignonne, or Bœuf Fondue Bourguignonne. Sometimes this is called just Bœuf Bourguignonne, but that can be confusing since this is also the name of a classic French dish, which you will find on page 96.

Bœuf Fondue Bourguignonne

Beef Fondue Burgundy Style
Serves 4–6
Cooking Time: 2–3 minutes
plus time to prepare sauces
and heat the oil

INGREDIENTS

fillet steak: 2 lb
to garnish:
watercress: to taste
Béarnaise Sauce: as page 64
Curry Sauce: as page 85
Tomato Sauce: as page 96
for frying:
oil: see method

The secret of serving this is to have prime-quality meat and an interesting selection of sauces in which to dip the cooked beef.

Each person spears a piece of beef with a fondue fork, then holds it in the very hot oil until cooked to personal taste. They then remove the meat, put an ordinary fork into it, remove the fondue fork, dip the meat into a sauce, and eat at once.

Serve side salads and crusty French bread with the meat.

It is essential to replace the fondue fork with an ordinary one before eating the meat, for you could burn your mouth very seriously with the very hot fondue fork.

In Bœuf Fondue always choose a metal fondue pan, as the oil has to be raised to a very high temperature. On the other hand, you should cook a cheese fondue in a ceramic pan, to prevent the possibility of the mixture becoming too hot, or sticking to the pan, as it might do if the pan were metal.

When cooking fondues, take sensible 'safety-first' precautions:
(i) Put heat-resistant mats under the table heater, if you are using this on a dining-room table.
(ii) Make sure the heater is nowhere near curtains or anything which can catch fire.
(iii) Check that the oil does not become over-heated.

1 Cut the steak into neat portions about 1 inch square. Keep covered and in the refrigerator until ready to arrange on the table, so the cut surfaces do not dry; garnish the uncooked steak with watercress.

2 Prepare the various sauces, put these in small dishes round the main dish, or better still, on a table hotplate, so that they keep pleasantly warm. (There are suggestions for sauces to serve cold on this page.)

3 Use enough oil to come a *little under* two-thirds of the depth of a metal fondue pan. Heat this on a cooker, then transfer to a table heater, so that the temperature remains constant. The oil should be sufficiently hot to start cooking the meat as soon as it is put into it.

4 Spear one piece of meat with the fondue fork and hold in the hot oil until cooked.

To vary:
Make a large quantity of mayonnaise, see page 139, or buy a thick mayonnaise and divide into 5 portions, flavour as below.
a) Herb mayonnaise: Add a little finely chopped tarragon, thyme, and chervil.
b) Mustard mayonnaise: Blend a generous amount of French mustard (Dijon or Bordeaux is a good choice) with the mayonnaise.
c) Blend concentrated tomato purée with the mayonnaise.
d) Blend a little curry powder and/or curry paste with the mayonnaise.
e) Add a generous amount of lemon juice to the mayonnaise.

Bœuf Fondue au Fromage

Beef in Cheese Fondue
Serves 4–6
Cooking Time: 3–5 minutes
plus time to melt cheese

INGREDIENTS

fillet steak: 1 lb
to garnish:
watercress: to taste
for the fondue:
butter: 2 tbsp ($\frac{1}{4}$ stick)
Gruyère cheese or use a mixture of Gruyère and Emmenthal: 1 lb
salt and pepper: to taste
dry white wine: $1\frac{1}{4}$ cup
brandy or Curaçao: 1–2 tbsp

1 Prepare the meat as for *Bœuf Fondue Bourguignonne*, stage 1.

2 Spread the butter over the base and sides of the ceramic fondue pot.

3 Grate the cheese and put into the pot with the other ingredients.

4 Heat over the fondue heater, stirring from time to time until a smooth sauce; do not allow the mixture to become over-heated, otherwise it may curdle. Another way to prevent curdling is to add 1 teaspoon cornstarch or arrowroot which you should blend with the wine. To shorten the heating time for the cheese mixture, you should heat the fondue over a *very low* heat on the stove, and then transfer it to the fondue heater.

As the temperature of the cheese mixture must not be too high, it is important that you choose really prime beef. The time given in this recipe is for very under-done meat. However, if you prefer to have meat that is cooked more, cut it into smaller portions and leave it in the mixture for a longer time.

To serve: Spear the beef on the fondue forks and cook in the hot cheese mixture. You may also like to spear pieces of French bread or toast on the fork after cooking the beef and eat cheese-coated meat and bread or toast together. If not, serve the meat with crusty bread and salad. As the cheese mixture itself is so satisfying, you tend to eat less meat, but the quantity is really a matter of personal taste.

To freeze: This dish is not suitable for freezing.

To vary:
(i) By using other good cooking cheeses, you may create most interesting flavours; for example, try blending crumbled Danish Blue cheese with Gruyère or Cheddar cheese; or try dicing Camembert with Gruyère or Cheddar cheese. A little finely grated Parmesan cheese may be used with other cheeses.
(ii) Use beer or cider in place of wine.
(iii) Add finely chopped herbs and/or a little prepared mustard.

Filete de Lomo con Coñac

Fillet Steak in Brandy
Serves 4
Cooking Time: 15–20 minutes

INGREDIENTS

fillet steaks: 4
flour: 1 tbsp
salt and pepper: to taste
onions: 8 small
button mushrooms: 6 oz
butter: generous $\frac{1}{3}$ cup ($\frac{3}{4}$ stick)
brandy: 3 tbsp
beef stock: $1\frac{1}{4}$ cup
tomato purée: 1–2 tbsp
paprika: pinch
cayenne pepper: pinch
heavy whipping cream: 3 tbsp
to garnish:
chopped parsley: to taste
tomatoes: 4–6

1 Press out the fillet steaks until very thin, then cut across the centre to make 2 small steaks for each person.

2 Blend the flour with the salt and pepper, and coat the steaks with this mixture.

3 Peel the onions but leave them whole; trim the ends of the mushroom stalks, wipe or wash, but do not peel.

4 Heat the butter in a large heavy frying pan and fry the steaks for a minute on either side, then remove from the pan.

5 Fry the onions until golden in any butter remaining in the pan; add the mushrooms towards the end of the cooking period and fry for 1–2 minutes.

6 There are two ways of igniting the brandy:
a) As shown in picture 6a, i.e., to add the brandy to the ingredients in the pan, heat thoroughly, then tilt the pan, so that the warm brandy comes in contact with the heat and ignites; allow it to burn for a few seconds, then add the stock.
b) Pour the brandy into a really large spoon or soup ladle; warm over the heat and then tilt slightly, so that it comes in contact with the heat and ignites. Allow it to flame for a few seconds, then pour it over the vegetables in the pan and add the beef stock, see picture 6b.
Note: It you are not cooking over a table cooker or gas you may need to ignite the brandy with a match.

7 Blend the tomato purée, paprika, and cayenne pepper with the liquid in the pan and simmer for 15 minutes.

8 Finally, add the steaks and cream; simmer for 5 minutes for a rare steak but for 10 minutes for a well-cooked one. Taste the sauce and add more salt and pepper, if desired.

To serve: Spoon the meat and vegetables onto a hot serving dish, or serve from the pan. Top the meat with chopped parsley; slice the tomatoes and arrange round the edge of the meat and sauce. The contrast between the cooked meat and raw tomatoes is very pleasant.

To freeze: This dish is better when freshly made.

To vary:
Steak Calvados: Follow the directions as the recipe above, but use Calvados in place of brandy and cider instead of beef stock.

Steak au Poivre

Pepper Steak
Serves 4
Cooking Time: 10–15 minutes

INGREDIENTS

peppercorns: 1–1½ teaspoons
salt and pepper: to taste
steaks (in this version, fillet or Chateaubriand steaks
– tournedos are ideal): 4
unsalted butter: generous ⅓ cup (¾ stick)
for the sauce:
beef consommé: generous ½ cup
heavy whipping cream: generous ½ cup
chopped chervil or parsley: 1–2 teaspoons
brandy or Armagnac: 3 tbsp
to garnish:
watercress: to taste

It is interesting how this dish can vary in restaurants, from a simple fried steak which has been studded with crushed peppercorns, to a more luxurious version in which pepper-flavoured steak is served in a cream and brandy, or Armagnac, flavoured sauce.

Each version is excellent, but before making this dish, ensure that your guests really do like hot-flavoured foods, for the amount of pepper used is large.

You may use black peppercorns, but the steak looks more interesting if coated with a mixture of black and white peppercorns.

The French cuts used for steaks are somewhat different from others, and the faux-filet often recommended by French cooks for this recipe is not a cut that is always reproduced exactly in other countries. You can, therefore, use very good quality top sirloin, rump, or fillet steak. The latter is better for the more elaborate version of this dish, also given on this page. First, here is the simple version.

1 Allow about 1½ teaspoons peppercorns for 4 average-sized steaks; this will produce a moderately hot flavour and may be increased slightly, if desired. Should you use appreciably fewer peppercorns though, you will not have sufficient for coating.

2 Crush the peppercorns into small fragments; a rolling pin is best for doing this, since blenders tend to give too fine a texture.

3 Season the steaks with a little salt and freshly ground white or black pepper.

4 Press the crushed peppercorns into both sides of the steaks; do this very firmly so that they do not fall away in cooking.

5 Heat a generous amount of butter in a frying pan and fry the steaks as per the directions given on page 33.

To serve: Lift onto a dish, top with any butter left in the pan, and garnish with watercress.

Version 2

1 Prepare the peppercorns and season the steaks, as above.

2 Heat the butter in a large frying pan and fry the steaks as on page 33.

3 When *nearly* ready, add the consommé and heat with the meat quite briskly, until reduced to about half the original volume.

4 Lift the steaks out of the pan onto a hot dish, then add the cream to the pan, stir over a low heat until this is blended with the butter and consommé, then add the herbs and a little salt and pepper to taste.

5 Flambé the brandy or Armagnac in a large spoon over heat, as shown opposite, then add to the ingredients in the pan, heat for a minute. Spoon the sauce over the steaks.

To serve: Garnish with watercress and serve with a green salad.

To freeze: The cooked dish is spoiled if frozen.

To vary:
(i) In France you may well have this dish with a few green peppercorns in the cream sauce. These are imported from Madagascar and are available on fine-food counters, but are not readily obtainable everywhere, so the sauce can be flavoured with a little extra ground pepper and a pinch of nutmeg to give more flavour.
(ii) *Veal au Poivre:* Use fillet of veal instead of steak, but, as the meat is more delicate in flavour, be rather more sparing with the pepper and peppercorns and cook more rapidly.

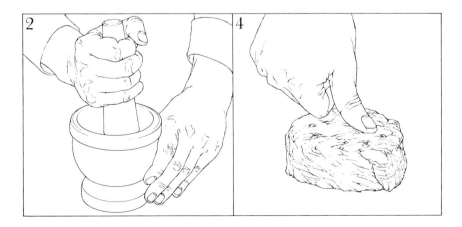

Bistecs a la Andaluza

Steak Andalusian Style
Serves 4
Cooking Time: 35–40 minutes

INGREDIENTS

onions: 4 medium
tomatoes: 6 large
eggplants: 2 medium
olive oil: 3 tbsp
salt and pepper: to taste
cooked ham: ¼ lb
cooked rice: 2 oz
rump or sirloin steaks: 4
to garnish:
olives: to taste

1 Peel and chop the onions; skin and chop 2 tomatoes.

2 Cut a slice from the remaining 4 tomatoes, scoop out the centre pulp, chop this and mix with the chopped tomatoes.

3 Halve the eggplants lengthways, brush with a little oil, and sprinkle with salt and pepper. Put into a dish, cover and bake for 15–20 minutes in a moderate oven, 350°F.

4 Scoop out the centre pulp of the eggplants, chop this finely, and chop the ham.

5 Heat half the remaining oil and fry the onions until soft, then blend half the onions with the chopped eggplant pulp.

6 Blend the eggplant and onion mixture and ham, and spoon into the eggplant cases.

7 Season the tomato cases with a little salt and pepper, and fill with the cooked rice.

8 Place the stuffed tomatoes and stuffed eggplants in a dish and bake for 10–15 minutes towards the top of a moderate oven.

9 Add the chopped tomatoes, with a little salt and pepper, to the onions left in the pan and continue cooking for 10 minutes.

10 Brush the steaks with the last of the oil and broil, see page 34.

To serve: Arrange the steaks on a hot dish, top with the onion and tomato mixture. Arrange the stuffed aubergines and tomatoes round the dish and garnish with the olives.

To freeze: Do not freeze this dish.

To vary:
Tournedos a la Andaluza: This is an interesting version which provides 2 sauces for the meat. Use the ingredients in the recipe above, but choose tournedos, prepared from fillet, see page 22, rather than rump steak, and add a sweet red pepper to the vegetables. Chop them all finely, discard the core and seeds from the pepper, and fry in the oil for 5 minutes; add a little wine and simmer until soft. This makes the first sauce.

If you dislike the bitter taste of eggplants, remember to follow the advice on page 58.

Fry, instead of broil, the steaks; lift out of the pan, add a little extra butter. Heat this for 2–3 minutes until golden brown, add several spoons of beef stock and the same amount of red wine, blend with the butter, boil hard for 1–2 minutes, then spoon over the steaks. Serve the first sauce separately.

Bistecca alla Pizzaiola

Steak with Tomato Sauce
Serves 4
Cooking Time: 35–40 minutes

INGREDIENTS

for the tomato sauce:
onions: 2 medium
garlic cloves: 2
plum tomatoes: 1 lb
oil: 2 tbsp
water: $\frac{1}{2}$–$\frac{2}{3}$ cup
chopped oregano or marjoram: $\frac{1}{2}$ teaspoon
chopped basil: $\frac{1}{2}$ teaspoon
salt and pepper: to taste
sugar: to taste
fillet, top sirloin, or boneless loin steaks: 4
butter or oil: to taste
to garnish:
mushrooms: $\frac{1}{4}$ lb or 4 oz can
butter: $\frac{1}{4}$ cup ($\frac{1}{2}$ stick)
artichoke hearts: 1 small can
chopped parsley: 2 tbsp

1 Peel and finely chop the onions and garlic.

2 Skin and chop the tomatoes; page 46 shows how to skin them.

3 Heat the oil, turn the vegetables in this, but do not allow them to brown.

4 Add the rest of the ingredients for the sauce and simmer for 10–15 minutes until a thick purée. This particular tomato sauce is not sieved.

5 Salt and pepper the steaks and fry in the butter or broil, see pages 33 and 34.

6 While the steaks are cooking, prepare the garnish. Trim the ends of the mushrooms, wipe or wash, and dry thoroughly, but do not peel.

7 Melt the butter and fry the mushrooms for 5–6 minutes in a separate frying pan.

8 Heat the artichokes, drain and blend with the mushrooms in the frying pan.

To serve: Arrange the steaks on a dish, top with the tomato sauce and chopped parsley. Spoon the mushrooms and artichokes round the meat.

To freeze: The steaks should not be frozen after cooking. This particular tomato sauce freezes well for 6 months.

Beiried-Doppelstücke auf Weinhändlerart

Austrian Wine Merchant's Steak
Serves 4
Cooking Time: 15–20 minutes

INGREDIENTS

onions: 1–2 medium
button mushrooms: 8–12
salt and pepper: to taste
top sirloin or porterhouse steaks: 4
butter: $\frac{1}{4}$ cup ($\frac{1}{2}$ stick)
oil: 1–2 tbsp
chopped parsley: 1 tbsp
fine breadcrumbs: scant $\frac{1}{4}$ cup
Gruyère cheese, grated: 4 tbsp
red wine: 1 cup

In order to have both topping and steaks perfectly cooked, I would use two frying pans for this dish.

1 Peel the onions and cut into thin rings.

2 Wipe the mushrooms, but do not peel; trim the ends of the stalks and slice thinly.

3 Add a little salt and pepper to the steaks.

4 Divide the butter and oil between the pans, heat the one pan, and start to cook the onions and mushrooms together until a soft purée; add the parsley, with salt and pepper to taste.

5 Meanwhile, heat the remaining butter and oil in the second pan and fry the steaks to personal taste, as per the timing on page 33. Heat the broiler at this stage.

6 Lift the steaks onto a flame-proof serving dish, and spoon the onion and mushroom mixture on top.

7 Blend the breadcrumbs and cheese, sprinkle over the topping, and brown under the broiler for a few minutes.

8 Pour the wine into the pan in which the steaks were cooked, bring just to boiling point, stir well to absorb any meat juices.

To serve: Pour the wine sauce round the steaks. These are excellent with cooked noodles.

To freeze: Does not freeze well.

To vary:
(i) This dish is even more delicious if the marrow from beef bones is extracted and added to the onion mixture and if a squeeze of lemon juice is blended with the purée.
(ii) Omit the crumb-and-cheese topping.
(iii) *Lamb – Wine-Merchant's Style:* Substitute noisettes of lamb (boned and rolled lamb cutlets) for the steaks.

Tatranské Medailjonky

Giant Mountains Medallions
Serves 4–6
Cooking Time: 15–20 minutes

INGREDIENTS

very small button mushrooms: 6 oz
white wine or white malt vinegar: $\frac{1}{2}$–$\frac{2}{3}$ cup
salt and pepper: to taste
fillet of veal: 1 lb
fillet or boneless loin steak: 1 lb
flour: 1 tbsp
butter: $\frac{1}{4}$ cup ($\frac{1}{2}$ stick)
heavy whipping cream: $\frac{1}{2}$–$\frac{2}{3}$ cup

This Czechoslovakian recipe combines veal and beef very happily and I have also used lean pork with the beef to make an interesting change.

Pickled mushrooms, generally used in Czechoslovakia, are not always available, so this recipe uses fresh mushrooms and vinegar instead.

1 Wash or wipe the mushrooms; trim the ends of the stalks and put into a saucepan with the vinegar, salt, and pepper.

2 Bring the vinegar to the boil, then leave the mushrooms in the vinegar for 30 minutes.

3 Pound and roll the veal and beef until very thin, then cut each piece of meat into 4 neat portions and sprinkle with the flour and a generous amount of salt and pepper.

4 Heat the butter in the pan, fry the veal for 3–4 minutes, then add the beef and continue frying for 2 minutes.

5 Lift half the mushrooms from the vinegar, add to the pan, and fry for just a minute.

6 Stir in the cream and heat gently.

To serve: Arrange the meat and sauce on a hot dish. Reheat the rest of the mushrooms in the vinegar, then spoon them over the top of the meat. Any vinegar left can be cooled and used as a dressing in a salad.

To freeze: This dish is unsuitable for freezing.

To vary:
(i) To give a sharper flavour use sour cream instead of fresh cream at stage 6.
(ii) Use fillet of lean pork with the beef, or blend pork and veal and omit the beef.
(iii) This method of cooking meat, with the combination of the sharp-flavoured mushrooms and cream, could be used with noisettes of lamb, (lean cutlets of lamb which are boned and rolled to look like tournedos of beef).

Fried Steak and Onions

To many Britons, a fried steak is not worth eating without a lavish helping of fried onions. What kind of fried onion? There is the problem – no one has exactly the same idea as to what constitutes the perfect way of cooking this vegetable.

To some people the rings should be soft and moist, to others dry and beautifully crisp, with each onion ring quite separate.

Whichever type is preferred, it is important to fry them *before* the steak.

1 Peel the onions and cut into slices, then separate the slices into rings.

2 *For soft onions:* Heat a generous amount of butter in the frying pan and fry the onions steadily until soft and pale golden in colour. If the butter seems to be getting a little hot and the onions in danger of becoming too brown, add 1 tbsp of stock or water. When the onions are cooked, add a little salt and pepper; remove and keep hot while frying the steak, see page 33. You may use the same pan for cooking the steak, which will then acquire some of the onion taste.

3 *For crisp onions:* Dip the onion rings in either milk or lightly whisked egg white, then coat in flour or cornstarch. You must have a very light coating only, so shake away any surplus.

4 Heat enough oil in the frying pan to give a depth of about $\frac{1}{2}$ inch and fry the onions quickly until golden brown and crisp.

5 Drain on absorbent paper and keep hot until ready to serve with the steak.

You can fry the steak in the same frying pan, see page 33, using any oil left, or use two separate pans, one for the onion rings, the other for the steak. *Do not use too much oil* in cooking the steaks, for this could harden them.

If cooking a large quantity of onion rings, it is better to use a deep pan with a frying basket, as described on page 86.

The crisp onion rings can be flavoured with a light dusting of garlic or celery salt and finely chopped fresh sage. This is a strong-flavoured herb, so use it sparingly.

Filets Mignons Piémontaise

Mignon Fillet Steaks Italian Style
Serves 4
Cooking Time: 8–12 minutes

INGREDIENTS

filet mignon steaks, see pages 22 and 23: 4
salt and pepper: to taste
butter: $\frac{1}{4}$ cup ($\frac{1}{2}$ stick)
white wine: 3 tbsp
tomato juice or fresh tomato purée (see method): 3 tbsp

1 Sprinkle the steaks with a little salt and pepper.

2 Heat the butter in a frying pan and fry the steaks until cooked to personal taste, see page 33. These small and very tender cuts of beef are cooked within a very short time.

3 Lift the meat onto a hot serving dish.

4 Add the wine and tomato juice or purée to the pan; stir and heat to absorb any butter left in the pan and spoon over the steaks.

To make the purée: rub 2–3 large ripe tomatoes through a sieve.

To serve: Either with rice blended with truffles, or, when these are not available, with cooked peas and fried sliced mushrooms.

To vary:
(i) *Filets Mignons à la Dijon:* Omit the tomato juice or purée in the basic recipe on this page. Cook the steaks as in stage 2, remove from the pan. Stir 1–2 tbsp Dijon mustard and $\frac{1}{2}$–$\frac{2}{3}$ cup white Burgundy into the pan. Blend with the butter remaining in the pan. Add several tablespoons of heavy whipping cream and heat gently. Spoon the sauce over the steaks.
(ii) *Medallions de Boeuf du Barry:* Omit the tomato juice or purée in the basic recipe here. Cook the steaks as in stage 2, but allow them to remain in the pan and add a little wine towards the end of the cooking period. Serve garnished with florets of cooked cauliflower, topped with a cheese sauce, made as follows:
Heat 2 tbsp butter in a saucepan; stir in 2 tbsp flour and stir over a low heat for several minutes. Blend in $1\frac{1}{4}$ cup milk with a little salt, pepper, and mustard. Bring the liquid to the boil and stir until the sauce has thickened. Add $\frac{1}{4}$ lb finely grated Gruyère, Cheddar, or other good cooking cheese. Heat the sauce gently, without boiling, until the cheese has melted.

The Chinese have perfected a technique, known as 'stir-frying', in which thin shreds of food are cooked in a frying pan for a very short time.

Tender steak is ideal for this method of cooking. Choose any cuts of steak you prefer.

Bamboo shoots are the shoots of an Oriental plant and very rarely obtainable as a fresh vegetable. They are easily purchased in the canned form. Their taste and texture are delicious. They are slightly sweet and crisp, even after canning.

1 Drain the canned bamboo shoots and cut these into very narrow strips.

2 Peel and chop the carrots and onion into the same-sized pieces.

3 Wash the leek and mushrooms, and cut these in a similar manner, together with the flesh of the sweet red pepper; discard the core and seeds.

4 Cut the steak into narrow strips.

5 Blend the cornstarch with a little salt and pepper, and toss the meat in this.

Chinese Beef with Bamboo Shoots

Serves 4–6
Cooking Time: 8–11 minutes

INGREDIENTS

canned bamboo shoots: about 8 oz
carrots: 2 medium
onion: 1 small
leek: 1 small
mushrooms: 6 small
sweet red pepper: 1
steak, see above: 12 oz
cornstarch: 1 tbsp
salt and pepper: to taste
vegetable oil: 2 tbsp
bean sprouts: $\frac{1}{4}$ lb or 4-oz can
soy sauce: 1 tbsp
dry sherry: 2 tbsp
fresh green ginger root: 1 piece
beef stock: scant $\frac{2}{3}$ cup

6 Heat half the oil in a large frying pan or table cooker, fry the meat for 1–2 minutes only, *no longer;* remove to a plate.

7 Heat the remaining oil and fry the prepared vegetables; if using canned bean sprouts, add at the end of stage 8, but fresh ones should be put in here.

8 Cook for 3–4 minutes, then add the soy sauce and sherry.

9 Dice the ginger, put into the pan with the stock, and simmer for 4–5 minutes.

10 Return the beef to the pan and heat for another 2 minutes.

To serve: With rice. This is an ideal dish for table cookery; it can be served from the pan.

To freeze: This is a dish which should not be frozen.

Mørbradsteg

Grilled Steak with Blue Cheese
Serves 4
Cooking Time: 10–15 minutes

INGREDIENTS

butter: generous ⅓ cup (¾ stick)
Danish Blue cheese: ¼ lb
salt and pepper: to taste
rump or sirloin steaks: 4
to garnish:
parsley: few sprigs
radishes: 12

1 Melt about 2 tbsp of the butter.

2 Cream the rest of the butter and blend with the cheese and a little salt and pepper.

3 Brush the steaks with the melted butter and broil, see page 34, but remove the steaks for the last 1–2 minutes and spread with the cheese mixture.

4 Return to the broiler and heat until the cheese mixture bubbles and is really hot.

To serve: Garnish with the parsley and radishes and serve with new potatoes and green salad.

To freeze: Do not freeze.

To vary:
(i) Use Gruyère or another good cooking cheese instead of the Danish Blue.
(ii) Use the butter and cheese topping on veal or *lean* pork fillets.

Chateaubriand

A Chateaubriand steak is really a double fillet steak, cut from the very centre of the whole fillet of beef. A Chateaubriand weighs about 1¼ lb and serves 2 to 3 people. The steak is cooked whole and carved, see page 26. Apparently, the method of cutting the meat and the ways of cooking and serving it were created by Montmireil, chef to Chateaubriand, hence the name.

In some books of reference a Chateaubriand is described as being the same as a Porterhouse steak; this is not correct. A Porterhouse steak is similar to a T-bone steak, but larger. While it certainly includes the fillet, it also incorporates the loin, which the Chateaubriand does not do.

Fillet steak, like any other, may be frozen uncooked, but you will need to defrost the meat before it can be formed into the traditional Chateaubriand shape, unless you do this before you freeze it.

1 Make the thick piece of steak into a much thinner one, as shown on page 23.

2 Fry or broil the steak; although it has now become much thinner, a Chateaubriand is still a large steak which must be cooked carefully, so that it does not become over-brown on the outside before it is cooked to personal taste in the centre. The timings on pages 33 and 34 may need to be increased by a minute or so, but not much more, for it is essential that the steak is not dried. Obviously, where people share the steak, they must agree upon how long it should be cooked.

It is possible to roast the steak in the oven, and the timings given on pages 35 and 36 should be reduced by a few minutes, since fillet steak is so very tender and this particular cut has been made thinner.

3 When the steak is cooked, lift onto a board or dish, and add any juices still in the pan.

To serve: Garnish with a selection of vegetables, and Chateaubriand Sauce.

To freeze: Cooked fillet steak should never be frozen.

To vary:
(i) Serve the Chateaubriand with a Béarnaise Sauce, page 64, or with any of the garnishes or accompaniments given for other steaks in this chapter.
(ii) *Planked Steak:* A Chateaubriand lends itself to this method of presentation. A board on which a steak is to be partially cooked, and then served, must be chosen with care. It must be of well-dried oak and really so solid that it is suitable for placing under the broiler. It is often recommended that the steak is cooked in the usual manner on one side, then lifted onto the oiled plank and placed under the broiler to finish cooking. In this way the board becomes less charred.

Another suggestion is to cover any exposed part of the board with a border of piped Pommes Duchesse, see page 107; the potato mixture browns while the steak finishes cooking. If this is not convenient, then exposed parts of the board should be covered in foil. Undoubtedly, the contact with the oak while cooking gives the meat a very excellent flavour.

Chateaubriand Sauce

1 Peel and halve or slice a shallot or very small onion.

2 Put into a pan with a small sprig of thyme, a bay leaf, 2–3 sliced mushrooms, 1¼ cup beef stock, and scant ⅔ cup white wine.

2 Add a little salt and pepper, and allow the liquid to simmer in an open pan until reduced to about ½–⅔ cup. This means that the flavour is very concentrated.

4 Strain the mixture and return the liquid to the saucepan.

5 Add ¼ cup (½ stick) butter, 1 tbsp chopped parsley, and a squeeze of lemon juice.

6 Heat well, then spoon over the sliced steak when serving.

To freeze: This sauce is better freshly made.

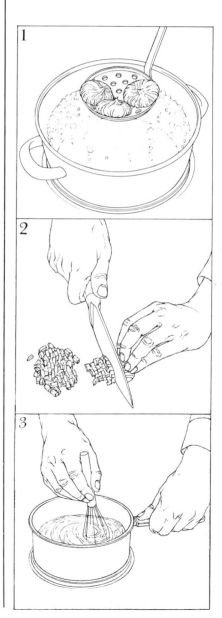

Entrecôte Bercy

Entrecôte in White Wine Sauce
Serves 4
Cooking Time: 10–15 minutes

INGREDIENTS

for the sauce:
shallots: 3
white wine: $\frac{1}{2}$–$\frac{2}{3}$ cup
lemon juice: 1 tbsp
unsalted butter: generous $\frac{1}{3}$ cup ($\frac{3}{4}$ stick)
salt and pepper: to taste
chopped parsley: 1 tbsp
boneless rib or loin steaks: 4
for broiling:
butter or oil: to taste
to garnish:
watercress: to taste

The recipe below and the one that follows illustrate the ability of the French to create a delicious sauce from very simple ingredients. These particular sauces are based on a process known as 'de-glazing'. This means incorporating a very generous amount of butter into liquid, which is generally wine.

The secret of the creamy sauce is to have the butter at room temperature, so that it is easily blended with the liquid, without using excessive heat or a prolonged cooking period.

Shallots are better in these recipes than onions, since they have a more delicate flavour.

1 Peel and chop the shallots very finely; pictures 1 and 2 shows how best to do this. Put into a saucepan with the white wine and lemon juice.

2 Heat for a few minutes until the liquid is reduced to about half the original volume.

3 Whisk or beat in the butter for the sauce gradually, do not add this too quickly; the butter should not become oily or melt completely, but be soft and creamy.

4 Add the salt, pepper, and parsley.

5 *While the sauce is cooking,* season the steaks and broil to personal taste, see page 34, basting with a little butter or oil; it is important that the sauce is not kept waiting.

To serve: Spoon the sauce over the steaks and garnish with watercress.

To vary:
1 tbsp beef glaze could be added to the ingredients to give a stronger sauce.

This beef glaze forms beneath real beef drippings and should never be wasted, see page 35.

Entrecôte Marchand de Vin

Entrecôte in Red Wine Sauce
Serves 4
Cooking Time: 10–15 minutes

INGREDIENTS

for frying:
salt and pepper: to taste
entrecôte steaks: 4
butter or oil: to taste
for the sauce:
shallots: 3–4
red wine: $1\frac{1}{4}$ cup
chopped parsley: 1 tbsp
lemon juice: 2 teaspoons
butter: generous $\frac{1}{3}$ cup ($\frac{3}{4}$ stick)
to garnish:
chopped parsley: to taste

This recipe is similar in many ways to Entrecôte Bercy, but the steaks are fried, rather than broiled. It is important that any butter or oil left in the pan from frying the steaks and shallots should be poured away, so that the sauce will not become cloudy. It is possible, though, to make the sauce in the same pan as that in which the steaks were cooked, provided the meat is not kept waiting too long on the hot dish before being served. You can, of course, use two frying pans or a frying pan and a shallow saucepan, and cook the steaks and sauce simultaneously.

1 Add a little salt and pepper to the steaks and fry in the butter or oil, see page 33, but do not over-cook the meat, if it is to be kept hot while you make the sauce.

2 Peel and chop the shallots for the sauce, as in pictures 1 and 2; it is better to do this before cooking the meat, so that there is no time-lag.

3 If you are using the same pan for making the sauce, lift the meat onto a hot serving dish.

4 Add the shallots to the pan and very gently sauté in the butter or oil left, stir well so that they do not discolour. When these are nearly soft, check that there is no surplus butter left; if there is, then lift the shallots onto a plate, pour away the butter or oil, then replace the shallots in the pan.

5 If, on the other hand, you are using two pans, then you will need a little extra butter or oil in which to cook the shallots.

6 Add the wine to the shallots and simmer to half the original volume, then stir in the parsley, lemon juice, and a little salt and pepper.

7 Finally, incorporate the butter as described in Entrecôte Bercy, stage 3.

To serve: Coat the steaks with the sauce and garnish with some chopped parsley. This dish is excellent served with cooked artichoke hearts.

Mixed Grill

This is an interesting way of blending steak with other meats and vegetables. Fried eggs are often part of the mixed grill, too.

There is no classic recipe for this dish, for the choice of ingredients depends very much upon personal taste, but the grill should consist of a good selection, if not all, of the following. Naturally the portions of each are relatively small.

Bacon slices – allow 1 per portion
Calves' or lambs' liver – allow a small slice per person
Lamb cutlets – allow just 1 cutlet per person
Lambs' kidneys – allow 1 or 2 kidneys per person
Sausages – allow 1 large or 2 small sausages per person
Steaks – allow about a third of the usual amount of steak
Butter or oil, where necessary
Salt and pepper to taste
Flavourings, see method
Mushrooms – allow several per person

Tomatoes – allow 1 or 2 per person
Fried eggs – allow 1 per person

To garnish:
watercress,
maître d'hôtel butter, recipe on page 67; this serves 4 people.

The important secret of a good Mixed Grill is to cook the various foods in such a way that they are all ready together.

1 Cut any rind from the bacon, brush the liver with melted butter or oil, and season with a little salt and pepper; do not coat in flour, for this hardens the outside. A very little French mustard can be spread on the liver, if desired.

2 The cutlets do not need any butter or oil, unless very lean; just season lightly with salt and pepper.

3 Remove any white fat from the kidneys, then skin and halve if desired, brush with plenty of melted butter or oil, and season lightly; a

squeeze of lemon juice adds an interesting flavour.

4 Prick the sausages. There is no need to add fat to the 'breakfast' type of sausage, but brush Frankfurter sausages with a little melted butter or oil.

5 Make sure you use a generous amount of butter or oil on the steak; season lightly.

6 Prepare the mushrooms, trim the ends of the stalks, but do not peel; halve and season the tomatoes, or leave whole. The vegetables can be placed in the pan with a little melted butter or oil, and the meat on a broiler above the vegetables, so that they cook simultaneously. Naturally, this depends upon the type of broiler available; if this is not possible, then you must add the vegetables to the meat during cooking.

7 Start cooking the food that needs most time, generally the lamb cutlets and kidneys, and add the meat

gradually to the broiler pan, keeping it moist with melted butter or oil as you do so.

8 Towards the end of the cooking period, heat a little butter or oil in a frying pan and cook the eggs.

To serve: Arrange the foods on a large dish; garnish with the watercress and maître d'hôtel butter, and serve at once.

To vary:
A Czech mixed grill combines small pork chops, lamb chops, veal, and steaks to give a very sustaining dish; obviously, the portions of each kind of meat are relatively small in comparison to the normal portions.

Carpet Bag Steak

Serves 6–8

If you imagine that a combination of shell fish and steak is odd, you might be right, but it is delicious. I first tasted this dish some years ago in Sydney, Australia, and found it both a simple and appetizing way of cooking steak.

The coast of New South Wales is famous for shell fish, particularly oysters, which are small, but incredibly sweet in taste. A Carpet Bag Steak is one which is stuffed with, among other ingredients, oysters.

Australians eat a lot of meat, so the portions are generous. The amount of meat may be reduced, but you must still purchase a thick piece of steak in order to make adequate pockets.

1 *To make the stuffing:* Slice ¼ lb mushrooms, chop enough parsley to give at least 1 tbsp.

2 Heat ¼ cup (½ stick) butter in a frying pan and fry the mushrooms until nearly tender, then add about 18 small oysters. If the oysters are large, you will need fewer, but they should be sliced, not left whole.

3 Continue cooking gently for 2–3 minutes, then blend the mushrooms and oysters with ½–⅔ cup fine breadcrumbs, the parsley, and salt and pepper to taste.

4 Add the finely grated peel and juice of a small lemon; bind with an egg.

5 Take a flat piece of rump steak, or top sirloin, weighing just about 3½–4 lb; insert the tip of a sharp knife into the meat and make fairly deep pockets; you need one for each person.

6 Push the stuffing into each pocket with a small spoon.

7 Sew up the pockets with a needle and fine thread, or secure with wooden cocktail picks.

8 Spread the steak with butter and roast for 40 minutes to 1 hour, depending on personal taste. Start with a hot oven, 425°F, for the first 20 minutes, then reduce the heat slightly to complete the cooking.

To serve: With green salad.

To vary:
(i) Make pockets in individual steaks and grill or fry.
(ii) Use mussels instead of oysters.

Nadivana Hovesi Pecene S Omackou
(Stuffed Steak Czech Style)
The Czechoslovakian cuisine includes a steak that is not unlike the Australian Carpet Bag Steak, but the stuffing is quite different, and the tender steak is rolled round the filling. You could, however, make a pocket and insert the stuffing, if preferred.

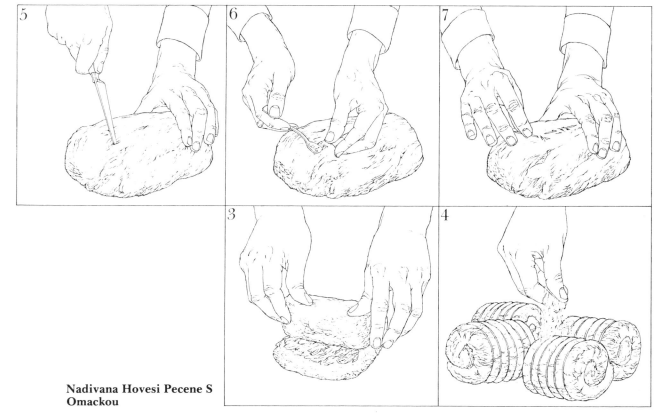

Nadivana Hovesi Pecene S Omackou

82

Biftec al Horno

Baked Steak
Serves 4
Cooking Time: 40 minutes

1 *To make the stuffing:* Peel and chop 2 medium onions, fry in 2 tbsp butter or lard until soft; blend with ¼ lb finely chopped cooked sausage, salami, or ham, and ½–⅔ cup breadcrumbs (the traditional recipe often uses rye or black bread).

2 Add salt, pepper, and a shake of paprika to taste; bind with an egg.

3 Roll 4 fillet steaks until very thin, spread with the stuffing and roll firmly, tie with cotton or secure with wooden cocktail picks.

4 Dust the rolls with a very little flour, blended with salt and pepper.

5 Heat generous ⅓ cup (¾ stick) butter in a heavy frying pan and fry the steaks, turning over once or twice until cooked to your personal taste; remember, they will take longer than usual, as they are filled and rolled. Information on frying steak is on page 33.

6 While the sauce is cooking, slice ¼ lb mushrooms.

7 Heat 2 tbsp butter in another pan, fry the mushrooms until just tender, then blend in 1¼ cup cream, blended with salt and pepper, a good pinch of paprika, and either a pinch of powdered caraway or a few caraway seeds.

To serve: Arrange the cooked steaks on a dish, top with the sauce and garnish with chopped parsley.

This method of frying and then baking the steak in the oven is only suitable for those people who like their meat well cooked. It is rather pointless to remove the meat from the frying pan and transfer it to the oven, if you like it to be 'rare' or even moderately underdone.

Remember this dish has a really hot flavour, with the combination of cayenne pepper and chilli powder.

I have learned that chilli powder can vary quite appreciably in its strength, so *always* add it gradually to any dish and make certain that everyone will enjoy its potency.

1 Peel and crush the garlic, put half to one side to add to the vegetable topping.

2 Blend the remaining garlic with the flour, cayenne pepper, a pinch of the chilli powder, and a little salt and pepper.

3 Lay the steaks on a flat surface, sprinkle the flour mixture on the meat and press this firmly into the flesh with the back of a metal spoon.

4 Leave for about 1 hour in a cool place, so that the meat absorbs the various flavourings.

5 Heat half the oil in a large frying pan and cook the steaks for 2 minutes on either side, then transfer them to a large oven-proof dish.

6 Peel the onions and cut into neat slices, separate these into rings; skin and slice the tomatoes and chop the olives.

7 Heat the rest of the oil in the frying pan and add the vegetables with the remainder of the garlic and chilli powder and a little salt.

INGREDIENTS

garlic cloves: 3–4
flour: 1 tbsp
cayenne pepper: pinch
chilli powder: ½–1 teaspoon
salt and pepper: to taste
rump or sirloin steaks: 4
oil: 3 tbsp
onions: 3 medium
tomatoes: 4 medium
stuffed olives: 8–12
beef stock: 4 tbsp

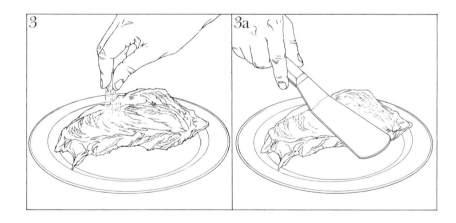

8 Fry in the oil for a minute only, then add the stock, and simmer for 5 minutes or until the stock is virtually absorbed.

9 Spoon the mixture over the steaks and cover the dish.

10 Bake towards the top of a moderately hot oven, 400°F, for 25 minutes.

To serve: With new or creamed potatoes and peas.

To freeze: This dish is better freshly made.

To vary:
This method is also very suitable for thick lamb chops.

Beef Stroganoff

Serves 4–6
Cooking Time: 15–20 minutes

INGREDIENTS

fillet steak: 1½–2 lb
salt and pepper: to taste
butter: ½ cup (1 stick)
flour: 1 tbsp
beef stock: generous ½ cup
tomato purée: 1 tbsp
prepared mustard: ½ teaspoon
button mushrooms: ¼ lb or 4-oz can
onion: 1 medium
sour cream: 1¼ cup

This Russian dish has become so much part of international cookery that one finds it on menus throughout the world. Sadly, the version often served bears no resemblance to the original, named after a Russian, Count Stroganov. A true Beef Stroganoff is not a stew, but a way of serving prime fillet steak in a sour cream sauce.

To make Beef Stroganoff well, you must prepare the ingredients a good time beforehand, and then cook the food for a very limited time only, allowing it to stand before being served, so that the flavours may blend. This means that the dish is an ideal choice for entertaining and an admirable dish for table cookery.

1 Cut the fillet beef into neat strips; do not have these too thin, otherwise the beef is easily over-cooked.

2 Sprinkle the meat with a generous amount of salt and pepper, cover and leave in the refrigerator for 2–3 hours.

3 Heat 2 tbsp (¼ stick) of the butter in a pan, stir in the flour, and allow this to turn a pale golden brown, then gradually blend in the stock, tomato purée, and prepared mustard. Stir until thickened.

4 Remove the sauce from the pan and leave in a cool place; if you put the sauce into the blender after cooking, it will have a very velvety, smooth texture.

5 Wash or wipe the mushrooms, do not peel, and cut into wafer-thin slices.

6 Heat another 2 tbsp (¼ stick) of the butter, and cook the mushrooms for a few minutes until soft.

7 Peel and chop the onion very finely before the dish is to be cooked.

8 Heat the remaining butter in a large frying pan and fry the steak and onion for 4–5 minutes only; stir continually and turn the beef after 2 minutes so that it does not become too well cooked; the onion should still retain a certain amount of its texture and not become too soft.

9 Add the sauce, heat for a minute, then stir in the cooked mushrooms and sour cream; add a little extra salt and pepper if required.

10 Put a lid on the frying pan, and keep the dish warm over a table heater or near the cooker, but do not allow the food to continue cooking. Bring to boiling point just before serving.

To serve: With rice and a green salad.

To freeze: This dish is spoiled if frozen.

To vary:
(i) Less expensive steak or good-quality round or rump steak may be used. As this requires a longer cooking period at stages 8 and 9, use double the amount of stock to make the sauce, at stage 3.
(ii) If you prefer a rather drier mixture, use only half the quantity of sour cream.
(iii) Add a liqueur glass of brandy to the meat and onion at the end of stage 8. Warm for a minute, then ignite and continue as the recipe above.

Sauces

Sauces to Serve with Steaks

These classic sauces add flavour to broiled or fried steaks.

Espagnole Sauce

1 Peel and chop 1 small onion, slice 2 large mushrooms, and slice 2 large tomatoes; remove the rind and chop a small strip of bacon.

2 Melt 2 tbsp butter or beef drippings in a pan, add the bacon and the bacon rind, and fry for 2–3 minutes. Put in the vegetables and continue cooking for another 5 minutes, stirring well; remove the bacon rind.

3 Blend in 2 tbsp flour and stir over a low heat for 3–4 minutes.

4 Gradually blend in 1¼ cups of beef stock, add a bouquet garni of parsley, thyme, and a bay leaf.

5 Bring the sauce to the boil, stir continuously, and add salt and pepper to taste.

6 Cover the pan and simmer for 30–40 minutes.

7 Sieve the sauce, reheat, and add 2 tbsp of sherry.

To serve: With fried or broiled meats.

To freeze: The sauce freezes well; add the sherry when reheating.

To vary:
(i) *Creole Sauce:* This is particularly good with broiled T-bone steaks. Add a crushed clove of garlic at stage 1, together with 2 extra tomatoes. Add a diced sweet green pepper (discard the core and seeds) at the end of stage 7. The garlic can also be added at stage 7, so that it is stronger in taste.

(ii) *Poivrade Sauce:* Add a generous amount of pepper or peppercorns at stage 5 and 1–2 tbsp red wine vinegar and the same amount of brandy at the end of stage 7.

Brown Sauce

1 Use a really good beef stock and infuse in this an onion or carrot for extra flavour, then strain.

2 Heat 2 tbsp (¼ stick) butter or beef drippings in a pan. Stir in 2 tbsp flour, and allow this 'roux' to brown over a low heat, stirring all the time, so that it does not burn.

3 Blend in a *generous* 1¼ cup stock, bring to the boil and allow to cook until it has a coating consistency.

4 Add salt and pepper to taste, plus a little prepared mustard if desired.

To serve: This sauce blends well with beef but can be made more interesting as described under the variations.

To freeze: It is better to freeze the stock, rather than the sauce.

To vary:
(i) Add a little port wine or sherry to the brown sauce.
(ii) Use double the amount of butter or drippings and fry 1 or 2 sliced onions, 1 sliced carrot, and a little sliced celery in it at stage 2. Proceed through stage 4, then sieve or put through a blender.
(iii) *Madeira Sauce:* Use half stock and half Madeira wine; a little fresh sieved tomato purée can be added, if desired.
(iv) *Indienne Sauce:* Simply add a little curry powder with the flour.

Curry Sauce

This particular curry sauce is not only one of the accompaniments to Bœuf Fondue Bourguignonne on page 68, but a classic sauce to serve with steak. Do not cook the steak in the sauce, but fry or broil it in the usual manner, then top with a portion of sauce. You could then entitle the dish 'Tournedos Indienne' or preface the word 'Indienne' with the particular steak you have selected.

This sauce has only a delicate touch of curry flavour. The quantity given below is sufficient to serve with 4–6 steaks or as one of the sauces on page 68.

1 Peel and chop a small onion.

2 Heat 3 tbsp (scant ½ stick) butter in a pan and fry the onion until just golden.

3 Add 2 tbsp flour, blended with 1–2 teaspoons curry powder.

4 Stir in 1¼ cup milk, bring steadily to the boil, stirring all the time; simmer for 8–10 minutes.

5 Add salt and pepper to taste, with a very little sugar, if desired; stir 4 tbsp heavy whipping cream into the hot sauce just before serving.

To serve: With the cooked steak, rice, and a green salad.

To freeze: The sauce can be frozen for 2–3 weeks, but much of the flavour of curry is lost.

To vary:
(i) For a less creamy sauce, use all beef stock, or half beef stock and half milk, at stage 4.
(ii) For a more interesting sauce add a few sultanas and a little finely grated coconut; increase the amount of curry used.

Potatoes

Pommes de Terre Pont-neuf

In most countries fried potatoes, or 'French fries', are popular as an accompaniment to grilled or fried steaks. The potatoes can be cut into slices or shaped as shown in the pictures. A good fried potato should be crisp, golden brown, and never greasy. Peel the potatoes, shape, and keep in cold water until ready to fry. Dry the potatoes well before frying.

Picture 1 Cutting potatoes to shape; the ends of the potatoes are removed, then the flesh cut into narrow finger shapes. There are special gadgets to do this easily and quickly.

Picture 2 A narrow match-shaped potato known as 'allumettes' and even thinner straw-shaped potatoes, Pommes de Terre Paille.

Picture 3 How to make round balls or 'noisettes'. Insert a vegetable scoop into the flesh of the potato, turn carefully until you have cut a perfect ball. Any potato flesh left over can be cooked and creamed.

Picture 4 Ribbon-shaped potatoes. Make by peeling the potato flesh carefully until you have a thin ribbon.

Picture 5 Heat the fat or oil in a deep pan; if you are using oil it should be sufficiently hot for a cube of day-old bread to turn golden within just over half a minute. Never have the pan more than half filled with fat or oil, for it will rise appreciably when frying the potatoes.

Picture 6 Heat the frying basket in the hot fat or oil; this prevents the potatoes sticking to the basket. Put some of the potatoes into the basket and lower into the hot fat or oil. Fry steadily until the potatoes are just soft, then remove from the pan, and stand the potatoes and basket on a plate or metal tray.

Picture 7 Reheat the fat or oil, then fry the potatoes again for a very short time. This will turn them golden brown.

Picture 8 Drain on absorbent paper, sprinkle with a little salt, and serve.

Roast Potatoes

Roast potatoes are an excellent accompaniment to roast beef or to many of the beef dishes in this book.

1 Peel old potatoes; if large, cut into equal-sized pieces; the smaller the size, the greater the proportion of crisp outside to soft centres. Keep in cold water until ready to cook, then dry well.

2 It is ideal if you can roast the potatoes in the same pan as the beef, for they absorb the flavour of the meat; whether roasting in the meat pan or separately, you need approximately $\frac{1}{4}$ cup extra fat.

3 Make sure the fat is very hot, then turn the potatoes round in it so that they are well coated.

4 Cook for about 1 hour, unless they are very small, in a moderately hot oven, 400°F.

To vary:
(i) For a more 'floury' potato, boil in salted water for about 10–15 minutes, drain, dry well, then roast.
(ii) Small new potatoes should be roasted with their skins on; just scrub these well.

CLASSIC ROASTS

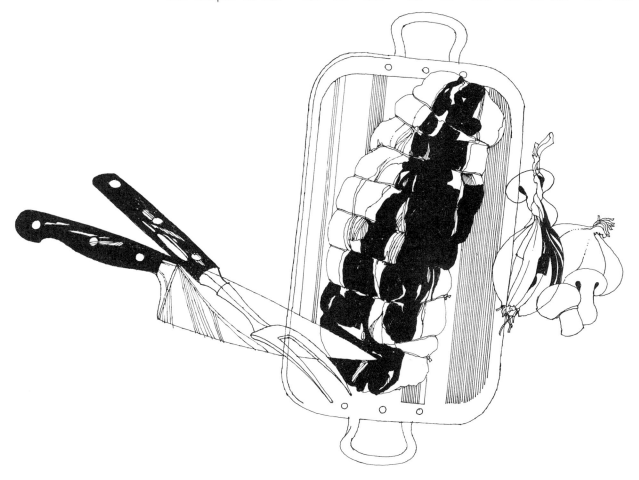

Nobody is quite sure about how roasting as a method of cooking originated. It may well have been that someone once dropped a large piece of meat into a fire, left it there for a while, and then found that it was appetizing. The ancient and primitive method of cooking food in a pit covered with leaves and soil is, of course, not unlike the roasting process in a modern oven.

Roasts, especially of beef, have always been associated with prosperity; a third-century BC Chinese poem, listing a number of luxuries, emphasizes that only the rich can eat beef! One line of this poem runs, 'Ribs of the fatted ox, cooked tender and succulent'. One cannot ask for a better definition of good roast beef.

The bones of ribs of beef have been found in a third-century BC Egyptian tomb, but, unfortunately, nothing was found that could indicate how they were cooked.

Perhaps the greatest of all the French chefs, Carême, has left us a description of the preparations for a banquet given at the French foreign ministry at the beginning of the nineteenth century. This took place during the time when Talleyrand-Périgord, the statesman who survived the perils of the French Revolution to serve under Napoleon, was foreign minister. Carême describes the scene of activity before the banquet and highlights the sight of the great wood fire over which a sirloin, weighing between 45–60 lb, was being roasted on a spit.

The term 'sirloin' comes, of course, from the French *sur longe* ('on the loin'), but a pleasant anecdote relates that Charles II of England was so pleased with the taste of a cooked *sur longe* that he knighted this portion of meat, calling it 'Sir Loin'.

For centuries, spit roasting has been the accepted method of roasting meat. Children were often given the task of turning the spit, and sometimes, even dogs were made to do this; but however the spit is turned, the method produces the finest flavoured roast beef, and we are fortunate that, today, electricity enables us to continue using the method.

Filete Vascongado

Roast Fillet Basque Style
Serves 6–8
Cooking Time: See method

INGREDIENTS

fillet of beef: 3 lb
to baste:
beef drippings or butter: $\frac{1}{4}$ cup ($\frac{1}{2}$ stick)
for the topping:
onions: 2 small
button mushrooms: $\frac{1}{2}$ lb
smoked and cooked sausage or cooked ham: $\frac{1}{4}$ lb
bread: 3–4 large slices
butter: $\frac{1}{4}$ cup ($\frac{1}{2}$ stick)
olive oil: 1 tbsp
salt and pepper: to taste
chopped parsley: to taste

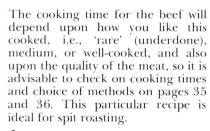

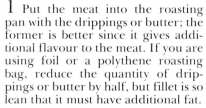

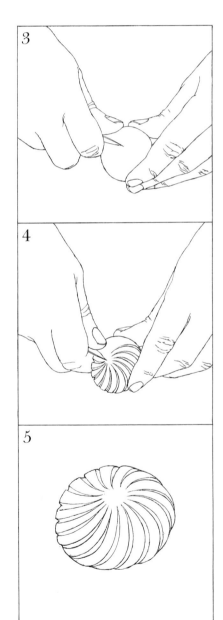

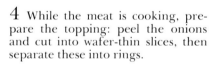

The cooking time for the beef will depend upon how you like this cooked, i.e., 'rare' (underdone), medium, or well-cooked, and also upon the quality of the meat, so it is advisable to check on cooking times and choice of methods on pages 35 and 36. This particular recipe is ideal for spit roasting.

1 Put the meat into the roasting pan with the drippings or butter; the former is better since it gives additional flavour to the meat. If you are using foil or a polythene roasting bag, reduce the quantity of drippings or butter by half, but fillet is so lean that it must have additional fat.

2 Roast as the method selected, until cooked to your personal taste.

3 If using an open roasting pan, 'baste' the meat 2 or 3 times during the cooking period to make quite certain it is kept moist. It is also an advantage to turn the meat.

4 While the meat is cooking, prepare the topping: peel the onions and cut into wafer-thin slices, then separate these into rings.

5 Trim the ends of the mushrooms and either slice them or, if they are very small, keep them whole and 'flute' the caps. The word so often used to describe this attractive finish is 'turning', and the pictures on the right show how this is done.

6 Cut the sausage or ham into narrow strips.

7 Cut 6–8 neat small rounds (croûtons) from the bread.

8 Heat the butter and oil together; the oil helps to prevent the butter from over-heating. Fry the croûtons until golden brown on both sides, drain on absorbent paper. If you do this some time before the meat is cooked, put the croûtons back into the oven to heat again for 1–2 minutes before serving the dish.

9 Fry the vegetables in the remaining butter and oil mixture until just soft, add the sausage or ham, salt, pepper, and a little parsley.

To serve: The meat on this roast should be carved thickly, so that each person has a slice rather like a steak. Put a croûton on each portion and top with the mushroom mixture.

To freeze: Larger quantities of the topping can be prepared and frozen for up to 6 months. Fried croûtons freeze well; wrap after freezing and use within 6 weeks.

To Flute Mushrooms
This takes considerable practice, so do not be depressed if your first efforts are less than perfect.

1 In this case the mushrooms must be skinned (normally the skin is left on, to give additional flavour). Remove the stalk.

2 Insert the tip of a sharp knife under the skin and pull away a strip; do this carefully and gently, so that the mushroom cap keeps a perfect shape.

3 Hold the cap, skinned side uppermost, in your left hand (if you are right-handed) and a small sharp vegetable knife in your right hand; the picture illustrates how the right thumb helps to rotate the mushroom.

4 Start in the very centre of the mushroom cap and begin to cut out shallow pieces to give a fluted effect. The secret of success is to move the mushroom cap *slowly* in an anti-clockwise direction, using the fingers of the left hand, while pushing against the edge with the right thumb to give sufficient strength to cut out these tiny pieces of mushroom flesh.

5 The completed mushroom cap.

New Zealand Savoury Roast

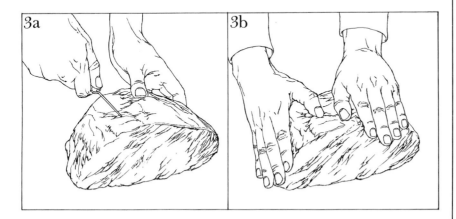

3a   3b

This is an unusual and interesting way of flavouring the meat before it is roasted.

Choose whatever cut you require and prepare the following mixture, which is suitable for up to a 4 lb piece of meat.

1 Blend a little flour with 2 teaspoons brown sugar, 2 teaspoons instant coffee powder, 2 teaspoons dry mustard powder, a generous shake of salt, black pepper, and cayenne pepper.

2 Put the mixture on top of the meat, then press it in with the back of a wooden spoon or spatula.

3 Take a metal skewer and pierce holes in the meat, then press the flour mixture down into these holes, so that it penetrates the meat.

4 Roast as per the directions on pages 35–36.

To serve: With roast potatoes, and roast peeled and diced pumpkin. In New Zealand you may have roast quinces with roast beef. Peel the fruit, cut into halves or quarters. Poach for 15 minutes in water to which is added a small amount of sugar. Drain the fruit, pat dry on absorbent paper, then roast round the meat for about 45 minutes.

To vary:
When quinces are not available, add soaked and cooked prunes to the roasting pan a short time before the end of the cooking period, or roast small dessert apples instead of quinces.

Würstelbraten

Austrian Stuffed Roast Beef

In most countries where prime beef cuts are available for roasting, it is not usual to stuff the meat before it is cooked, the theory being, of course, that *good* roasted beef has such a superb flavour that any additions are unnecessary.

One very simple but very excellent way to add flavour to the meat comes from Austria, where frankfurters are added. Choose top round or rump for this method of cooking, or for special occasions, a boned and rolled loin of beef.

1 Dry the meat well, then pierce it with a large skewer (or if this is not available, a thick knitting needle) in about 6 places.

2 Move the skewer or needle in the holes until they have opened sufficiently to allow a frankfurter sausage to be inserted in each.

3 Calculate the increased weight of the meat and roast as pages 35–36.

Lomo Relleno (Spanish Stuffed Roast Beef)

A more elaborate method of stuffing beef is based upon a traditional Spanish dish. You can choose top round or boned rib of beef. Boned sirloin does not give the right shape.

1 Pound and roll the meat until it has been made thinner and as nearly oblong as possible; this takes time, but the pounding will help to

Würstelbraten

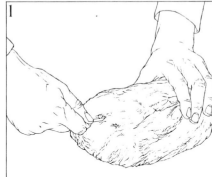

1

Lomo Relleno

2

5

tenderize the fibres of a not-so-tender round.

2 Prepare the stuffing; the amount given here is sufficient for up to a 4 lb piece of meat. Peel and chop 2 medium onions; skin, de-seed, and chop 3 medium tomatoes. Page 47 shows how to skin a tomato, and we show here how to de-seed the tomatoes with a small spoon.

3 Fry the vegetables in 2 tbsp (¼ stick) butter.

4 Blend the vegetables with ¾ lb pork sausage-meat or finely ground pork. Add salt, pepper, and a little mustard.

5 Spread evenly over the meat.

6 Roll the meat firmly and form into a neat roast, then tie or skewer.

7 Weigh the stuffed meat and roast it, see pages 35 and 36.

To serve: With mixed vegetables.

To freeze: The roast can be prepared and frozen, to be cooked at a later date. Use within 3 months.

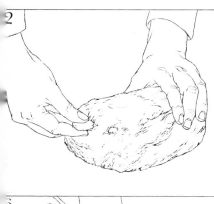

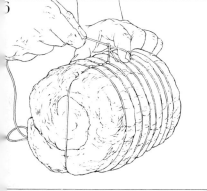

Roast Beef and Yorkshire Pudding

Yorkshire Pudding
Serves 4–5
Cooking Time: 30–35 minutes

Yorkshire Pudding is eaten in all parts of Britain, although it is believed to have originated in that northern county.

Originally, this pudding, made from a batter similar to that used for pancakes, was served with gravy as a prelude to the meat course, rather than as an accompaniment to the meat, but that tradition has now ceased.

Roast the meat, see pages 35 and 36, and then bake the pudding so that it is ready to serve with the meat.

To serve: The accompaniment to the meat is an unthickened gravy and horseradish sauce or cream. Unfortunately, fresh horseradish is becoming difficult to obtain in many places, so commercially prepared horseradish cream or English mustard is often served instead.

1 Sieve ½ cup flour and a good pinch salt together into a basin, drop in 1 egg, then beat the mixture well.

2 From 1¼ cup milk, gradually beat in just enough milk to make a stiff batter.

3 Beat until smooth, leave for about 5 minutes, then gradually beat in the rest of the milk. A batter like this can be left for some time in a cool place before being cooked, although the belief that this makes a better pudding has now been proved to be incorrect.

4 When ready to cook, put a walnut-sized knob of lard or drippings into a Yorkshire Pudding pan, measuring about 7×5 inches, and heat in the oven for a few minutes,

raising the temperature of the oven to that given in stage 5.

5 Pour in the batter and cook for 25–30 minutes towards the top of a very hot oven, 450°F, but after 15 minutes, lower the heat again to that required for roasting the beef.

6 You may, if you wish, cook the batter in small pot pie pans. Heat a piece of fat (the size of a large pea) in each tin, then pour in the batter and cook for about 15–20 minutes towards the top of a very hot oven, see stage 5. You need this high heat, if you require a well-risen pudding.

7 Another way of cooking Yorkshire Pudding is in the meat pan. Pour away most of the beef drippings but leave about 1 tbsp. Pour the batter into the pan.

8 Stand the meat on a rack or an oven shelf *above* the meat pan, so that any juice from the beef drops into the batter, so flavouring the pudding.

Although the flavour of the Yorkshire Pudding is infinitely better when cooked in this way, the pudding itself does not rise as in the previous method, but it has a wonderful taste.

This method can also be used if you are following the slower method of roasting described on page 36, but the pudding will then take about 40 minutes to cook.

To serve: With the beef; the larger pudding is generally cut in portions and put round the meat.

To freeze: The cooked pudding cannot be frozen, but the *uncooked* batter can be stored in the freezer for a month.

To vary:
(i) This is an economical pudding; you will improve the flavour and texture if you use 2 eggs and omit 2 tbsp milk.
(ii) Strong flour (the type used in bread making) gives a pudding which rises particularly well.

Gravy
The sauce called 'gravy' and served with roast beef and Yorkshire Pudding is based on the drippings and sediment left in the roasting pan after cooking the beef.

This amount serves 4–6 people and should be freshly made; it does not freeze well.

1 Pour all the drippings, except 2 tbsp, into a container; page 35 deals with the value of beef drippings.

2 If cooking the gravy in the roasting pan, blend just 1 tbsp flour with the drippings and sediment; stir over a low heat until it turns golden brown. Modern cooks often dispense with this stage and use a gravy browning powder instead. If you prefer to make the gravy in a separate container, then spoon the drippings and sediment into a saucepan.

3 Gradually blend in scant 2 cups beef stock or the liquid from cooking green vegetables (recommended by nutritionists, as it retains the mineral salts and certain vitamins from the vegetables).

4 Stir over a low heat until the liquid is boiling and the sediment absorbed; simmer for 4–5 minutes, strain into a sauce boat.

To vary:
(i) Some cooks prefer not to make a gravy but serve rare beef just with the juices that run from the beef.
(ii) Omit the flour (this is too small an amount to act as a true thickening); retain only 1 tbsp drippings. Heat the liquid with this and the delicious sediment from the meat, then strain and serve.
(iii) Add 1–2 tbsp port to the gravy just before serving.

Sweet and Sour Ribs of Beef

Serves 6–8
Cooking Time: As per pages 35–36

INGREDIENTS

for the sauce:
fresh pineapple: 1 medium
water: 1¼ cup
brown sugar: 2 tbsp
beef stock: scant ⅔ cup
oil: 2 tbsp
prepared mustard: 1–2 teaspoons
white malt or wine vinegar: ½–⅔ cup
salt and pepper: to taste
cornstarch: 1 tbsp
prime ribs of beef: 4–5½ lb
drippings or fat: ¼ cup
sweet potatoes: 2–3 lb

This recipe blends the fresh sharpness of pineapple with the taste of beef. It is a recipe that is as suitable for spit roasting or cooking over a barbecue as it is for roasting in the oven.

Although a tender rib roast of beef is given on this page, you could use a less expensive top round or eye, for pineapple is sufficiently acid to help the vinegar tenderize the meat.

1 First, wash and dry the pineapple and cut it in 6–8 slices across the fruit.

2 Cut away the skin with kitchen scissors; do this over a dish so no juice is wasted. Save the skins, see stage 4.

3 Lay the pineapple slices on a flat surface and remove the hard centre core; this can be done with the tip of a sharp knife, but an apple corer is ideal. Stamp out the very centre of the pineapple ring, then move the corer around slightly until all the hard part of the pineapple is removed.

4 Put the pineapple skins and cores into a saucepan with the water and simmer until the liquid is reduced to a generous ½ cup. Strain this and dissolve the sugar in the hot liquid.

5 Pour the pineapple liquid into a large flat dish, add the rest of the sauce ingredients, except 2 tbsp of the stock, and the cornstarch. Keep the pineapple rings for garnish.

6 Dry the meat well, so that it will absorb the marinating sauce, add to the dish and leave for several hours, turning about every hour.

7 Lift the meat from the marinade but keep this to make the final sauce. Allow the meat to drain over the container for a few minutes, then roast in the manner selected, see pages 35 and 36.

8 Add the drippings or fat to the pan, and heat this before putting in the sweet potatoes. Peel these, cut into neat and even-sized pieces, arrange round the roast and cook for about 40–45 minutes, if roasting by the quicker method, or longer, if

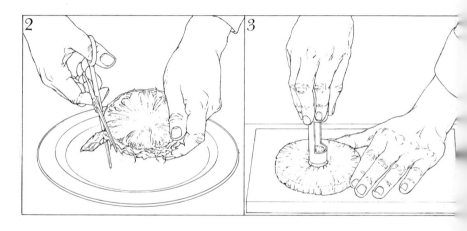

using the slower method; check that the potatoes do not burn, for they brown easily, due to their high sugar content.

9 Tip the remaining marinade liquid into a saucepan, blend the cornstarch with the last of the beef stock, add to the liquid in the saucepan, and stir over a low heat until thickened.

10 Taste the sauce, adjust the flavourings of sugar, vinegar, salt, and pepper to your personal taste. Add the pineapple rings to the hot sauce while carving the meat.

To serve: Carve the ribs of beef, arrange on a hot serving dish, and top each serving with the sauce and a pineapple ring. Garnish with watercress and the roast sweet potatoes.

To freeze: The sauce does not freeze well.

1 Peel and chop the onions and garlic; skin and chop the tomatoes.

2 Heat the butter in a pan and fry the vegetables until just soft.

3 Blend the vegetables with the rest of the stuffing ingredients.

4 Mark a slit halfway down the meat, then continue cutting carefully to make a pocket.

5 Press the stuffing into this pocket.

6 Either sew the cut with a needle and strong thread or secure with a wooden or metal meat skewer; as you do this, form the meat into a neat shape to fit into a saucepan for pot roasting.

7 Heat the fat or drippings in the bottom of this saucepan and brown the meat on both sides; remove from the saucepan onto a plate.

8 Add a selection of vegetables: whole onions and carrots, sliced peppers and celery, etc.; brown these in the fat.

9 Pour in just enough water to cover the vegetables, add salt and pepper to taste.

10 Replace the meat in the pan, so that it 'sits' on the vegetables; cover the pan and pot roast, see page 37.

To serve: Lift the meat onto the serving dish, and spoon the vegetables round the meat. Strain the liquid and use for a gravy.

Stuffed Pot Roast of Beef

Serves 6–8
Cooking Time: $2\frac{1}{2}$–$2\frac{3}{4}$ hours

INGREDIENTS

for the stuffing:
onions: 2 medium
garlic: 1 clove
tomatoes: 2 large
butter: $\frac{1}{4}$ cup ($\frac{1}{2}$ stick)
breadcrumbs: 4 oz
chopped parsley: 1 tbsp
chopped thyme: 1 teaspoon
salt and pepper: to taste
egg: 1
top round or fresh brisket beef: 3–4 lb
fat or drippings: $\frac{1}{4}$ cup
vegetables: see stage 8

Carne Asado
Spanish Marinated Beef

This Spanish method of preparing beef is ideal for meat whose quality is not as perfect as one would wish. It can, however, be used with all cuts of beef, no matter how tender they may be.

The secret of the good flavour and texture of the cooked dish is that the beef is marinated for at least 12 hours.

If the ingredients for a marinade are chosen carefully, they give a pleasant flavour to the meat. As the marinade includes oil, it will keep lean beef moist during cooking.

One of the advantages of marinating meat is that at least one of the ingredients in the liquid tenderizes the food. The reason for this is that the mixture contains, or should contain, some form of acid, e.g., vinegar, wine, or fruit juice.

To make enough marinade for a 3–4 lb roast:

1 Peel and chop 2 medium onions and 2–3 cloves of garlic. Put these into a large shallow dish with 1–2 bay leaves, 2 tbsp oil, 4 tbsp red wine vinegar, and $\frac{1}{2}$–$\frac{2}{3}$ cup red wine.

2 Add a good pinch of salt, and a shake of black and cayenne peppers.

3 Dry the meat thoroughly, so that it will absorb the marinade. Place it in the dish.

4 Leave for about 2 hours, then turn; do this consistently, so that the meat absorbs the marinade.

5 When ready to cook the beef, lift it from the dish and hold it for 2–3 minutes so that any marinade not absorbed runs back into the container.

6 Roast the beef as described on pages 35–36, choosing the method of cooking according to the cut of meat, i.e., if not a prime cut, choose the slower method of cooking.

7 Spoon a little marinade over the meat from time to time, if you are cooking it in an open roasting pan.

To serve: With mixed vegetables and Espagnole Sauce, page 85. You can add any marinade left to the sauce before it is sieved.

To freeze: The marinade does not freeze well.

To vary:
(i) Add a generous amount of chopped herbs to the marinade, e.g., 1–2 tbsp parsley and the same amount of chives and tarragon.
(ii) Flavour the marinade with mustard; the type of mustard you choose will give a subtle change to the taste of the meat.

Lambata di Manzo Chateau al Cartoccio
Roast Beef Italian Style
Serves 6–8
Cooking Time: As pages 35–36

INGREDIENTS

marrow: from 3–4 beef bones
button mushrooms: $\frac{1}{4}$ lb or 4 oz can
onions: 2
butter or beef drippings: $\frac{1}{2}$ cup (1 stick)
red wine: scant $\frac{2}{3}$ cup
chopped parsley: 2 tbsp
chopped thyme: 1 teaspoon
salt and pepper: to taste
boned loin or other roasting cut, see pages 35–36: 3–4 lb
oil: 1 tbsp

1 Remove the marrow from the beef bones with a fine skewer.

2 Slice the mushrooms thinly; peel and chop the onions very finely.

3 Heat three-quarters of the butter in a pan and turn the marrow, mushrooms, and onions in this for 10 minutes, stirring well, so that the mixture does not burn.

4 Add the wine, herbs, salt, and pepper, then allow the mixture to simmer until fairly thick.

5 Meanwhile, heat the remaining butter in the roasting pan, brown the beef on either side, and cook for 25 minutes, if using the quick method of cooking, or about 40 minutes, if using the slower method; both are described in full on page 36.

6 Remove the meat from the oven.

7 Take a large piece of aluminium foil and brush this with the oil.

8 Place the beef in the centre of this and top with the marrow and vegetable mixture.

9 Wrap the foil securely round the meat and continue cooking as per the timings on pages 35 and 36.

To serve: Unwrap the foil; do this carefully, for it holds the steam. Lift the beef onto a hot serving dish, and carve in the usual way. You may need to spoon the topping to one side of the dish to carve neatly.

STEWS AND CASSEROLES

The variety of dishes that can be cooked in a saucepan under the title 'stew', or in a covered dish in the oven and named 'casserole', is endless.

If you consult a dictionary, you will find a considerable number of interpretations of the term 'stew'. We talk of 'being in a stew' when we are bothered. The expression 'to stew in his own juice' or *'cuire dans son jus'* is a familiar one which means 'to undergo the consequences of his own actions'. Since medieval times, it has been used as a slang term to denote that someone is shut up in a confined space, generally for the purpose of work and study.'

The last meaning really has the most relevance to cooking, for isn't that what we do when we create a stew, a casserole dish, or a ragoût? The food is prepared and then closely covered to cook slowly and gently in a confined space.

It is important to examine the secret of creating successful stews of all kinds. The answer lies partly in the long, slow cooking, which not only tenderizes the meat, but allows the flavours to blend. I still believe the best stews are those cooked on one day, left for twenty-four hours, and then reheated.

It is the combinations of flavours that make a stew or casserole so interesting. These can range from the spice mixtures of the curries of India, the Far East, and Africa to the subtle blend of herbs and wine of France and other European countries. Have we lost the art of using herbs cleverly and, indeed, of growing our own? In the sixteenth century, it was quite usual to have over forty different herbs in one's garden; some were for medicinal purposes, but most were used to add interest and variety to food.

Bœuf à la Bourguignonne

Burgundy Style Beef
Serves 4–6
Cooking Time: $1\frac{3}{4}$–2 hours

INGREDIENTS

top round or chuck: $1\frac{1}{2}$–2 lb
salt and pepper: to taste
onions: 3 large
garlic cloves: 1–2
fresh thyme: 1 sprig
bay leaf: 1
parsley: 1–2 sprigs
lemon peel: 1–2 strips
red Burgundy: $1\frac{1}{4}$ cup
oil: 4 tbsp
fairly fat bacon slices: 2–3
flour: 2 tbsp
beef stock: scant $\frac{2}{3}$ cup
button mushrooms: 4–6 oz
to garnish:
lemons: 1–2

1 Cut the meat into neat, fairly large cubes and put into a dish. Add salt and pepper to taste.

2 Peel and slice the onions and garlic very thinly, sprinkle 1 onion and the garlic over the meat, and add the thyme, bay leaf, and parsley; remember that the stalk of parsley gives more flavour than the leaves.

3 Add the lemon peel and Burgundy together with about a quarter of the oil.

4 Leave the meat to marinate for at least 2 hours – preferably 3–4 hours – turning once or twice and pressing the herbs, to extract as much flavour as possible.

5 Cut any rind from the bacon and dice it.

6 Heat the remaining oil in a heavy pan and gently fry the rest of the onions and the bacon until just pale golden.

7 Lift the meat from the marinade with a perforated spoon or strain the liquid from the meat, retaining the liquid, of course; toss the meat in the flour, then fry for several minutes with the onions and bacon.

8 Strain the wine marinade into the pan, stir well to blend, add the beef stock with a little more salt and pepper, bring to the boil, lower the heat, and cover the pan tightly.

9 Simmer gently for $1\frac{1}{2}$–$1\frac{3}{4}$ hours, or until the meat is very tender, adding the mushrooms in the last 5–10 minutes.

To serve: Spoon onto a hot dish, cut the lemon(s) into thick wedges and arrange round the meat.

To freeze: With the high percentage of wine used, you will find that although the cooked dish can be frozen, it tends to lose much of the delicious wine flavour.

To vary:
This very well known French stew is capable of infinite variety.
(i) You can make the dish with cheaper stewing beef, in which case increase the amount of liquid by scant $\frac{2}{3}$ cup and allow at least $2\frac{1}{4}$ hours cooking time.
(ii) Some recipes use all wine and omit the beef stock, but in my opinion, the blending of flavours makes the dish more interesting.
(iii) A chopped calf's foot can be added to the beef to give a richer flavour; this can be marinated with the beef, but that is not essential; it can be fried in the oil at stage 6. As the calf's foot produces a richer taste, it is advisable to cook the dish one day, allow it to cool, then skim away any surplus fat and reheat the following day.
(iv) Perhaps the nicest variation is to increase the amount of herbs used in cooking the dish, i.e., to add a little finely chopped thyme, chervil, parsley, and garlic at stage 8.
(v) 1–2 tbsp concentrated tomato purée can be incorporated at stage 8.
(vi) *Poulet à la Bourguignonne:* Use jointed chicken in place of beef. The cooking time will vary with the age of the chicken; a fairly young bird takes about 1 hour at stage 9.

1 Cut off the bacon rinds but keep them to flavour the sauce. Finely dice the bacon.

2 Peel the onion and garlic, and chop these very finely; or, if you do not intend to sieve the sauce, grate the onion and crush the garlic.

3 Skin the fresh tomatoes. There are three ways of doing this:
a) Put into boiling water for some seconds, then plunge into cold water.
b) Insert a fine skewer in the tomatoes and hold over a gas ring or heated electric plate until the skin breaks.
c) Run the back of a knife firmly over the fruit.
In each of these cases the skin can be removed very easily.

4 Cut the tomatoes into small pieces.

5 Heat the butter and bacon rinds in a pan. Fry the bacon, onion, and garlic for about 5 minutes, stirring all the time to prevent browning.

6 Remove the bacon rinds, add the tomatoes, nearly all the stock, bay leaf, and salt and pepper to taste.

7 Simmer gently for about 20 minutes.

8 Blend the cornstarch with the rest of the stock, stir into the hot mixture, and continue stirring over a low heat until the mixture thickens.

9 Taste, and add the sugar, if desired.

10 Tomato sauce is generally sieved or put through a blender to

Stufatino di Bue

Beef Stew with Fennel and Tomato Sauce
Serves 4–6
Cooking Time: 3 hours

INGREDIENTS

for the tomato sauce:
fat slab bacon: 2 slices
onion: 1 small
garlic clove: 1
plum tomatoes, fresh or canned: 1 lb
butter: 2 tbsp ($\frac{1}{4}$ stick)
white stock: scant $\frac{2}{3}$ cup
bay leaf: 1
salt and pepper: to taste
cornstarch: $\frac{1}{2}$ oz
sugar (optional): 1 teaspoon
chuck or other stewing meat, see page 37: 2 lb
fatback (in one piece): $\frac{1}{4}$ lb
onions: 2 large
lard or fat: 2 tbsp
white wine: $1\frac{1}{4}$ cup
oregano (wild marjoram): 1 teaspoon
fennel seeds: 1 tbsp
to garnish:
head of fennel: 1 medium

make a smoother mixture, but in this particular recipe it is not necessary. Simply remove the bay leaf.

11 Cube the beef and pork.

12 Peel and slice the onions.

13 Heat the lard or fat in a saucepan, fry the pork for 3–4 minutes, add the onions, and continue cooking for a further 5 minutes.

14 Finally, add the meat and cook steadily until golden brown.

15 Pour the white wine into the pan, add the oregano and fennel seeds, then stir in the tomato sauce.

16 Cover the pan, lower the heat, simmer gently for $2\frac{1}{4}$ hours, until the meat is tender.

17 Meanwhile, cut off the leaves and the hard outer part of the stalk of the fennel and cut the head into thin rings.

18 Cook steadily in a little boiling salted water for 15 minutes, then strain.

To serve: Spoon the stew into a dish. Garnish with the fennel. Serve with boiled noodles.

To freeze: The stew freezes well for 3 months.

Bœuf en Daube à la Provençale

Marinated Beef Provence Style
Serves 4–6
Cooking Time: 2½ hours

INGREDIENTS

fat bacon: ½ lb
lean stewing beef or round steak: 1½–2 lb
garlic cloves: 1–2
chopped parsley: 1–2 tbsp
ground cloves: good pinch
allspice: good pinch
red wine vinegar: 3 tbsp
red wine: 2¼ cup
onions: 6 medium
carrots: 6 medium
salt and pepper: to taste
oil: 3 tbsp
brandy (optional): 1–2 tbsp
bouquet garni:
parsley: 2 sprigs
thyme: 1 sprig or pinch
rosemary: very small sprig or pinch
orange: 1 small

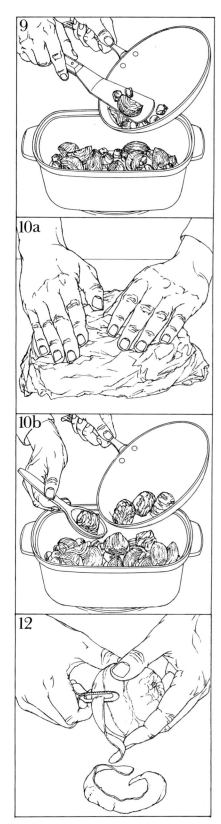

1 Cut half the bacon into 8–12 thin strips and dice the remainder.

2 Divide the meat into 8–12 portions.

3 Skin and crush the garlic, using the tip of a firm knife, in a pinch of salt on the chopping board, or use a garlic press; blend with the chopped parsley cloves, and allspice.

4 Roll the strips of bacon in the parsley mixture, thread onto a larding needle with a large eye, and lard the pieces of meat.

5 Put the meat into a dish, and add the wine vinegar and the wine.

6 Peel 2 onions and 2 carrots, slice thinly, and add to the marinade with a little salt and pepper.

7 Leave for about 12 hours, turning once or twice.

8 Peel the remaining onions and carrots; quarter the onions but leave the carrots whole.

9 Heat the oil in a saucepan, fry the diced bacon and quartered onions until golden brown, and spoon into a casserole.

10 Remove the meat from the marinade, drain well, brown in the oil remaining in the pan, and add to the onions.

11 Pour the marinade liquid and vegetables into the pan and stir well to absorb the last of the oil remaining in the pan; add the whole carrots, brandy, and herbs.

12 Cut away the very top peel from the orange, use only the golden zest, i.e., the top part of the peel, avoid any bitter white pith; squeeze out a little orange juice and add this and the peel to the sauce.

13 Season the sauce with a little salt and pepper, pour over the meat and onions, cover the casserole; cook in the centre of a slow oven, 300 °F, for 2¼ hours.

To serve: Remove the bouquet garni. This dish is particularly good when served with spaghetti, macaroni, or noodles, topped with butter, grated cheese, and a little chopped parsley.

To freeze: The vinegar and wine content make this slightly disappointing after freezing.

To vary:
Bœuf en Daube à la Marseillaise:
This is an interesting variation of the better-known dish on this page.

Prepare the dish as stages 1–13, then top the beef mixture with 1 lb skinned, halved, and de-seeded tomatoes before covering the casserole. Cook as the basic recipe and garnish with black olives. Sometimes, this version has several peeled and chopped cloves of garlic added to the wine sauce.

Karjalan Paisti

Karelian Ragoût
Serves 8–10
Cooking Time: 5–6 hours

INGREDIENTS

chuck or other stewing beef, see page 38: 1 lb
shoulder or leg of lamb (weight without bone): 1 lb
shoulder or loin of pork (weight without bone): 1 lb
onions: 1½ lb
salt: to taste
ground allspice: 2–3 teaspoons
beef stock: 2¼ cups

The secret of the good flavour of this simple casserole dish is the blending of the three meats and the very slow cooking. Obviously, it makes a good-sized casserole, but like most casserole dishes, it is good the day it is cooked but even better if cooked, cooled, then heated again. If cooking for a small family, therefore, it is a good idea to prepare the given quantity and then to freeze it in suitable portions.

1 Cut the meats into neat cubes and mix together.

2 Peel and cut the onions into thin slices; the quantity given can be increased, if desired.

3 Arrange layers of meat and onions in a casserole, adding salt and allspice to each layer; when adding the salt, check on the flavour of the beef stock; if this has been well seasoned, be sparing with the salt. Obviously, the amount of allspice used depends upon personal taste, but this dish should be well spiced.

4 Add the stock, cover the casserole, and cook in the coolest part of a very slow oven, 275 °F, for 5–6 hours.

To serve: This dish is excellent with the casserole of sweetened potatoes, given on this page.

To freeze: This dish freezes well for up to 3 months.

Kropsu

Potato Casserole
Serves 8–10
Cooking Time: 5–6 hours

INGREDIENTS

old potatoes, weight when peeled: 3 lb
salt and pepper: to taste
butter: generous ⅓ cup (¾ stick)
flour: 2 tbsp
milk: to mix
corn or golden syrup: 2–3 tbsp

Many meat dishes go well with a sweet accompaniment, and this potato dish will provide just the right contrast to complement the meat dish on this page. The potato casserole can be baked for the same length of time as the meat, then browned under a hot broiler if it is not convenient to raise the temperature in the oven.

1 Cook the potatoes in boiling salted water until soft, then strain and mash.

2 Add a little pepper, half the butter and the flour, then beat until very light and fluffy; use a wooden spoon first, then a whisk as you gradually add a little milk to make a soft consistency.

3 Stir in the syrup; taste as you do so, for it may be a little over-sweet for some people, but remember that it is an accompaniment to a savoury meat dish.

4 Use a little of the remaining butter to spread round a casserole.

5 Spoon in the potato mixture, spread flat on top, and cover.

6 Bake for 5 hours in a very slow oven, 275 °F.

7 Take the lid off the casserole and put the rest of the butter in small knobs over the top of the potato mixture.

8 Raise the heat of the oven for 10–15 minutes to brown the potatoes, or put them under a broiler.

To freeze: This does not freeze well, it is better freshly cooked.

Lingonberry Preserve
Lingonberries or cranberries are excellent with the meat dish on this page. To make a preserve:–

1 Wash and dry 1 lb of the fruit.

2 Put 1¼ cup water and 1 lb sugar into a saucepan, stir until the sugar has dissolved, then add the finely grated peel from a small lemon, and ¼ teaspoon each of ground cinnamon, nutmeg, and cloves.

3 Tip the fruit into the syrup, simmer gently until just soft, remove the fruit from the liquid with a perforated spoon, and put into a bowl.

4 Boil the syrup until reduced to half the original volume, pour over the fruit, and allow to cool.

Beef Curry

This is probably the most difficult recipe to give, for how can one select just one curry from the range of recipes made throughout the Far East and Africa?

One way to vary your curry dishes is to blend your own curry powder. In order to do this, you need to choose and mix: ground chilli powder, ground turmeric, ground ginger, mustard powder, ground coriander, ground cardamon, ground cumin, plus a little black and/or cayenne pepper.

Obviously, you need not use all the above at one time, but it allows you to have a good variation of flavour. If you do not want to prepare your own curry flavouring, then experiment and find the brand of curry powder that pleases you most. I generally use both a curry powder and curry paste, when not making my own mixture of spices.

1 Peel and chop 2 medium onions and 1–2 cloves of garlic. You may add a small diced apple, a diced sweet green pepper, and 1–2 skinned chopped tomatoes; these are not essential but blend well with beef.

2 Heat either 2 tbsp oil or ghee in a good-sized saucepan. Ghee is clarified butter and used in many curries.

3 Turn the ingredients listed in stage 1 in the oil or ghee; add 1 tbsp curry powder, or your own blending of spices, and 1–2 teaspoons curry paste.

4 Dice 1–1½ lb beef; this can be good-quality uncooked stewing beef or round steak, or it can be cooked meat. Stir the beef into the ingredients in the saucepan. If time allows, stand for about an hour, so the meat absorbs some of the flavourings.

5 Gradually blend in the liquid. If cooking fresh meat, allow 1¼ cup for a fairly dry curry or at least 2 cups for a more moist curry. If using cooked meat, you can halve the above quantities.

The liquid can be half coconut milk, see page 122, and half stock, or vary the proportions to taste.

6 Bring the liquid to boiling point, taste, and add a little salt, lemon juice, or vinegar to sharpen the sauce and a little sugar to balance this, if you like a sweet curry. You may like to add a few raisins or other dried fruit.

7 Cover the pan tightly; simmer gently for 2–3 hours, if using raw meat, and at least an hour if using cooked meat. The flavour of a curry is improved if you cook it one day, allow it to cool, then reheat on the following day.

To serve: With chutney or the Lemon Pickle given opposite; Bombay duck (a dried fish); poppadums or chapatis; dishes of sliced pineapple or banana; sliced tomatoes and sweet green pepper (discard the core and seeds); salted nuts; gherkins; sliced or tiny raw onions.

To freeze: A curry freezes quite well for up to 2 months. It may lose a little flavour.

Lemon Pickle

1 Wash and dry 1 lb firm lemons (use fruit with perfect peels).

2 Chop the lemons very finely, just discard the pips, use any juice on the chopping board.

3 Blend the chopped lemons with approximately $\frac{1}{2}$ teaspoon of each of the following: turmeric, curry powder, and chilli powder.

4 Add salt to taste and 6 tbsp soft brown sugar.

5 Spoon into a jar and leave in a warm place for 2–3 days before using, stir regularly.

To serve: With curries.

To freeze: This freezes well for 3 months.

To Cook Rice

1 Choose long-grain, Patna-type rice to serve with a curry.

2 Wash the rice if not already cleaned; do this only just before cooking.

3 Measure the rice. It is considered that $\frac{2}{3}$ cup is sufficient rice for 2 people.

4 Put the desired amount of rice into a saucepan.

5 Measure the water. Allow exactly twice the volume of water to rice, unless you are cooking the type of rice known as 'par-boiled', when you allow exactly $2\frac{1}{2}$ times the volume.

6 Pour the cold water over the rice, add salt to taste.

7 Bring the liquid to boiling point, cover the pan, lower the heat. Simmer for 15 minutes with ordinary long-grain rice or 20 minutes for the 'par-boiled' type.

   At the end of the time, the rice will be cooked, yet will not be sticky, and the liquid will have been absorbed.

To serve: As soon as possible after cooking.

'Mousaka' is used to describe a range of dishes made in most Balkan countries, but particularly in Greece.

The basic ingredients vary as much as the spelling of the name 'Mousaka'; some are based upon vegetables alone, others combine vegetables and meat, but in most recipes the ingredients are blended with a sauce flavoured with cheese.

As lamb and mutton are the most plentiful meats in the Balkan countries, you will find that these are generally used in Mousakas which contain meat, but this recipe is particularly good when made with beef.

1 Heat the milk with the celery and onion, allow this to stand in a warm place to infuse for 30 minutes, then strain. If time does not permit, this stage can be omitted and the un-flavoured milk used.

2 Heat the butter in a pan, add the flour, and stir over a low heat for 2–3 minutes; gradually blend in the milk, bring to the boil, stirring all the time, and cook until a coating consistency; add a little salt, pepper, and the mustard.

3 Stir in the cheese and remove from the heat. Any good cooking cheese could be used, such as Gruyère or Cheddar.

4 Whisk the eggs into the sauce, together with the nutmeg.

5 If you dislike the slightly bitter taste of eggplant, score the skin with a knife and sprinkle with a little salt. Leave for 30 minutes, then pour away the liquid; there will then be no bitter flavour.

Melitzanes Mousakas

Beef and Eggplant Mousaka
Serves 4–6
Cooking Time: 1¼ hours

INGREDIENTS

for the cheese sauce:
milk: 2½ cups
celery: small piece
onion: small piece
butter: ¼ cup (½ stick)
flour: ¼ cup
salt and pepper: to taste
prepared mustard: to taste
grated cheese (see method): ¼ lb
eggs: 2
grated nutmeg: ½–1 teaspoon
eggplant: 1½ lb
onions: 2 medium
tomatoes: 4 medium
oil: ¼ cup
ground beef: 1–1½ lb
butter: 2 tbsp
fine breadcrumbs: scant ½ cup

6 Cut the eggplants into thin slices, peel the onions and chop finely, and slice the tomatoes.

7 Heat half the oil and fry the onions until pale golden, blend with the minced beef, tomatoes, and salt and pepper to taste.

8 Heat the remainder of the oil and fry the eggplant until just tender, turn the slices at least once to prevent their discolouring.

9 Arrange layers of eggplant, meat mixture, and sauce in the dish, ending with a layer of sauce.

10 Heat the butter, turn the breadcrumbs in this, and sprinkle over the sauce.

11 Cover the casserole, making sure the lid or foil does not press down on the sauce.

12 Cook for an hour in the centre of a very moderate oven, 325 °F, then lift the lid and continue cooking for another 15 minutes.

To serve: With a green vegetable or salad.

To freeze: This dish freezes well for up to 6 weeks.

To vary:
This recipe contains a high percentage of sauce; the quantity can be reduced if you prefer a less moist mixture. Many Mousakas are so firm that they can be cut into slices, rather like a cake. An example of this is the Turkish recipe given on page 109.

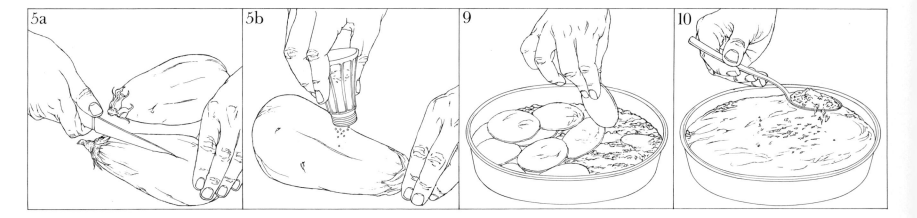

5a 5b 9 10

Gulyás

Hungarian Goulash
Serves 4–6
Cooking Time: $2\frac{1}{4}$–$2\frac{1}{2}$ hours

INGREDIENTS

tomatoes, preferably plum type: $1\frac{1}{2}$ lb
water: scant $\frac{1}{3}$ cup
salt and pepper: to taste
sugar: 1 teaspoon
meat – use chuck or other stewing beef see page 38,
stewing veal, and lean pork: $1\frac{1}{2}$ lb
paprika: 1–2 tbsp
onions: 1 lb
fat or butter: $\frac{1}{4}$ cup ($\frac{1}{2}$ stick)
potatoes, weight when peeled or scraped: 1 lb
to garnish:
yoghourt or sour cream: $\frac{2}{3}$–$1\frac{1}{4}$ cup
chopped parsley: to taste

If asked about Hungarian cuisine, most people would reply that they have enjoyed eating Goulash, the paprika-flavoured stew; but the conception of Gulyás as a stew is not quite correct. It is really a very satisfying soup, but the stew has now developed into a favourite international dish. There are countless versions of this dish, but this one is my favourite.

While you can make Gulyás with one meat only, a more interesting result is obtained by using the three meats.

1 First make the tomato purée: chop the tomatoes and simmer with the water, salt, pepper, and sugar until quite soft, then sieve. If they are put into a blender you do not get rid of every particle of skin or the very hardest seeds, but this is relatively unimportant in this recipe. There is no comparison between plum and other type tomatoes, plum tomatoes are so much better.

2 Dice the meats neatly, sprinkle with salt, pepper, and paprika; peel and slice the onions.

3 Heat the fat or butter in a large heavy pan; fry the meat and onions together (do this carefully and slowly, as paprika has a tendency to burn); make sure you have added sufficient paprika.

4 Blend in the tomato purée made in stage 1, cover the pan tightly, simmer gently for $1\frac{1}{2}$–$1\frac{1}{4}$ hours, depending on the tenderness of the meat.

5 When the meat is nearly tender, peel or scrape the potatoes; cut into thick slices, or leave whole.

6 Check that there is sufficient liquid in the pan, if necessary add a little, but this version of Goulash produces a thick stew. Add the potatoes and cook for a further 30 minutes, or until just soft.

To serve: Top with the yoghourt or sour cream, and parsley.

To freeze: This freezes for no more than 1–2 weeks, as the potatoes lose their texture and the paprika its flavour, if frozen longer.

Znojemsky Gelas

This goulash is a speciality of Czechoslovakia. It varies from the better-known Hungarian dish in that prime beef is used.

It is important that the paprika, the essential flavouring in both these dishes, is fresh. When stale, it has a 'musty' flavour.

1 Blend 2 tbsp flour with a good pinch of salt and a shake of black and cayenne peppers.

2 Dice $1\frac{1}{2}$–2 lb sirloin hip or loin steak and coat in the seasoned flour.

3 Peel and slice 4 medium onions.

4 Heat $\frac{1}{4}$ cup ($\frac{1}{2}$ stick) butter in a saucepan, fry the meat for 5–6 minutes, then remove from the pan.

5 Heat another $\frac{1}{4}$ cup ($\frac{1}{2}$ stick) butter in it and cook the onions until golden.

6 Blend 1–2 tbsp paprika with $2\frac{1}{2}$ cups beef stock, add to the onions together with 3 tbsp tomato purée, and bring the liquid to the boil.

7 Peel and slice 2 medium old potatoes; add to the liquid and cook for 20 minutes, then beat well, so that the potatoes thicken the liquid.

8 Finally, return the meat to the sauce; heat for about 5 minutes for rare meat and up to 15 minutes if you like it well cooked.

To serve: With pickled cucumbers, given on this page, rice or noodles, and salad.

To freeze: This dish is better freshly made.

To Pickle Cucumbers

1 First make a brine by dissolving $\frac{1}{4}$ cup coarse *kitchen* salt (not refined table salt) in $2\frac{1}{2}$ cups boiling water. Allow this to become quite cold; this is very important, so that the cucumbers are not over-softened.

2 Put 1 lb small pickling cucumbers into a container and add the cold brine. Leave for 48 hours.

3 Prepare the spiced vinegar: bring to the boil $2\frac{1}{2}$ cups pure malt vinegar, which can be white or brown, with $\frac{1}{2}$–1 tbsp mixed pickling spices. If you like a mild flavour, strain the liquid at once. For a stronger flavour, either simmer for a few minutes, or let the spices stand in the vinegar until cold, and then strain.

4 Lift the cucumbers from the brine, rinse in plenty of cold water, pat dry on paper towels.

5 Pack the cucumbers in the jars and cover with the cold vinegar.

6 Seal down carefully, if you intend to store the pickles for any time. Always put waxed paper or cardboard *under* metal covers, otherwise the metal will impart a bad taste to the pickles.

Chilli con Carne

Beef and Chilli
Serves 4–6
Cooking Time: $2\frac{3}{4}$–$3\frac{1}{4}$ hours

INGREDIENTS

navy beans: $\frac{1}{2}$ lb
salt and pepper: to taste
onions: 2 medium
garlic cloves: 1–2
sweet green pepper (optional): 1
tomatoes: 3 medium
butter or bacon or beef drippings: $\frac{1}{4}$ cup
ground chuck or other lean beef: 1–1$\frac{1}{2}$ lb
chopped oregano: 1 teaspoon
dried cumin: good pinch
beef stock: scant 2 cups
chilli powder (see method): $\frac{1}{2}$–2 tbsp

If your previous experience of Chilli con Carne has consisted of eating a beef and bean dish with a faintly hot flavour, you certainly have not experienced a true Chilli con Carne. Unless you are familiar with dishes flavoured with chilli, it is difficult to realize just how hot and fiery this taste can be.

The chilli powder comes from very hot peppers, which are bright red when ripe. They should not be confused with sweet peppers, often called capsicums.

Different brands of chilli powder vary in their potency, so always add this gradually and taste as you do so.

1 Put the navy beans into a container, cover with cold water, and leave soaking overnight.

2 Add a little salt and pepper to taste and simmer gently until tender; this takes 1$\frac{1}{2}$–2 hours. Strain and discard the liquid.

3 Peel and chop the onions and garlic.

4 Dice the pepper, discard the core and seeds, and chop the tomatoes. If you wish to skin these, page 96 suggests various methods.

5 Heat the butter or drippings and fry the onions and garlic until just a pale golden brown.

6 Add the meat, stir over a low heat for a few minutes, then blend in the rest of the ingredients, including the beans; add only a pinch of the chilli powder at this point.

7 Bring the liquid to the boil, stir well; taste the mixture and add a little extra quantity of chilli powder, together with salt and pepper.

8 Cover the pan and simmer gently for about an hour; taste the mixture once or twice and increase the chilli powder as desired; check on the amount of liquid towards the end of the cooking time and add a little more, if the stew becomes too dry.

To serve: With rice or noodles; this is excellent served with a Tortilla, shown on this page.

To freeze: This dish freezes well for 3 months but loses a little potency.

To vary:
(i) Use diced, rather than minced beef; this means increasing the cooking time, unless you have chosen really tender beef.
(ii) Use canned beans and, instead of navy beans, choose dried kidney, red, or pinto beans.
(iii) Use fresh broad beans instead of navy beans.

Tortilla
(Spanish Omelette)

1 Peel 2 medium onions and chop these very finely; dice 2 or 3 cooked potatoes.

2 Heat $\frac{1}{4}$ cup ($\frac{1}{2}$ stick) butter or a generous 2 tbsp oil in a frying or omelette pan, fry the onions until soft.

3 Add another 2 tbsp ($\frac{1}{4}$ stick) butter or a little more oil, if necessary, and heat the potatoes with the onions.

4 Beat 4–5 eggs, add salt and pepper to taste; pour over the vegetables and cook until just set.

To serve: Cut the Tortilla into slices and serve on the meat dish.

Estofado de Vaca a la Catalana

Catalan Beef and Sausage Stew
Serves 4–6
Cooking Time: 2½ hours

INGREDIENTS

chuck or other stewing beef, see page 38: 1½ lb
sweet red pepper: 1 large
onions: 3 medium
garlic cloves: 1–2
tomatoes: 4 medium
flour: 2 tbsp
salt and pepper: to taste
olive oil: 2 tbsp
beef stock: 1¼ cup
red wine: 1¼ cup
new potatoes (optional): 1 lb
choriza or garlic sausage: ½ lb

1 Cube the beef neatly. Dice the pepper and discard the core and seeds.

2 Peel and slice the onions and crush the garlic; skin and chop the tomatoes, see page 96.

3 Blend the flour with the salt and pepper, then coat the meat.

4 Heat the oil in a saucepan and fry the meat for several minutes, then remove; add the vegetables and fry in any oil remaining in the pan, taking care they do not discolour.

5 Return the beef to the pan and gradually add the stock and wine.

6 Bring the liquid just to boiling point, stir until slightly thickened, then lower the heat and cover the pan; simmer gently for 1½ hours.

7 If adding the new potatoes, scrape these to remove the skins; add to the pan and check that there is plenty of liquid to cover the potatoes; if not, add a little more stock or wine.

8 Cook gently for about 25 minutes, then spoon into a heated oven-proof serving dish.

9 Dice or slice the choriza; if this Spanish spiced sausage is not available, then use a garlic sausage. Arrange around the edge of the food in the casserole.

To serve: This is excellent with cooked rice.

To freeze: This stew freezes well for 3 months, but the wine tends to lose its potency. It is better to add the choriza when reheating the dish.

To vary:
(i) *Cazuela a la Catalana:* Transfer the food to a casserole at the end of stage 6 and cover; cook for the same time as the recipe above in a slow oven, 300 °F.
(ii) Other vegetables can be used: grated raw carrots give an attractive colour to the sauce; add diced sweet green pepper as well as red.
(iii) This dish can be made with ground beef instead of diced beef; obviously the cooking time will be shortened by an hour. Do not add potatoes to this version.

Beef Olives

Serves 4
Cooking Time: 2¼ hours

1 Flatten the slices of beef with a rolling pin until they become very thin, then cut each slice into two portions; this will give 8 olives.

2 Blend all the ingredients for the stuffing together and divide between the slices of meat.

3 Older recipes gather the meat together to form a round or olive shape, as picture 3a, but nowadays, one generally finds the meat rolled round the stuffing, as picture 3b.

4 Tie the round or roll with fine thread or cotton.

5 Put the flour, with a little salt and pepper, onto a plate or a sheet of grease-proof parchment or into a polythene bag. Coat the meat. Do this by turning the meat in the flour with the help of two small knives or by dropping it into the bag and gently shaking until the meat is evenly coated, and all the flour absorbed.

6 Heat the fat or drippings in a pan and fry the olives until golden brown, do not over-cook and so harden the meat.

7 Lift the meat into a casserole, then stir the stock into any fat remaining in the pan, continue stirring until slightly thickened; flavourings can be added, as suggested under the variations at the end of the recipe.

8 Pour the sauce over the beef olives, add the bay leaves, cover the casserole, and cook in the centre of a slow oven, 300 °F, for 2 hours.

9 While the meat is cooking, prepare the macédoine of vegetables and potatoes.

To serve: Pipe the potatoes round the heated serving dish, as picture 5 on page 107. Lift the beef olives into the centre of the dish, coat with some of the sauce, serve the remainder in a separate sauce boat, first removing the bay leaves. Garnish the olives with the macédoine of vegetables.

To freeze: Beef Olives freeze well; use within 3 months.

To vary:
(i) Add a little tomato purée and a small amount of finely diced bacon or ham to the sauce at stage 7.

INGREDIENTS

top round or good-quality stewing beef: 4 large slices
for the stuffing:
fine breadcrumbs: scant 2 cups
chopped or shredded suet: 1 oz
chopped mixed herbs: 1 teaspoon
chopped parsley: 1 tbsp
finely grated lemon peel: ½ teaspoon
lemon juice: 1 tbsp
salt and pepper: to taste

egg: 1
flour: 2 tbsp
fat or drippings: ¼ cup
beef stock: scant 2 cups
bay leaves: 1–2
to garnish:
macédoine of vegetables, see this page;
Pommes Duchesse, see page 107

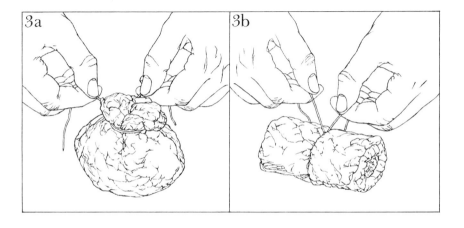

3a   3b

(ii) Increase the amount of fat or drippings to 6 tbsp and sauté 1 or 2 peeled and chopped onions and ¼ lb small button mushrooms in this before browning the meat, then continue as stage 6.
(iii) In a number of countries suet, the hard animal fat, is not readily available. Use melted butter or margarine in the stuffing instead of suet.

Macédoine of Vegetables
This is the term given to diced cooked root vegetables, i.e., carrots, turnips, parsnips, and rutabagas, together with diced green beans.
   The vegetables should be cooked in a little boiling salted water until just tender, but sufficiently firm to retain a good shape.
   Strain the vegetables and blend in a little butter and chopped parsley.

Niños Envueltos
(Argentinian Beef Rolls)
As one might expect from such a beef-producing country as the Argentine, the cut of meat used in this recipe is a somewhat luxurious one, and this means a relatively short cooking time.

1 Flatten 6 slices of boneless loin and marinate for 2–3 hours in a little well-seasoned wine vinegar, to which a crushed clove of garlic is added.

2 Remove the meat from the marinade, drain, and fill with a stuffing similar to that used in Beef Olives on this page.

3 Proceed as stages 3 and 6.

4 Prepare a sauce; this is what makes these rolls quite different from the European recipes: peel and chop 2 medium onions very finely, crush 1–2 cloves of garlic and fry in a little hot oil, then add 1 lb skinned, chopped tomatoes, 1 medium diced sweet green pepper (discard core and seeds), and 1¼ cup red or white wine.

5 Simmer until a thin purée, sieve or put through a blender if desired, pour over the beef rolls, and cook as the Beef Olives, but only for 1 hour.
   Diced potatoes and peas can be added during the cooking period to give a complete and colourful meal in one dish.

This is a more luxurious version of Beef Olives, so do not over-cook the meat.

1 Flatten the meat to make thinner and larger slices, cut each slice into 2 portions.

2 Blend the ground beef with salt, pepper, half the spices, and all the parsley.

3 Divide the mixture between the slices.

4 Cut the fatback into tiny pieces and put on top of the stuffing.

5 Roll the meat and tie with fine thread or string.

6 Blend the flour, a little salt and pepper, and the rest of the spices, and coat the rolls, as in stage 5 in Beef Olives.

7 Heat the butter or drippings in a large shallow saucepan or a deep frying pan with a well-fitting lid.

8 Fry the rolls until golden brown, then add the stock.

9 Cover the pan and simmer gently for about 45 minutes or until the meat is tender, check once or twice on the quantity of liquid and add more, if necessary.

10 Lift the rolls onto a hot serving dish.

To serve: Spoon the sauce over the birds; these can be garnished as the Beef Olives.

To freeze: As Beef Olives.

Benløse Fugle

Norwegian Beef Birds
Serves 4
Cooking Time: 1 hour

INGREDIENTS

boneless loin of beef: 4 large slices
for the stuffing:
ground loin or other beef: $\frac{1}{4}$ lb
salt and pepper: to taste
ground ginger: $\frac{1}{4}$ teaspoon
ground cloves: $\frac{1}{4}$–$\frac{1}{2}$ teaspoon
chopped parsley: 2 tbsp
fatback: $\frac{1}{4}$ lb
flour: 1 tbsp
butter or beef drippings: $\frac{1}{4}$ cup ($\frac{1}{2}$ stick)
beef stock: scant 2 cup

To vary:
(i) Instead of using fatback in the stuffing, add pieces of suet or the marrow from beef marrow bones (these bones makes a superb stock).
(ii) If you dislike the flavour of cloves, and many people do, then substitute ground cinnamon instead.
(iii) *Blinde Vinken:* The Dutch version of Beef Birds is shown below left. The slices of beef are covered with a strip of fatback and a gherkin (sweet dill pickle). Spices are not used in this version.

(iv) Stir a little fresh or sour cream into the sauce at the end of stage 9.

Pommes Duchesse

1 Cook sufficient old potatoes to give about 1 lb; do not allow the water to boil rapidly during the process of cooking. There is a saying, 'A potato boiled is a potato spoiled', and undoubtedly, this is true, for rapid boiling breaks the outside before the centre is adequately cooked.

2 Strain, mash lightly, then rub through a sieve, so that the potatoes are perfectly smooth.

3 Beat in $\frac{1}{4}$ cup ($\frac{1}{2}$ stick) butter and the yolks of 2 eggs; do not add milk, for this makes the potatoes too soft and they lose their good shape when piped and browned.

4 Insert a $\frac{1}{2}$ inch rose-shaped potato pipe into a large piping bag and fill with the potatoes; picture 4 shows how to support the bag in a jug or jar when filling with the hot potato mixture.

5 Hold the piping bag firmly at the top and pipe rosettes onto a baking dish, or make a flowing design round the edge of a dish.

It is not essential to brown the potatoes for garnishing Beef Olives, as the white border forms a pleasing contrast to the meat and colourful macedoine.

To brown the potatoes, brush with a little egg white and heat for a short time in the oven or under the broiler.

To freeze: Freeze and then cover; use within 3 months.

Perdices de Cappellán
Although the name means 'Veal Birds', I sometimes make this Spanish dish with lean top round; as a change from veal fillet, it is excellent.

1 Flatten 8 small slices of beef, or use 4 larger slices and halve these. Page 106, stage 1, gives suggestions for doing this.

2 Cook 8 pork sausages until just golden brown, do not over-cook.

3 Lay 8 slices of ham on the slices of beef, roll the two meats round the sausages.

4 Proceed as for Beef Olives, stages 4–8, but use half red or white wine and half stock, instead of all stock; this can be flavoured with 1 or 2 crushed cloves of garlic, or use a little garlic salt.

5 The cooking time at stage 8 should be reduced to 1$\frac{1}{2}$ hours.

To serve: As Beef Olives, page 106.

Blinde Vinken

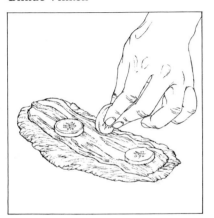

Pommes Duchesse

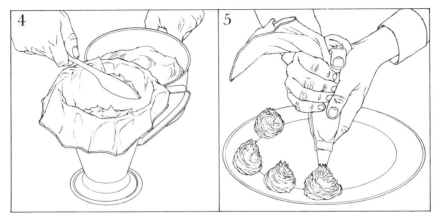

Vothino me Makaronaki

Beef with Macaroni, Corfu Style
Serves 4–6
Cooking Time: 2 hours

1 Cut 1½–2 lb round steak into slices, then divide into 4–6 portions. Sprinkle with a little salt and pepper.

2 Peel 3–4 medium onions and chop well. Skin and chop 1 lb tomatoes.

3 Fry the onions and meat in 2 tbsp olive oil in a saucepan until the onions are golden.

4 Add the chopped tomatoes, 1¼ cup white wine, and a scant ⅔ cup beef stock or water.

5 Cut some strips of the top peel of 1 lemon; add to the liquid together with 2 bay leaves, ½ teaspoon chopped oregano, some lemon juice, and salt and pepper.

6 Cover the pan and simmer gently for 1½ hours.

7 Meanwhile, cook 12 oz–1 lb macaroni in boiling salted water, strain, and tip back into the dry saucepan with 2 tbsp (¼ stick) butter.

8 Spoon most of the sauce from the stew into the macaroni, then transfer this into a heated shallow casserole.

9 Arrange the portions of meat and any remaining sauce on top of the macaroni; remove the lemon peel and bay leaves as you do so.

10 Place towards the top of a moderately hot oven, 400° F, for 10–15 minutes, so that the meat colours slightly.

To serve: With plenty of grated Parmesan cheese and a green vegetable or salad.

To freeze: The meat mixture freezes well, but not so the macaroni.

To vary:
Veal is used more often than beef in this dish, but lamb or mutton chops may also be used; the cooking time would then be about 30 minutes less.

Carbonades de Bœuf à la Flamande

Flemish Style Beef
Serves 4–6
Cooking Time: 2½ hours

INGREDIENTS

onions: 4 large
lean stewing beef: 1½–2 lb
lean bacon slices: 3
flour: 2 tbsp
salt and pepper: to taste
beef drippings or fat: ¼ cup
beer: 1¼ cup
beef stock: 1¼ cup
French mustard: 2 teaspoons
brown sugar: 2 tbsp
bouquet garni:
parsley: 2 sprigs or pinch
thyme: 1 sprig or pinch
chives: small bunch
sage: 1 small sprig or pinch

1 Peel the onions and slice thinly.

2 Cut the beef into narrow strips; remove the rinds from the bacon and dice it.

3 Blend the flour with a little salt and pepper, and coat the beef.

4 Heat the drippings or fat in a frying pan and fry the onions until golden; remove from the pan into a casserole.

5 Add the coated beef to the pan and fry until pale golden, then blend with the onions.

6 Pour the beer and stock into the pan, stir well to absorb any fat and thickening left; bring the sauce to boiling point and cook until thickened.

7 Add the bacon, mustard, brown sugar, and bouquet garni; pour over the meat and onions.

8 Cover the casserole and cook in the centre of a slow oven, 300 °F, for 2¼ hours.

To serve: Remove the bouquet garni and serve from the casserole with boiled potatoes. Cooked red cabbage or pickled red cabbage makes an excellent accompaniment.

To freeze: The dish freezes moderately well, although the special flavour imparted by the beer is somewhat lost in freezing. Use within 2 months.

To vary:
(i) Use all beer instead of half beer and half stock.
(ii) Often, the flour is omitted in the basic recipe at stage 3. To thicken the sauce, blend several tablespoons breadcrumbs with the liquid at the end of stage 8, then replace the casserole in the oven for 10–15 minutes to soften the crumbs.

Carbonada

Spanish Beef and Fruit Stew

Patlican Musakası

Turkish Mousaka

It is interesting to note how recipes and recipe titles travel and often become quite different on reaching another country.

For instance, there is a world of difference between South American Carbonada, the recipe for which is given in the barbecue section, and Spanish Carbonada, as given here. Obviously, the South American dish originates from the Spanish, but somehow, over the years, it has changed into something quite different.

We have become accustomed to sweet and sour flavour from Chinese cookery, but other countries also combine the savoury and sweet in some of their dishes.

A simple but appetizing Spanish dish with inexpensive ground beef is given a sweeter taste by the addition of fresh and dried fruits. The dish gives 4–6 generous portions.

1 Peel and chop 2 large onions; skin and chop 2 large tomatoes.

2 Heat ¼ cup (½ stick) butter in a saucepan and fry the vegetables for 5–6 minutes only.

3 Add 1½ lb ground chuck steak and blend with the vegetables.

4 Add 1¼ cup well-strained beef stock and stir well, so that the beef does not form into large lumps.

5 Add a little salt and pepper and simmer gently for 40 minutes.

6 Peel and dice 3 large old potatoes, add to the beef and continue cooking for 15–20 minutes or until the potatoes are soft.

7 Peel, halve, and dice 2 dessert pears, 2–3 ripe peaches, and 4–6 ripe apricots or plums; stir into the beef with ¼ cup seedless raisins.

8 Heat for a few minutes only.

To serve: With a green salad.

To freeze: Does not freeze well.

This is one of the Turkish recipes for a mousaka, and it is quite different from the Greek version on page 102. It uses cooked meat, and this can be mutton, instead of the beef used in this recipe.

There is no sauce in this recipe, so it will appeal to those people who like food that is not over-moist.

The eggplants are generally peeled, although this is a matter of personal taste. If you do peel them, the advice given on page 102, to combat the slightly bitter taste, is less important.

1 Peel and slice 4 medium eggplants, 6 medium potatoes, and 4 medium onions.

2 Fry the vegetables individually in 4 tbsp of oil or butter. Cook the onions first, then the potatoes, and the eggplants last. Salt and pepper to taste.

3 Slice 1–1½ lb tomatoes, blend with a little chopped parsley, salt, and pepper.

4 Grind enough cooked beef to give ¾ lb.

5 Arrange layers of the mixed vegetables, meat, and tomatoes in an oven-proof dish, finishing with a layer of tomatoes.

6 Cover the dish; bake for 1 hour in the centre of a very moderate oven, 325 °F.

To serve: Cut into wedges, like a cake, and serve with a green salad.

To freeze: This freezes well for up to 3 months.

To vary:
A little grated cheese can be added to the dish a short time before it is finally cooked.

Oxtail Ragoût

Serves 4–6
Cooking Time: 3¼ hours

INGREDIENTS

oxtails: 2 medium
flour: ¼ cup
salt and pepper: to taste
slab bacon, cut in a thick slice: ¼ lb
onions: 4 medium
garlic cloves (optional): 2
carrots: 6 medium
turnips: 1–2 medium
celery stalks: 2–3
leeks: 2 medium
tomatoes: 2 medium
butter or fat: ¼ cup (½ stick)
beef stock: 3¾ cups
bay leaves: 2
parsley: small bunch
port wine: 2–3 tbsp

This dish is generally served in cold weather, for the animal stores more fat in its tail in winter, and therefore the tail is more 'meaty'.

1 Wipe and dry the tails, cut away any surplus fat, then cut the tails into sections; this is quite easy to do between the bones.

2 Blend the flour with the salt and pepper and coat the pieces of oxtail in this.

3 Cut the rind from the bacon and divide into neat pieces.

4 Peel and chop 1 onion quite finely, but cut the others in fairly thick slices; crush the cloves of garlic, if using these.

5 Peel and slice the carrots and dice the turnip(s); chop the celery into short pieces.

6 Cut the green tops from the leeks; wash and chop the white part of the leeks.

7 Skin the tomatoes, see page 96, and cut into slices.

8 Heat the butter or fat in a large pan and fry the pieces of oxtail until pale golden; remove from the pan and separate the sizes; some pieces are very small, others of moderate thickness, and the top part of the tail is considerably thicker and, therefore, will take longer to cook.

9 Add the diced bacon, chopped onion, the garlic, and 1 carrot to the fat in the pan, fry steadily for 2–3 minutes, then blend in the stock and bring to the boil.

10 Put the large pieces of oxtail and the herbs into the thickened sauce and simmer for about 30 minutes, then add the medium-sized pieces and cook for another 30 minutes. Taste the sauce and adjust the seasoning.

11 Finally, add the small pieces of oxtail and continue cooking for another 2 hours, or until the meat is very tender; add the vegetables about an hour before serving the dish, so that they retain colour, flavour, and texture.

12 Remove the bay leaves and parsley, add the port wine, and heat for a few minutes.

To serve: While you can serve the oxtail the day it is cooked, the flavour is better if the ragoût is prepared to the end of stage 11, allowed to cool for 12 hours, the surplus fat removed, and the dish reheated.

To freeze: While you can freeze oxtail ragoût, the meat loses some of its rich and 'sticky' taste. If freezing, use within a month.

To vary:
(i) Soak ¼ lb navy beans overnight, drain and cook with the meat at stage 10. Increase the amount of liquid by almost 2½ cups or by as much as is absorbed by the beans.
(ii) *Coda di Bue alla Vaccinara* (Oxtail in Wine Sauce): Proceed as stages 1–11 of the recipe on this page; allow only 1 hour's cooking at stage 11. Lift the portions of oxtail from the original saucepan into a second pan, with 1¼ cup white wine, the same amount of stock from the original cooking process and several spoons of the diced vegetables. Add 1 lb skinned chopped tomatoes. Simmer until the oxtail is tender; add 2–3 tbsp raisins and the same amount of pine nuts. Add a little ground allspice and cinnamon.

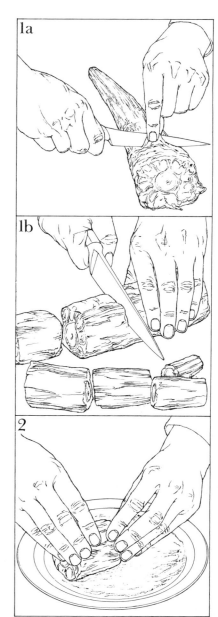

MINCED BEEF

I think that most people consider the hamburger to be a totally American creation. This is not true, of course, for, as James Beard points out in his *Delights and Prejudices*, 'the hamburger has now become an international dish, after shuttling back and forth between continents'. He also adds, 'It is now a mainstay of the American diet and many children do not know there is any meat but chopped meat'.

It is odd that this dish is called 'hamburger'; after all, it is made entirely with ground beef. I found the derivation of the word in *The American Heritage Cookbook*, a book which has always given me great pleasure and which has taught me much about the traditions of true American cookery. Apparently, in the German city of Hamburg, the citizens had an exceptional fondness for raw beef, such as in Steak Tartare; this led eventually to the creation of cooked meat cakes, which came to be called after the city. Thence, the dish travelled to the United States. Long before the hamburger recrossed the Atlantic to

become popular in Britain and the rest of Europe, the British enjoyed what were known as 'Swiss steaks', which are similar to hamburgers but have additionally grated onions, herbs, and Worcestershire sauce, the cooked 'steak' being topped with a fried egg.

I give here the generally accepted best method for cooking hamburgers, but do not let this limit your own inspiration. You may add, for instance, grated onion, garlic, herbs, or even grated Cheddar cheese. In the days when meat was rationed, we used to add grated raw potato or rolled oats, and these provide very acceptable variations of the dish.

You will also find many other meat cake recipes in this chapter, for in every country the value of grinding meat to make it go further and to give a more tender mixture has been realized. It is the method of preparation and the flavourings used that make the meat cakes of different countries so interesting; they indicate something of the way of life in that particular part of the world.

Hamburgers

This is the simplest and, to many people, the *only* true recipe for hamburgers.

1 Blend salt and pepper with the freshly ground beef, or see stage 4 below.

2 Form into the famous round flat cakes; it is possible to purchase utensils that press out the meat for you, so that you have a perfect shape.

3 The method of cooking depends upon the quality of the meat used. If there is a fair distribution of fat and lean, then you may cook the hamburgers in an ungreased, but heavy, frying pan. Heat the pan steadily, then put in the hamburgers; these should start to sizzle as they touch the metal. If the meat is very lean, then use a small amount of butter or a piece of fat pork or suet to give a thin film of fat over the base of the pan when it is heated. Heat the fat so that it begins to cook the meat the moment this goes into the pan.

4 Add the hamburgers, cook on one side for 2–3 minutes, turn, and cook for the same time on the other side. Many people advise that you do not season the hamburgers until they are cooked on the first side and turned, the theory behind this being that the salt 'draws out' the juices from the meat. This may be so if you use a large amount of seasoning but is not very evident with a small quantity of salt and pepper.

To serve: Top split, toasted hamburger rolls with the hot meat cakes, or serve the cakes with salad or a selection of vegetables.

To freeze: Freeze the uncooked hamburgers on open trays, then pack the firm meat cakes with squares of waxed paper in between and give them a final wrapping. This prevents the hamburgers sticking together. Cook from the frozen state within 3 months.

To vary:
Many of the flavourings and toppings for hamburgers are mentioned on page 111. The meat cakes can be broiled or baked, if this is a more convenient way of cooking.

Hamburger im Stehkragen
(Hamburger in a Collar)
The Germans have adapted hamburgers in this way.

1 Prepare the hamburgers as per the recipe on this page.

2 Take thin strips of bacon, remove the rinds, then stretch the bacon; halve the strips if too long.

3 Wrap each strip round a hamburger to form the 'collar' of the recipe title; secure with a wooden cocktail pick or toothpick.

4 Put the hamburgers and bacon on an oven-proof dish and place towards the top of a hot oven, 425°F, for 5–6 minutes or until the bacon is crisp and the hamburgers cooked; then remove the cocktail picks.

To serve: On toasted hamburger rolls or with mixed vegetables.

To freeze: See the comments in the hamburger recipe. It is better to freeze the hamburgers raw and then to add the 'collars' after defrosting, for the salt bacon limits the freezer storage time to 6 weeks.

1 Hard-boil 3 eggs and shell. Keep in cold water.

2 Peel the onion; if you are grinding the beef at home, grind the onion too, otherwise chop very finely or grate.

3 Mix the onion with the beef, parsley, and breadcrumbs.

4 Separate the white from the yolk of the raw egg and blend the yolk with the meat mixture.

5 Add salt and pepper; mix the ingredients very thoroughly.

6 Dust a flat surface with the flour, place the meat mixture on this, spread out to an oblong shape with a flat-bladed knife or your fingers.

7 Lift the eggs from the water, dry on absorbent paper, and place in the centre of the meat mixture. Form this into a roll round the eggs.

8 Brush the roll with the egg white; this helps it to remain quite firm on the outside during cooking.

9 Heat the oil or the butter in a large frying pan with a lid or in a flame-proof casserole, and fry the meat roll, turning it carefully during this process, so that it browns on all sides.

10 Skin the tomatoes, see page 96, halve, remove the seeds, then chop the pulp.

11 Blend the tomato pulp, wine, and a little salt and pepper together with enough water to give approximately 2½ cups; tip into the pan or casserole.

12 Cover the container, lower the heat, and continue cooking very

Hamburger im Stehkragen

Roulé

Greek Meat Roll
Serves 4–6
Cooking Time: 55–60 minutes

INGREDIENTS

for the roll:
eggs: 4
onion: 1 medium
ground beef: 1½ lb
chopped parsley: 1 tbsp
fine breadcrumbs: 3 oz (about 1 cup)
salt and pepper: to taste
flour: 1 tbsp
for frying:
oil: 5 tbsp
or butter: ¼ cup (½ stick).
tomatoes: 4 large
red wine: 1¼ cup

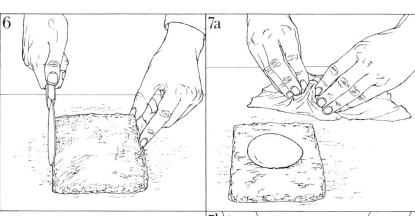

slowly for a further 40 minutes. Do not turn the roll during this process.

To serve: Lift the meat roll onto a serving dish and cut into thick slices. Serve with mixed vegetables and noodles. Pour the tomato and wine sauce over the meat and vegetables.

To freeze: This dish cannot be frozen because the hard-boiled eggs become 'leathery'.

Tefteli

Russian Meat Balls
Serves 4
Cooking Time: 30–35 minutes

INGREDIENTS

onion: 1 medium
butter: generous ⅓ cup (¾ stick)
ground beef: 1 lb
fine breadcrumbs: 2 oz, ½–⅔ cup
milk: 2 tbsp
salt and pepper: to taste
egg yolk: 1
flour: 3 tbsp
garlic clove: 1
beef stock: 1¼ cup
tomato purée: 2 tbsp
bay leaves: 2

1 Peel and chop the onion finely; heat 2 tbsp (¼ stick) of the butter and fry the onion until just soft.

2 Blend with the ground beef.

3 Put the breadcrumbs into a mixing bowl, add the milk, and beat until soft. Blend with the meat. Add salt and pepper to taste.

4 Bind the soft mixture with an egg yolk, form into about 24 small balls with the help of 2 spoons.

5 Add a little salt and pepper to the flour and coat the meat balls.

6 Heat the remaining butter in a heavy frying pan and fry the meat balls for a few minutes until golden; lift into a casserole.

7 Peel and crush the garlic and blend with the stock; pour into the frying pan, stir to absorb any butter left, then add the tomato purée, bay leaves, and a little salt and pepper. Pour over the meat balls.

8 Cover the casserole and bake towards the top of a moderately hot oven, 400°F, for 20 minutes.

To serve: Remove the bay leaves and spoon over cooked rice and mixed vegetables.

To freeze: These meat balls freeze well for 3 months.

To vary:
(i) Use half beef and half pork.
(ii) *Bitki* (Meat Balls with Sour Cream Sauce): Prepare the meat ball mixture to the end of stage 6, lift the meat balls into a casserole.
Make a sour-cream sauce: Heat 3 tbsp (generous ⅓ stick) butter in the pan the meat balls were cooked in.
   Blend in 2 tbsp flour; add 1 scant cup sour cream and stir over a low heat to thicken. Add salt and pepper, a pinch of paprika, and a few capers. Pour over the meat balls and cook as stage 8. Top with paprika and chopped parsley just before serving.

Note: Sour cream is not always readily available and you can substitute fresh cream plus 3 tbsp lemon juice. To achieve the correct consistency, blend 1¼ cup heavy whipping cream with scant ⅔ cup light cream.

Köttbullar

Swedish Meat Balls

Each Scandinavian country has its own way of making meat balls or meat cakes. It may consist of a specially subtle way of blending the flavours in the meat mixture, or of cooking the meat in different shapes.

The Swedish recipe that I enjoy is made as follows:

1 First soak ½–⅔ cups fine breadcrumbs in scant ⅔ cup water or beef stock until very soft; this takes at least 15 minutes.

2 Grind ¾ lb good-quality beef and ¼ lb pork fat together. If time permits, you can scrape the meats to give fine soft particles.

3 Finely chop or grate a medium onion; fry in 2 tbsp (¼ stick) butter until soft.

4 Blend the meats, onion, softened crumbs, 1 egg, 2 tbsp flour, with salt and pepper to taste.

5 Gradually blend in scant ⅔ cup heavy whipping cream. The mixture will seem very soft as you do this, but the cream thickens as you stir the ingredients together. This recipe does, however, produce particularly soft-textured meat balls.

6 Form into round balls with two teaspoons, or use one spoon and the palm of your hand to shape the mixture. If you make tiny balls, you will have about 36 and will need to fry them in two batches.

7 Heat 3 tbsp (scant ⅜ stick) butter in a frying pan and cook the first batch of meat balls until golden, turning them very carefully so that they remain a good round shape, then lift onto a hot dish.

8 Repeat stage 7 with the remainder of the meat balls, remove to the dish, and keep hot.

9 Blend 1 tbsp flour with the butter remaining in the frying pan, then add scant ⅔ cup heavy whipping cream and scant ⅔ cup milk, or use all light cream.

10 Heat for a few minutes, add salt and pepper to taste plus a little water if the mixture is too thick; pour over the meat balls.

To serve: With mixed vegetables.

To freeze: These freeze well for 2 months.

To vary:
(i) Use 1 lb beef and omit the pork.
(ii) Flavour with a little allspice.

Biff à la Lindström

Beef Cakes à la Lindström
Serves 4
Cooking Time: 5–6 minutes

INGREDIENTS

lean meat, see below: 1 lb
onion: 1 medium
cooked potatoes: 2–3 medium
cooked beet: 1–2 medium
capers: 1–2 teaspoons
egg yolks: 2
heavy whipping cream: approximately 4 tbsp
salt and pepper: to taste
for frying:
butter: ¼ cup (½ stick)

This recipe is so renowned internationally that you may well find variations, each claiming to be *the* correct method of making the dish.

It is important that the beef is ground very finely, so it may well be advisable to do this yourself. In this recipe, top round steak would be a good choice, or an even better would be a *lean* sirloin, rib, or rump steak.

1 Put the meat through a grinder two or three times until very fine in texture. If you have no grinder, scrape the meat with a sharp knife to bring away small particles, then put these into a bowl and pound until very smooth. A pestle and mortar would be ideal for this purpose.

2 Peel the onion and chop very finely or put through the grinder; blend with the meat.

3 Dry the cooked potatoes on absorbent paper to make quite sure they are not over-moist on the outside; dice finely. You need 3 oz.

4 Skin and dice the cooked beet finely also, and dry very well if it is moist; you should have about 2 oz.

5 Blend the diced vegetables with the meat and onion; add the capers and egg yolks.

6 Stir the mixture gently and carefully to mix, so you do not break the pieces of potato and beet, gradually blend in enough cream to give a soft consistency, but one you can handle. Add salt and pepper to taste.

7 Form into small round or rectangular cakes, allowing 2 or 3 per person.

8 Heat the butter in a large frying pan and cook the small meat cakes on either side until brown.

To serve: At once with vegetables or a salad.

To freeze: These are better fresh.

To vary:
(i) The onion can be chopped and fried in a little butter until just soft, then added to the meat. This gives a softer texture to the meat.
(ii) While beet is always included in these Swedish meat cakes, the potato is sometimes omitted.

Kefta is the Moroccan term for ground meat, which is used in that country in many different ways.

The meat balls made from Kefta bear no resemblance to the milder-flavoured mixtures of Europe. Sometimes, they are made with camel meat (a speciality of the 'souks' – the Moroccan markets), sometimes with mutton, and sometimes with beef. It is the spices and herbs which give the subtle taste so characteristic of this part of the world.

Although the Kefta balls could be called a Kebab, if cooked as the recipe below, they really are too delicate to cook over a barbecue fire, unless you can handle the skewers with great care.

The sauce that accompanies the meat balls adds a further flavour.

*Note: Ras el Hanout is an Arabic spice containing an almost unbelievable blending of mixed spice, cinnamon, pimento, black pepper, ground ginger, and other ingredients. You may be able to buy it, but I find a good substitute is a little curry powder plus ground ginger and mixed spice.

When I was first taught about making this dish by an enchanting Moroccan lady, she stressed that the amount of pepper used must be so generous that 'it almost takes your breath away' – obviously it must be a question of how much you prefer.

Kefta
Moroccan Meat Balls
Serves 4–6
Cooking Time: 25–30 minutes

INGREDIENTS

for the sauce:
tomatoes: 4 large
onion: 1 medium
garlic cloves: 1–2
olive oil: 3 tbsp
powdered ginger: pinch
salt and cayenne pepper: to taste
water: 1¼ cup
chopped parsley: 1 tbsp
chopped mint: ½–1 teaspoon
for the meat balls:
lean beef: 1 lb
onion: 1 medium
mint leaves: 2–3
parsley: sprig
marjoram leaves: 2–3
Ras el Hanout* see note: ½–1 teaspoon
ground cumin: to taste
salt and cayenne pepper: to taste
egg (optional): 1
oil: a trace

1 *To make the sauce.* Skin the tomatoes, see page 96, halve, and chop neatly, having discarded the seeds; skin and chop the onion finely.

2 Skin and crush the garlic.

3 Put all the ingredients except the parsley and mint into a saucepan and simmer for 20 minutes, then add the herbs.

4 *To make the meat balls.* Put the beef, onion, and herbs through a grinder.

5 Blend all the ingredients together; the egg is not essential but makes the mixture easier to mould. Divide into about 16–18 portions.

6 Take 4–6 metal skewers and press the beef mixture round these to make small balls.

7 Brush the meat balls with a little oil and cook under the broiler until golden brown.

To serve: With the sauce and rice.

To freeze: Much of the potency is lost, but you can freeze these. Protect other packages in the freezer against the skewers by wrapping the sharp ends securely.

To vary:
Poach in boiling water for 15 minutes. Add the balls gradually to the water, keeping it boiling all the time. Lift out, drain, and serve.

115

Kjøttkaker med Geitost-saus

Norwegian Meat Cakes with Cheese Sauce

Norwegian meat cakes can be served with an interesting cheese sauce. The cheese used in the sauce is the unusual brown-coloured goat cheese, known as geitost (or often given as gjetost). No other cheese will give quite the same taste, so try to obtain this. It is exported from Norway and is reasonably easy to buy in shops which specialize in a wide variety of cheeses.

These patties, with the satisfying sauce, serve 6–8 people.

To make meat cakes:

1 Grind together $\frac{1}{2}$ lb good-quality beef, $\frac{1}{2}$ lb veal, and $\frac{1}{2}$ lb lean pork.

2 Peel and grind, or grate, 2 medium onions, and chop or grind about 12 capers.

3 Mix the onions and capers with the meat, add 3 eggs, a little salt and pepper, a pinch of ground ginger, a pinch of ground mace, and approximately 4 tbsp heavy whipping cream.

4 Finally, stir in 1 tbsp cornstarch.

5 Form the mixture into about 36 small flat cakes.

6 To cook the meat cakes initially you heat $\frac{1}{4}$ cup ($\frac{1}{2}$ stick) butter in a frying pan and fry the cakes on either side until just brown, but as they are then simmered in the sauce, it is generally more convenient to leave this frying stage until the sauce is ready.

To make the sauce:

7 Heat $\frac{1}{4}$ cup ($\frac{1}{2}$ stick) butter in a saucepan, add $\frac{1}{4}$ cup flour and stir over a low heat for a few minutes.

8 Gradually blend in 3 cups plus 2 tbsp chicken stock and stir until thickened.

9 Add 2 tbsp tomato ketchup, 1–2 tbsp paprika, scant $\frac{1}{2}$ cup grated geitost cheese, and a little salt and pepper.

10 Stir over a low heat until the cheese has melted, then pour the sauce over the meat cakes in the frying pan and simmer gently for 10–15 minutes.

To serve: With selected vegetables.

To freeze: The completed dish freezes well; use within 3 months.

To vary:
Use all veal instead of the mixture of meats.

Fricadelles

Dutch Meat Balls

I tasted the most delicious tiny meat balls on a visit to Holland some years ago. They were crisp and golden on the outside but very moist in the middle.

When I asked how they were made, I was given the secret; a little gelatine was added to the ultra-soft meat mixture. This 'tip' is certainly not given in standard recipes for meat balls, but it means a great improvement to the texture. The gelatine sets and so makes it possible to handle a soft mixture for the fricadelle.

As soon as the meat balls are cooked, the gelatine melts, so giving you once again a soft creamy centre. You can improve most very small meat balls by using this technique, provided the cooking time is brief, for the mixture would be too soft and would break if a longer cooking period were required.

The mixture will produce about 12–18 medium-sized meat balls or 36–38 miniature ones.

1 Grind together $\frac{1}{2}$ lb good-quality beef, $\frac{1}{2}$ lb veal, $\frac{1}{2}$ lb lean pork or lean bacon.

2 Peel and chop or grate 1 medium onion and a clove of garlic, add to the meat with 1 tbsp chopped parsley and $\frac{1}{2}$–$\frac{2}{3}$ cup very fine breadcrumbs.

3 Add 1 whole egg, 1 egg yolk, a little salt and pepper, a pinch of ground mace, and a pinch of sugar.

4 Soften 1 teaspoon gelatine in 2 tbsp good beef stock, then dissolve in a mixing bowl over hot water.

5 Add the hot gelatine liquid to the meat mixture, blend thoroughly, and chill the mixture. Omit the gelatine mixture if making larger balls, for, as explained above, the cooking time is then too long.

6 Form into balls; these can be large enough to serve for a main dish or 'bite-sized' to have as a pre-dinner appetizer with drinks.

7 Add a little salt and pepper to 2–4 tbsp flour; the amount used depends upon the size of the meat balls.

8 Coat the meat balls in the seasoned flour.

9 Heat 6 tbsp ($\frac{3}{4}$ stick) butter or fat and fry the meat balls until just golden brown; serve at once. Large balls take 7–8 minutes, tiny ones 3–4 minutes.

To serve: The tiny balls may be put on cocktail sticks when cooked. The larger ones should be served with vegetables.

To freeze: Cook and cool, then freeze on open trays, wrap when quite firm. Use within 3 months.

To vary:
(i) Use light or heavy cream instead of beef stock at stage 4.
(ii) *Keftaides Tiganiti* (Greek Meat Balls): Rather similar meat balls are made in Greece, but flavoured with 1 teaspoon finely chopped oregano, the wild marjoram which gives such a delicious flavour, together with 1 teaspoon finely chopped mint. When the meat balls are fried they can be served with Avgolemono Sauce.

To make this:

1 Beat 2 egg yolks with a little salt, pepper, and 3–4 tbsp lemon juice.

2 Pour approximately 1 cup boiling beef or chicken stock over the egg and lemon mixture, stirring all the time.

3 Tip into a saucepan, cook over a low heat until the mixture has thickened slightly. Never allow this sauce to boil.

BARBECUE COOKING

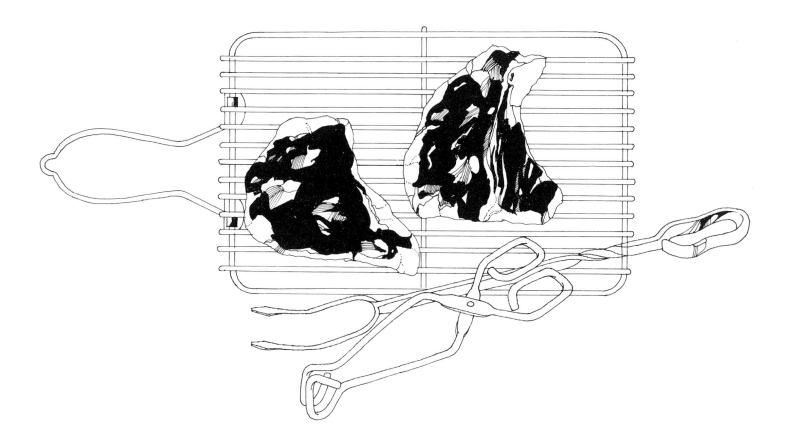

It is only in the last two decades that outdoor eating in the form of a barbecue has become popular throughout the world. The word seems to have originated in Britain in the middle of the seventeenth century but is usually associated with the United States. It is generally considered to derive from the Spanish *barbacoa* and the Haitian *barbacòa*, meaning a wooden frame on posts, but the art of cooking a whole animal from *barbe à la queue*, meaning literally from whiskers to tail, gives another explanation of the derivation of the word.

Communal outdoor eating has been a tradition on large estates when a special event, such as the birth of an heir or an important family marriage, was to be celebrated. At these festivities one could often see a whole ox being roasted over a huge fire.

The pleasures of outdoor eating had, of course, been known to nomads, warriors, and explorers all over the world.
It was Omar Khayyam who said:

Here with a loaf of bread beneath the bough,

A flask of wine, a book of verse – and thou
Beside me singing in the Wilderness –
and Wilderness is Paradise enow.

Few barbecues take place in the wilderness, for during this century most of us have made our gardens and patios an extension of our homes, to be enjoyed and lived in. An attractive barbecue area can enhance your garden.

Barbecue food has changed with the development of more sophisticated equipment; one can now cook a gourmet meal outdoors with the same ease as in the kitchen.

Whether you plan a simple barbecue over a charcoal fire, which, incidentally, probably gives the best flavour to the food, or on the most up-to-date equipment, the golden rule is to attain a good heat before you start cooking the steaks or other foods and to make as many essential preparations as you can beforehand, so that the barbecue is fun and in no sense a tiresome chore.

Barbecued Beef and Steak

There are many beef dishes that can be cooked over a barbecue fire; these range from joints and steaks to hamburgers and kebabs. Roasts are better cooked on a turning spit, while being basted with one of the savoury sauces given here. Allow the same cooking time as for roasting beef in the oven; this will vary according to whether you like the meat rare, medium, or well done. If you place the roast on the bars of the barbecue fire, or even in a roasting pan, it tends to become over-brown on the underside before it is ready in the middle. If you are prepared to turn this very frequently, it would then be successful, but a spit saves a great deal of labour.

Steaks, on the other hand, are relatively simple to cook over the barbecue, although once again they are better if turned over several times during cooking. The period of cooking will be similar to that for broiled meats, given in detail on page 34.

While you can cook the steaks with just a little oil or melted butter or fat to keep the meat moist, the whole essence of barbecue cooking is that the food should have a different taste from food cooked indoors, so try some of the following suggestions for preparing and flavouring the steaks during cooking. All recipes give enough flavouring for 4 good-sized steaks; remember that most of us develop a larger appetite than usual when we are eating out-of-doors.

Mustard Steaks: Blend 2 tbsp mustard and a peeled, chopped clove of garlic with 6 tbsp ($\frac{3}{4}$ stick) melted butter or fat; add 1 tbsp brown sugar. Brush the steaks with this before and during cooking.

Ginger Steaks: Melt $\frac{1}{4}$ cup ($\frac{1}{2}$ stick) butter, blend with 1–2 peeled and crushed cloves of garlic, 2 tbsp pow-dered ginger, 1 tbsp Tabasco sauce, 1 tbsp soy sauce, scant $\frac{2}{3}$ cup fresh or canned orange juice (pineapple juice makes a good alternative). Add salt and pepper to taste. Place the steaks in this mixture, leave for at least 3 hours, then lift the meat out of the marinade, drain, and cook over the barbecue; brush with the marinade throughout the cooking period.

To serve: Pour any marinade left into a saucepan, heat, and spoon over the steaks just before serving.

Sweet and Sour Steaks: Chop a large onion finely and fry in $\frac{1}{4}$ cup ($\frac{1}{2}$ stick) melted butter, until just soft. Add 2 tbsp vinegar, 2 tbsp honey, 1–2 tbsp mustard with salt and pepper to taste.

Brush the steaks with this mixture before and during cooking.

Jacket Potatoes
Scrub the potatoes well and prick the skins so that the potatoes will not burst during cooking. It is possible to cook them as they are on the bars of the barbecue fire, but there is a danger that they will be very burned on the outside before they are soft in the centre; it is, therefore, wiser to wrap each potato in foil, then place the package on the bars of the barbecue.

A large potato, wrapped in foil, takes about 45 minutes to 1 hour to cook, depending upon whether it is right over the heat or to the side of the barbecue.

When the potato is cooked, unwrap the foil carefully. Mark a cross on the top of the potato, top with butter or cottage cheese and chopped chives or parsley, and serve with the barbecued meat.

Barbecued Hamburgers
The hamburgers can be prepared as on page 112, but as these are inclined to be too fragile for handling over the barbecue fire, the following recipe may be more suitable. It also has a very definite flavour, in keeping with traditional barbecue food. Follow the ingredients for Şiş Köfte on this page, stages 1 and 2, then flavour the mixture with a little mustard and 2 tbsp tomato ketchup. This provides the blending of savoury and sweet tastes to the hamburgers. Form the mixture into traditional rounds, brush with oil, and cook for 10 minutes over the barbecue fire, basting with oil during the cooking process.

Şiş Köfte
(Turkish Meat-ball Kebabs)

These are a little less fragile than the Moroccan on page 115 and are, therefore, more suitable for barbecue meals.

1 Blend 1 lb beef with $\frac{1}{2}$–$\frac{2}{3}$ cup fine breadcrumbs.

2 Peel and grate a medium onion into the meat mixture, blend well, and add a generous amount of salt and pepper.

3 Divide into a number of portions which can be moulded round the skewers.

4 To make more interesting kebabs, put small pieces of suet or mutton fat, the diced pulp of sweet red and green peppers (capsicums), tiny mushrooms, and slices of eggplant on the skewers with the meat balls.

5 Brush the food with melted butter or oil and cook until tender.

To serve: Şiş Köfte are served with finely chopped raw onions and sprinkled with chopped parsley and lemon juice.

Mexican Steak Kebabs
These, like many Mexican dishes, are hot in flavour. Choose a good-quality beef steak with a reasonable distribution of fat, such as boneless loin, rib, or top sirloin.

1 Cut the meat into small cubes and put on skewers.

2 Brush with oil or melted butter, then sprinkle with finely chopped chillis or a very little chilli pepper. If preferred, you could blend the powder with the oil or butter to ensure an even distribution of this very hot flavouring.

3 Place the skewers over the barbecue, brushing with oil or melted butter throughout the cooking period.

To serve: With rice and a salad.

Barbecue Sauces
Steaks, roasts, and the dishes described on this page are more interesting if served with one of these typical barbecue sauces. Each recipe gives enough for 4–6 good portions. The beef should be basted with the sauce during the process of cooking; it then becomes impregnated with the various flavours.

I have chosen sauces that are equally as pleasant with lamb chops, slices of ham, or sausages, all of which are popular barbecue foods.

All the sauces are heated and brushed over the meat during cooking. Any sauce left should be spooned over the meat when it is served.

Apricot Sauce: Make a purée of canned or cooked apricots. For 1$\frac{1}{4}$ cup of the purée you need 2 tbsp of each of the following: oil, vinegar, tomato ketchup, grated onion, and brown sugar. Add salt, pepper, mustard, and Tabasco and Worcestershire sauces to taste. Heat the mixture.

Jamaican Sauce: Blend scant $\frac{2}{3}$ cup rum with scant $\frac{2}{3}$ cup pineapple juice and 2 tbsp each of oil, soy sauce, and brown sugar. Add a little powdered ginger, salt, pepper, and mustard to taste. Heat the mixture.

Barbecue Tomato Sauce: Prepare and cook the tomato sauce as given on page 96, stages 1 to 10. Add $\frac{1}{2}$–1 teaspoon of chilli powder, 1 tbsp Worcestershire sauce, 2 tbsp brown sugar, and 2 tbsp vinegar. Heat the mixture.

Carbonada

Argentinian Beef Stew
Serves 6–8
Cooking Time: 35–40 minutes

INGREDIENTS

dried apricots or peaches: ½ lb
garlic cloves (optional): 2
onions: ½ lb
tomatoes: ½ lb
potatoes: 6 oz
sweet potatoes: ½ lb
pumpkin or squash: ½ lb
sweet green peppers: 2 medium
rump or sirloin steak: 2½ lb
butter or beef drippings: ¼ cup (½ stick)
salt and pepper: to taste
paprika: 1 teaspoon
saffron powder: pinch
ground cinnamon: ½ teaspoon
white wine: 1¼ cup
long-grain rice: generous ⅓ cup
canned sweetcorn: ¾ cup
egg yolks (optional): 2

You will find various versions of this dish in Spain, Portugal, and the South American countries, particularly the Argentine. It is at its best in that country, where the availability of high-quality beef enables one to use a prime cut. This dish is suitable for an informal party, hence the large quantity given here.

I have tried many different versions over the years, but this is my particular favourite when pumpkin or summer squash are in season. I have given the weight of most of the vegetables, since the balance of flavours in this dish is very important.

Although it is very suitable for a barbecue dish, you can make this in the kitchen.

1 Cut the dried fruit into neat pieces, soak for an hour or longer, then strain.

2 Skin the garlic, but leave the cloves whole, for they are not left in the stew.

3 Peel or skin the onions, tomatoes, potatoes, and pumpkin or squash, and dice neatly.

4 Dice the peppers; discard the core and seeds.

5 Cut the meat into neat squares.

6 When these preparations are made, pack the various foods into polythene containers and carry out to the barbecue.

7 Choose a really strong and large saucepan to heat over the barbecue fire; melt the butter or drippings in this, and fry the garlic cloves and remove them.

8 Add all the vegetables, except the pumpkin or squash, together with the beef, and turn in the butter or drippings for 10 minutes; it is advisable to do this towards the side of the barbecue, so that the heat is not too great.

9 Stir the salt, pepper, paprika, saffron, dried fruit, and cinnamon into the mixture towards the end of the cooking time.

10 Add the wine, cover the pan, and simmer gently for 10 minutes; add the pumpkin or squash and continue cooking for another 15 minutes.

11 Meanwhile, cook the rice in boiling salted water, see page 108; this method is ideal for a barbecue meal, as there is no straining to be done.

12 Add the canned corn to the ingredients in the saucepan.

13 Take the pan off the heat, or move to the very edge of the barbecue fire to keep hot.

14 Whisk the egg yolks into the mixture just before serving; this stage could well be omitted for an informal barbecue meal, but it does make the mixture rather richer.

To serve: Blend the rice with the other ingredients, then spoon from the cooking saucepan and serve with a salad.

To freeze: This dish is better freshly made.

To vary:
In the Argentine you may find this dish served or even cooked in a hollowed-out pumpkin shell.

Meat that is cooked on skewers is generally known as kebabs or brochettes, but there are, of course, other names for this popular dish.

Shashlyk and Shish Kebab are two of the better known, but these terms are used to describe portions of mutton, lamb, buffalo, or kid cooked on the skewers.

Many kebab recipes do use beef, and some of the most interesting are included on page 121. Skewer-cooking is a method used throughout history by tribesmen and soldiers, who would spear their food on their swords and cook this over the camp fires.

Although modern stoves frequently provide facilities for cooking kebabs in the oven or under the broiler, nothing can compare with the flavour of the meat when cooked over a glowing charcoal barbecue. This is a rapid method of cooking, and it requires good-quality beef steak.

One word of warning: always pull the meat off the skewer with a fork before you try to eat it; the skewers become almost red-hot and may

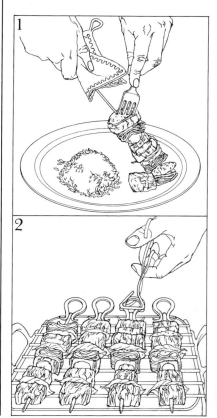

burn your mouth badly. If you hold the end of the skewer with a napkin, insert the prongs of the fork at the end by the napkin, and pull the fork down firmly, you thus remove all the food from the skewer onto the serving plate in one swift movement, see picture 1.

The method of cooking the kebabs is described under each recipe and the quantities given are sufficient for 4–6 people. The number of kebab skewers used will depend upon their length.

Do not pack the skewers too tightly with the food, otherwise this will not cook evenly.

You will need to turn the kebabs as they cook; kitchen tongs are the best way of doing this, see picture 2.

To serve: Cooked rice is an ideal accompaniment to kebabs, but jacket potatoes are an excellent alternative, see page 118.

The selection of ingredients used in kebabs makes them very colourful. One interesting way to present kebabs is the following. A loaf is put in the oven and warmed or is wrapped in foil and heated over the barbecue, then all the skewers of food are pushed into the loaf. The fresh hot bread can be served with the beef and the accompaniments. This is ideal if you do not want to cook rice.

To freeze: It is advisable to freeze the raw, diced beef for kebabs on open trays, then pack after freezing. This prevents the cubes of beef sticking

Kebabs from Many Countries

together. If you decide to prepare completed uncooked kebabs ready for freezing, remember that some ingredients, tomatoes in particular, cannot be frozen as they lose their firm texture. Protect the sharp tips of metal skewers with cotton wool or a thick pad of foil, so that they do not pierce the other packages in the freezer.

Kaduckievap
(Yugoslavian Kebabs)
Although lamb is often used in Kaduckievap, you can substitute beef, which blends well with the kidney and bacon.

1 Dice ½ lb lean beef, skin and halve 8–12 lambs' kidneys.

2 Cut the rinds (if necessary) from 6–8 long slices of fairly fat bacon, then stretch the bacon by sweeping a blunt knife along the strips; this makes the bacon longer and thinner, also more pliable. Cut each slice into 2 or 3 pieces and form into rolls.

3 Peel several medium-sized onions and cut into rings.

4 Thread the diced meat, kidneys, bacon, and onion rings onto skewers; brush the meats and onions with a little oil and a light sprinkling of salt and pepper.

5 Cook over the barbecue fire for about 10 minutes, or until the food is tender, brushing this with the oil once or twice during the cooking period.

To serve: Warm 1¼ cup yoghourt, flavour this with a skinned and finely chopped onion and 2 or 3 chopped chillis. The authentic recipe uses pickled chillis, but as they are not readily available, you may care to prepare your own.

Follow the recipe given for pickled cucumbers on page 103, but use chillis.

As an alternative, add a pinch of chilli powder to the yoghourt.

To freeze: General remarks on freezing meat for kebabs are given on this page, left.
The yoghourt sauce should not be frozen. It may be useful to freeze chilli peppers when in season. Blanch in boiling water for 2 minutes, cool, then pack. Use within a year.

Kababs
The secret of this Moroccan dish is the way the meat is marinated in the spice-flavoured butter for several hours before being cooked. As there is no wine or vinegar used, choose really tender beef.

1 Melt ¼ lb (1 stick) butter for each 1–1¼ lb beef; pour this into a dish.

2 Add to the quantity of butter above ½ teaspoon of each of the following: saffron powder, ground ginger, ground cumin, together with a generous pinch of cayenne pepper, ground cloves, and salt.

3 Cube the meat and put into the spiced butter; leave for several hours, turning regularly so that the meat becomes coated. Keep in a fairly warm place so that the butter does not solidify.

4 Lift the beef from the dish. In Morocco the meat is often impregnated with onion and garlic: take a medium-sized onion and 1–2 cloves of garlic for 1 lb meat. Peel these and chop very finely.

5 Put the meat onto the skewers, then press the onion and garlic into the flesh; you need to press quite hard.

6 Cook the kababs, basting once or twice with any butter that is left in the dish.

To serve: With cooked rice. The Kefta sauce on page 115 is an excellent accompaniment.

To vary:
The method of marinating the meat given in this recipe is ideal for lean veal, mutton, or lamb. The butter adds a richness to the meat. The accompaniments mentioned in stage 5 and 'To Serve' are equally good with other meats.

Kaduckievap

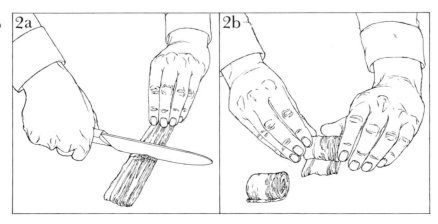

Balkan Kebabs

Meat on skewers (right) is one of the most popular dishes in the Balkan countries. Rarely will it be beef, for the beef there is not sufficiently tender for this method of cooking.

I think that all keen kebab cooks can learn from the way their Balkan counterparts marinate meat before cooking it. As beef is so lean, marinating is an excellent way to prepare it, but you may, of course, substitute other meats.

1 If cooking 1 lb lean beef, blend together:
3 tbsp olive or other first-class oil with the same amount of red or white wine.

2 Peel and chop a medium onion, 1–2 cloves of garlic, a small bunch of parsley, and a sprig of fresh marjoram (pinch of dry).

3 Add to the oil and wine, together with salt and pepper to taste.

4 Cut the meat in dice; these vary in size from 1 to 2 inches. Put into the marinade and allow to stand for several hours, turning regularly.

5 Put the meat on the skewers with other ingredients; these vary from country to country and include sliced pickled cucumbers, bay leaves, tiny sausages, diced fat bacon, and a selection of vegetables such as mushrooms, tomatoes, onions, and sliced eggplants.

6 Cook over the barbecue fire for about ten minutes until the meat is tender; baste several times with any marinade that may be left.

To serve: With rice and a green salad or jacket potatoes, cooked over the barbecue fire, as per the directions on page 118.

Kebabs from the Caribbean

These kebabs (far right) have an entirely different taste from those which are based upon the Balkan cuisine.

1 Cube 1 lb lean fillet beef and put on skewers with firm small tomatoes or quartered larger tomatoes, diced sweet red and green peppers (discard the core and seeds), peeled and quartered small onions, and diced fresh pineapple.

2 Make a sweet basting sauce for the kebabs; this recipe will give enough sauce for about 8 skewers.

3 Peel and chop a small onion and heat 2 tbsp oil in a pan.

4 Fry the onion until pale golden in colour, then add 2 tbsp of each of the following: tomato juice, vinegar, dark molasses, and water.

5 Heat together with a little salt, pepper, and sugar to taste.

6 Brush the food on the skewers with the sauce, then cook over the barbecue.

7 Continue to baste as the kebabs cook.

Sate Lembu

These Malaysian and Indonesian kebabs are probably the most interesting of all recipes, due to the marinade and the sauce, which combine to flavour the meat.

Unlike many other kebab recipes, which use beef only as an alternative to the more usual mutton or lamb, Sate Lembu is always based on beef, although similar satays are prepared from chicken and veal.

Choose a firm steak, such as rump, and cut it into really small cubes, no more than 1 inch in size.

The meat is put on bamboo skewers in the Far East, but, obviously, metal skewers can be used.

1 Before preparing the meat, make the marinade. For approximately 1 lb beef you need 1¼ cup coconut milk; this is not the liquid (which we often call 'milk') that runs from the fresh coconut but is made by pouring boiling water over the grated flesh of the coconut. To produce about 1¼ cup of milk, you need this amount of water and a scant ⅔ cup measure of finely grated coconut.

Leave for 4 hours, then pour through a fine muslin bag or a traditional flannel jelly bag, squeezing hard to extract the liquid. Or if you have a blender, then blend the coconut and water in it. This will give you a very thick mixture, but this can be diluted with extra water.

When fresh coconut is not available, use desiccated coconut.

2 Pour the coconut milk into a dish and add a good pinch of each of the

following spices: ground cardamom, cinnamon, cumin, curry powder, black pepper, and ginger, together with 1 or 2 peeled and crushed cloves of garlic.

3 Add the cubed meat to the marinade and leave for several hours.

4 Turn the meat once or twice, so that all the surfaces of the meat absorb the mixture, although this is a generous amount of liquid and all may not be absorbed.

5 Lift the beef from the marinade, drain well, put on the skewers, and cook over the barbecue fire until tender.

To serve: With cooked rice and Satay Sauce, see below.

Satay Sauce

1 Put ¼ lb shelled peanuts on a baking tray and put into the oven at a moderate heat, 375°F, for 5–6 minutes until roasted on the outside, then place in a bowl.

2 Peel and chop 1 medium onion, 1–2 cloves of garlic, add to the peanuts, together with 1 tbsp lemon or lime juice, 1 tbsp soy sauce, 2 tbsp peanut butter, a pinch of chilli powder, and a little salt and pepper.

3 Pound until very smooth or put into a blender until a smooth purée.

4 Gradually add up to scant ⅓ cup *thick* coconut milk (often known as coconut cream). This is made in exactly the same way as the milk in the marinade, but using a little less water so that the liquid from the coconut is like a cream, rather than a milk. The peanut sauce should have a fairly thick consistency.

5 Add 1–2 teaspoons sugar to taste.

To serve: With kebabs, such as the Sate Lembu opposite.

In this Indian recipe the beef is cut in fairly large pieces of at least 2 inches in width and the meat is cooked in a roasting pan over the barbecue or directly on the bars of the barbecue, exactly like steaks; the pieces of beef are too large to be placed on skewers.

The quality of the meat in India is not as good as in many countries and the lime juice marinade tenderizes it most successfully.

This beef dish is often served cold and would be equally successful cooked under a broiler.

1 Cut the beef into slices about 1 inch in thickness, then into portions of at least 2 inches square. Dry very thoroughly on absorbent paper.

2 Blend the ingredients for the marinade together and pour into a shallow dish.

3 Add the meat and leave for about 3 hours, turning over several times and pressing firmly to absorb the marinade.

4 Melt the butter or ghee when ready to cook the beef.

5 Lift the beef from the marinade and allow it to drip over the dish.

6 Blend the melted butter or ghee with the marinade and brush the meat with this.

7 Put the beef into a strong roasting pan (it has to withstand considerable heat over the barbecue fire) or onto the well-greased bars of the barbecue fire; cook for about 30 minutes, turning several times, and baste with the mixture as prepared at stage 6.

Indian Barbecued Beef
Serves 6–8
Cooking Time: 30 minutes

INGREDIENTS

top round: 2 lb
for the marinade:
lime juice: 6 tbsp
ground coriander: ½–1 teaspoon
chilli powder: ½ teaspoon
turmeric: ½ teaspoon
salt and pepper: to taste
for basting:
butter or ghee, see page 100: ¼ cup (½ stick)
eggs: 4
tomatoes: 4 large
cucumber: ½ medium

8 Towards the end of the cooking time, hard-boil the eggs; crack, shell, and slice these.

9 Slice the tomatoes and cucumber.

To serve: Arrange the beef on the serving dish with the eggs, tomatoes, and cucumber.

To freeze: Better freshly cooked.

Barbecued Spare Ribs

Pork spare ribs are generally selected for this dish, but beef ribs are equally enjoyable. As the bones are considerably longer in beef, you should request 'short ribs' if possible, or failing that, ask the butcher to cut the ribs into pieces. This makes the food easier to handle.

For 4–6 people you will need at least 4 lb of short ribs of beef. This sounds a large amount, but the bones are very heavy. The barbecue sauce is also used as a marinade in this recipe.

1 Wipe the meat, cut away any surplus fat, for this drops into the barbecue fire.

2 Prepare the barbecue sauce: blend together scant ⅓ cup red wine, 3 tbsp vegetable oil, 2 tbsp soy sauce, 1 tbsp honey or brown sugar, 1 or 2 peeled and crushed cloves of garlic, and salt and pepper to taste.

3 Pour the marinade into a large shallow dish, add the ribs of beef and leave overnight or, if this is not possible, for several hours.

4 Lift the ribs of beef from the marinade and place on the bars of the barbecue; cook until tender (this takes approximately 25 minutes).

5 Baste frequently with the sauce.

6 If you want the meat to be crisp, then cease basting for the last 7–8 minutes of the cooking time.

To serve: As a separate course with crisp radishes or other crudités.

To freeze: Fresh meat is better for this dish.

PIES AND PUDDINGS

To cook any kind of meat encased in pastry is to enhance its flavour, for the meat juices cannot escape but are kept sealed in by the pastry crust or are retained in the dish in which the pudding is cooked.

Many people imagine that meat pies and puddings are solely an Anglo-Saxon style of cooking; that is not true – just think of one of the most popular and delicious of all beef dishes, Bœuf en Croûte, a modern French dish consisting of tender fillet beef in a case of pastry – nothing could have a more interesting taste.

Certainly, pies have been known in Britain since medieval times, when moulded pastry cases known as 'coffins' or 'coffers' were filled with game or meat and cooked. The combination of beef and kidney seems to have been a British creation, and no two meats complement each other better. So fond are the British of this mixture that they put it in both a pudding and a pie. King Edward VII of England had a great liking for steak and kidney pudding, as indeed had many Victorians and Edwardians.

In the days when pudding basins and pie dishes were utilitarian, rather than elegant as they are today, it was traditional to serve the pudding with a white starched napkin round the container, and the pie dish was decorated with a pleated pie frill.

Americans share the British liking for beef and kidney pie, but as their recipe is similar to the British, I have given a lesser-known American dish.

The method of making pastry varies in different countries. The wafer-thin phyllo pastry of Greece is now becoming well known and liked in other countries, and in this section you will find one of the typically Greek pies, using this.

Beef is a meat that blends with a great variety of ingredients, and the pies that come from South America combine the meat with a wider selection of foods than you find in European pie recipes.

Empañadas

Chilean Beef Patties
Serves 4
Cooking Time: 40 minutes

INGREDIENTS

for the suet crust pastry:
flour: 1 cup
salt: pinch
chopped or shredded suet: ¼ lb
eggs: 2 small
for the filling:
eggs: 2
onion: 1 medium
sweet green pepper: ½ medium
stuffed olives: 12
cooked beef: 1 lb
butter: ¼ cup (½ stick)
raisins: 2 oz
salt and pepper: to taste

1 Make the suet crust pastry as in the recipe on page 134, stages 1–3, but use eggs, instead of water, to bind the mixture to a rolling consistency.

2 Hard-boil the eggs for the filling, shell and chop.

3 Peel and chop the onion very finely; dice the pepper, discard the core and seeds; chop the olives.

4 Dice or grind the meat.

5 Heat the butter in a frying pan and fry the onion until nearly soft; stir in the pepper, olives, meat, and raisins and heat for 2 minutes; add salt, pepper, and the hard-boiled eggs.

6 Roll out the pastry dough until very thin and cut into eight 5-inch squares or rounds.

7 Place the beef mixture in the centre of each pastry shape; brush the edges with a little water, then fold the dough over the filling to cover.

8 Press the pastry edges together very firmly and lift the empañadas onto a lightly greased baking tray.

9 Bake for 30 minutes in the centre of a moderate oven, 375°F, or until golden brown.

To serve: Hot, as a snack.

To freeze: These cannot be frozen unless you omit the hard-boiled egg.

To vary:
(i) Use cooked chicken or other cooked meat.
(ii) Use uncooked tender beef; top round is a good choice. In this case, cook for a total of 45 minutes to 1 hour, reducing the heat slightly after 20–25 minutes.
(iii) Although this pastry is not generally brushed with beaten egg to glaze before baking, doing this gives a more attractive appearance.

Steak and Kidney Pudding

Serves 4–6
Cooking Time: 4 hours

INGREDIENTS

suet crust pastry made with: 1 cup flour, etc.
for the filling:
stewing beef, see page 37: 1–1¼ lb
ox kidney: ¼ lb
flour: 2 tbsp
salt and pepper: to taste
beef stock or water: 2 tbsp

This recipe typifies the kind of savoury pudding that has been famous for generations in Britain.

The version in which oysters are added was reputed to be a favourite dish, as was Steak, Kidney and Oyster Pie, of Doctor Samuel Johnson, the famous writer and lexicographer who lived in the eighteenth century.

If you imagine this to be a very solid dish, you are wrong – it is sustaining, but the pastry is very thin. The flavour of the cooked meat 'imprisoned' in the pastry is superb, as it virtually cooks in its own juice.

I have served Beef and Pheasant Pudding as a dish at many winter buffet parties, and, although my guests have had a fairly extensive choice of dishes, it has always been this pudding which is the prime favourite.

1 Make suet crust pastry, as per the recipe on page 134, and turn it onto a lightly floured board.

2 Take two-thirds of the dough, roll it out thinly, and line a lightly greased 1–1½ quart pudding mould.

3 Cut the steak and ox kidney into neat dice and mix together.

Alternatively: A more expert way of combining the meats is to cut thin narrow strips of steak and small cubes of kidney. You then place the kidney at one end of the steak and turn this to make a neat roll.

4 Blend the flour with salt and pepper to taste, and coat the meat in the mixture.

5 Put the meat into the lined mould with the stock or water.

6 Roll out the remaining pastry into a round to cover the top of the basin.

7 Moisten the edges of the pastry with a little water, put the pastry 'lid' in position, and press the edges of the pastry together.

8 Cover with greased grease-proof paper or foil.

9 Steam over rapidly boiling water for 2 hours (this makes sure the pastry is light), then lower the heat slightly and cook for a further 2 hours.

To serve: With Brown Sauce, see page 85, but use rather more stock to give a thinner consistency.

To freeze: The pudding can be frozen before cooking for a period of 2 months or after cooking for 3 months.

To vary:
(i) *Beef Steak, Kidney, and Oyster Pudding:* Add 6 sliced oysters to the filling above.
(ii) *Beef and Pheasant Pudding:* Allow 1 lb stewing beef to a good-sized pheasant. As this will produce a greater quantity of filling than given in the recipe above, increase the amount of suet crust pastry. Use 1½ cup flour, etc. Cut all the flesh from the pheasant, dice this neatly, mix with the diced steak, then proceed as stages 5–9. Simmer the pheasant bones for stock. Make the Brown Sauce, see page 85, but use the pheasant stock, and add a generous amount of port wine to flavour and give a thinner consistency. Use a 1½-quart mold.

Biscuit Meat Roll

Biscuit Meat Roll
Serves 4–6
Cooking Time: 25–30 minutes
plus time to make the sauce

INGREDIENTS

for the filling:
Espagnole Sauce: see page 85
ground cooked beef: ¾ lb
chopped parsley: 1 tbsp
for the biscuit crust:
flour: 1 cup
salt: ½ teaspoon
white pepper: shake
baking powder: 2 teaspoons
butter or fat: ¼ cup (½ stick)
milk: to mix

1 Prepare the sauce as per the recipe on page 85.

2 Blend approximately a quarter of the sauce with the meat. This is only one of the sauces that may be chosen: you might also use Brown, Cheese, or Tomato sauces, as given on pages 85, 75, and 96, respectively.

3 Add the parsley and allow the mixture to cool.

4 Sieve the flour, salt, pepper, and baking powder.

5 Rub in the butter or fat until the mixture looks like very fine crumbs.

6 Gradually stir in enough milk to make a soft rolling consistency.

7 Turn the biscuit dough onto a lightly floured board and roll out to a neat oblong, about ¼ inch in thickness.

8 Spread with the beef mixture, brush the ends with a little water, and roll. Do this lightly, so that there is space for the pastry to rise; if the dough is rolled too firmly, the roll will be heavy.

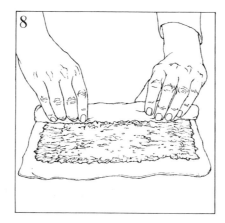

9 Turn so that the seam is underneath and bake in the centre of a moderately hot to hot oven, 400–425°F, for 25–30 minutes, reducing the heat slightly after 20 minutes if the outside is becoming too brown.

To serve: Serve the roll topped with the remaining sauce.

To freeze: This freezes well for 2 months.

Pierogi z Miesem

Polish Meat Patties
Serves 4
Cooking Time: 20 minutes

INGREDIENTS

for the dough:
high gluten flour: 1 lb
salt: ½ teaspoon
milk: 1 cup
yeast: 1 cake or 1 packet
butter: 1 oz
eggs: 2
for the filling:
onions: 2 medium
butter: 2 tbsp (¼ stick)
cooked beef: ¾ lb
fine breadcrumbs: ½–⅔ cup
chopped parsley: 1 tbsp
egg: 1
salt and pepper: to taste
milk: to bind
for the topping:
butter: ¼ lb (1 stick)
chopped parsley: to taste
Parmesan cheese, grated: to taste

1 Sieve the flour and salt into a bowl.

2 Warm the milk to body temperature, then blend with the yeast.

3 Make a well in the centre of the flour, pour in the yeast liquid, cover with a light sprinkling of flour, and leave until the surface is covered with bubbles.

4 Melt the butter and add to the yeast liquid and flour, together with the eggs.

5 Blend the dough with your hands to bind, then turn onto a working surface and knead until smooth. To test if the dough is sufficiently kneaded, press with a lightly floured finger and the impression should come out; if it does not, then the dough must be kneaded longer.

6 Cover the bowl with a cloth or put the yeast mixture into a large lightly oiled polythene bag and leave for about 1 hour, or until the dough doubles in bulk. While the dough is 'proving' (rising), prepare the meat filling, as per stages 9 and 10.

7 Return the dough to the working surface and knead once again.

8 Divide into about 12 small portions, roll out each to form a neat round.

9 Peel and chop the onions finely and fry in the butter until soft.

10 Grind the cooked beef or chop finely, blend with the cooked onions, breadcrumbs, and the rest of the filling ingredients; add only enough milk to form a firm mixture.

9 Peel and chop the onions finely and fry in the butter until soft.

10 Grind the cooked beef or chop finely, blend with the cooked onions, breadcrumbs, and the rest of the filling ingredients; add only enough milk to form a firm mixture.

11 Divide the filling between the portions of yeast dough, putting it into the centre of each round.

12 Moisten the edges of the dough with water, then gather up these edges and press together very firmly, so completely covering the filling.

13 Roll each patty very gently in your hands to form a round ball; if you handle it too roughly, the filling may break through the dough.

14 Place on a lightly greased baking sheet and leave for about 20 minutes, or until the balls have risen well.

15 Meanwhile, heat about 3–4 quarts water in a large saucepan and add salt to taste.

16 When the water is boiling, cook the balls in this for about 12–15 minutes; make certain that the water boils steadily during the whole period.

17 Lift the light balls from the water with a perforated spoon or spatula; hold over the saucepan as you do this.

18 Put on a hot serving dish.

To serve: Melt the butter, spoon over the balls, and top with the parsley and cheese.

To freeze: Cook and freeze. Use within a month. To reheat, tip the frozen balls into boiling salted water and cook gently until defrosted and hot.

To vary:
(i) Prepare the meat patties and cook them in a pan of deep fat (rather like you cook a doughnut), drain and top with parsley.
(ii) Make very small patties and cook them to serve as cocktail savouries.

Cornish Pasties

Serves 4
Cooking Time: 45–50 minutes

INGREDIENTS

for the short crust pastry:
flour: 1¼ cup
salt: good pinch
butter or fat: ¾ cup (1½ stick)
water: to mix
for the filling:
rump steak: ¾ lb
potatoes: 2 medium
onions: 2 medium
salt and pepper: to taste
beef stock: 2 tbsp
to glaze:
egg (optional): 1

The origin of the Cornish pasty goes back to the thriving days of the tin-mining industry in Cornwall, in the south-west of England. The miner used to have his complete meal in one large pasty. At one end of it was the meat mixture, as given in this recipe, and at the other end a fruit or preserve or other sweet filling.

While the short crust pastry recipe, as given, may be used for this dish, it is advisable to omit at least 2 tbsp butter or fat if you intend to make the pasties to carry on a picnic. This makes the pastry less light and delicate, and thus less likely to break. When the miner carried his Cornish pasty to work, the proportion of fat to flour was probably even slightly less than this, so that the pastry was strong and undoubtedly less appetizing than when a better proportion of fat is used. Savoury pasties can be made with a chicken, rabbit, or fish filling, but this recipe is the best known. The shape is also the traditional one.

1 Sieve the flour and salt, and rub in the butter or fat until the mixture looks like fine breadcrumbs.

2 Add cold water to bind to a firm rolling consistency.

3 Roll out the pastry and cut into 4 large rounds; you may need to do this by cutting round a small plate, since pastry cutters are rarely available in such a large size.

4 Cut the steak into very small dice; peel the potatoes and onions and cut into similar sizes.

5 Mix the vegetables with a little salt, pepper, and the stock.

6 Divide the mixture between the pastry rounds.

7 Moisten the edges of the pastry with a little water.

8 Bring the edges together and flute these with your forefinger and thumb, to form the traditional upright pasty shape.

9 Lift onto a lightly greased baking tray.

10 Beat the egg and brush over the pasties (this is not essential but gives a pleasant shine to the pastry).

11 Bake for 20–25 minutes in the centre of a moderately hot oven, 400°F, until the pastry begins to brown; lower the heat to moderate, 350°F, for a further 25 minutes to make sure that the filling is adequately cooked.

To serve: Hot or cold as a snack or main meal with salad or vegetables.

To freeze: Do not freeze.

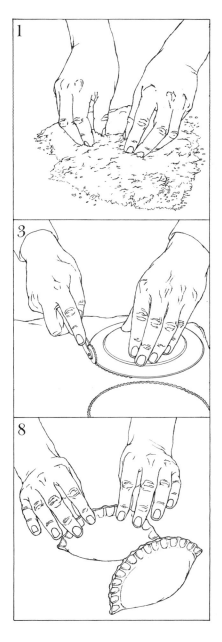

Bœuf en Croûte

Fillet Steak in Pastry
Serves 4–6
Cooking Time: 50 minutes to 1 hour 5 minutes

INGREDIENTS

puff pastry made with recipe, page 134: 1 cup flour, etc.
fillet steak cut in one piece: 1½ lb
butter: ¼ cup (½ stick)
for the stuffing:
mushrooms: ½ lb
onion: 1 small
chopped parsley: 2 teaspoons
salt and pepper: to taste
to glaze:
egg: 1

1 First make the pastry.

2 Even if you like rare steak, roast it until almost ready before putting it into the pastry case, which would become over-brown if raw steak was used. The steak will continue to cook while in the pastry in the oven.

3 Spread the steak with half the butter and roast in the centre of a hot oven, 425°F. Allow 10 minutes for rare steak, 15 minutes for medium steak, and 20–25 minutes for well-done meat; lift onto a plate and cool. Prepare the stuffing as the steak cools.

4 Chop the mushrooms and onion finely, blend with the remaining butter, parsley, salt, and pepper.

5 Roll out the pastry into a large square or oblong, large enough to envelop the meat; save a small amount of the pastry for decorating the pastry case.

6 Spread with the mushroom and onion mixture; leave a good margin of about ½ inch at the edges of the pastry without this stuffing.

7 Place the steak in the centre of the pastry and moisten the edges of the pastry with a little water.

8 Fold the pastry to cover the meat.

9 Seal the ends and the seam, turn so that the seam is underneath.

10 Cut leaves and make a pastry 'rose' from the odd pieces of pastry, as illustrated left; moisten with a little water, and place on the top of the pastry shape.

11 Place on a baking sheet. Make 2–3 slits to allow steam to escape.

12 Beat the egg and brush the pastry with this to glaze.

13 Bake for approximately 35–40 minutes in the centre of a hot oven, see stage 3, reducing the heat to moderate after 20 minutes, or when the pastry begins to brown.

To serve: Hot with an Espagnole, Brown, or Poivrade sauce (recipes all on page 85) and vegetables or salad.

To freeze: Prepare this and freeze rather than cook it before freezing. Always *defrost* before cooking. Use within 2 months.

To vary:
(i) Use 1 lb frozen puff pastry instead of making your own.
(ii) Spread the pastry with pâté instead of the mushroom mixture.
(iii) *Filets Mignons en Croûte:* The recipe on the left is one way of serving beef in a pastry coating. Another way to serve pastry round steaks is as follows:

1 Follow the directions for making puff pastry on page 134; put this in the refrigerator.

2 Prepare 4–6 small filets mignons, the very tender part of the fillet, and the stuffing given on the left. This cut of fillet is tender and the size small, so that pre-cooking is not necessary, unless you like steak well done, in which case allow 2 minutes on either side under the broiler, and then allow to cool.

3 Roll out the pastry until very thin, cut into 4–6 squares, spread with the filling, as in stage 6 left, and then continue as stages 7–9.

4 To make leaves, cut several diamond shapes from the remaining pastry, mark the 'veins' with a knife.

5 To make a rose, cut a long strip of pastry, turn this round loosely, depress at regular intervals to look like a rose, picture 5a. You may like to prepare a tassel, as picture 5b.

6 Complete the dish as the recipe on the left, stages 10–13, but allow a total of 25–30 minute cooking.

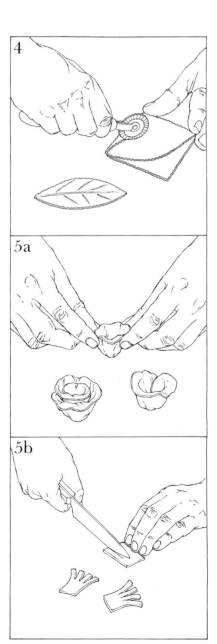

Bourekia apo Kima

Cypriot Fried Meat Pies
Serves 4–6
Cooking Time: 40 minutes

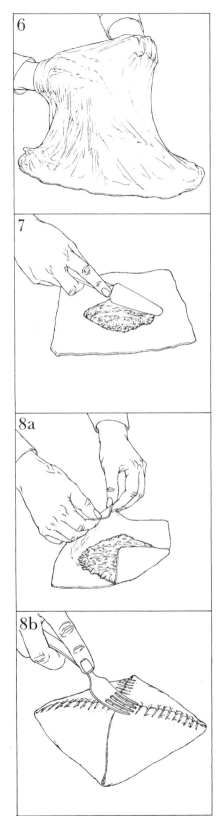

There is a variety of Bourekia recipes in Greece and Cyprus; these pies are filled with savoury meat mixtures.

Sometimes, the pies are baked, but these fried pies, which are very popular in Cyprus, are a pleasant change. The phyllo-type pastry is not difficult to make, but it needs firm kneading and rolling and must be very thin to be appetizing.

While mutton and lamb may well be the first choice in Greece, beef makes an excellent filling.

If you have really *good-quality* stewing beef, you can make the filling with this, but otherwise select top round or rib of beef.

INGREDIENTS

for the pastry:
flour: 1¼ cup
salt: ¼ teaspoon
olive oil: 4 tbsp
lemon juice: 1 tbsp
cold water: to blend
for the filling:
onions: 2 medium
beef – see remarks left: 1 lb
butter: ¼ cup (¼ stick)
chopped parsley: 1–2 tbsp
grated nutmeg: ½ teaspoon
ground cloves: ½ teaspoon
salt and pepper: to taste
beef stock or water: scant ½ cup
for frying:
oil: see method, stage 9

1 Sieve the flour and salt; add the oil, lemon juice, and then enough water to make a firm rolling consistency. Knead the dough with your finger-tips, then cover and leave for at least 1 hour.

2 Peel and chop the onions, and grind the meat or dice it very finely.

3 Heat the butter in a saucepan and fry the onions slowly until they become soft.

4 Mix with the meat, parsley, spices, and a fairly generous amount of salt and pepper.

5 Add the stock or water, cover the pan, and simmer steadily for 20 minutes. Then remove the lid of the pan and continue cooking for 10 minutes, until the meat is tender and the liquid has been absorbed. Stir quite frequently during the last part of the cooking period. Allow the meat mixture to cool.

6 Turn the dough onto a lightly floured surface. Knead until quite smooth, then roll out until it is an almost paper-thin oblong or square. This is easier if you pull gently, as well as rolling with a rolling pin.

7 Cut into about 8 large squares; divide the meat filling between the squares, placing this in the centre.

8 Brush the edges of the dough with water, then form into an envelope shape, sealing the edges with a fork.

9 Heat enough oil in a large shallow saucepan to give a depth of at least 2 inches. Test the heat with a cube of day-old bread: it should turn golden within 30 seconds.

10 Fry the meat pies steadily for approximately 8 minutes until golden brown. Drain on absorbent paper.

To serve: Hot with a mixed salad.

To freeze: While the filling can be frozen, the pies are better if freshly cooked.

To vary:
Add 2–3 tbsp grated Parmesan cheese to the meat filling, together with 1 tbsp tomato purée.

Instead of Parmesan cheese, you could use double the amount of grated Cheddar cheese and the pulp only of a large fresh tomato.

Vol-au-Vent en Bœuf

Beef Vol-au-vent

A vol-au-vent is, perhaps, a more interesting combination of puff pastry and beef than the usual pie, but the basic ingredients are very similar.

1 Make the puff pastry as on page 134 and roll out to about ½ inch in thickness; cut into a neat square, oval, or round shape; you may, if you prefer, make individual pastry cases; put on a baking tray.

2 To form the space to fill, mark the pastry first with the tip of a knife and then cut into the pastry to a depth of ¼ inch, leaving a margin all round the edge of the pastry.

3 Brush with beaten egg and bake in the centre of a very hot oven, 450°F, for 15 minutes until well risen, then remove from the oven and carefully lift out the centre pastry.

4 Return the case to the oven and dry out on a low heat for a few minutes.

To serve: Fill with the cooked steak and kidney mixture, see page 133, or the Bolognese Sauce, see page 146, and serve at once.

To freeze: Freeze the uncooked pastry case for a period of 3 months or the cooked, but empty, pastry case for up to 4 months.

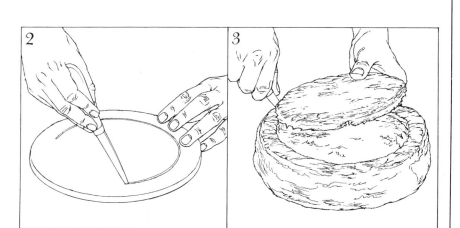

Hallacas

Venezuelan Meat Pies
Serves 4–6
Cooking Time: 35–40 minutes

INGREDIENTS

for the filling:
eggs: 3
onions: 2 large
sweet green pepper: 1 small
sweet red pepper: 1 small
fat: ¼ cup
salt and pepper: to taste
ground raw beef: ¾ lb
seedless raisins: generous ⅓ cup
pitted green olives: 14 medium
for the short crust pastry:
flour: 1½ cup
salt: good pinch
butter or fat: ¾ cup (1½ sticks)
water: to mix
to glaze:
egg: 1

These small pies are a speciality of Venezuela. They include a similar filling to that used in the Chilean Empañadas on page 126, but the pastry used is quite different; this is the more familiar short crust, whereas the pastry on page 126 is a richer form of the British suet crust pastry.

The combination of meat with vegetables, eggs, and dried fruit is a very pleasant one.

1 Hard-boil the eggs.

2 Peel and dice the onions; cut the pulp of the sweet peppers into small pieces; discard the core and seeds.

3 Heat the fat and fry the onions and peppers for just 3–4 minutes; add a little salt and pepper.

4 Stir the meat into the vegetable mixture and cook over a low heat for 6–7 minutes, stirring all the time.

5 Stir the raisins into the hot mixture, so that they become plump, then allow the mixture to cool.

Steak and Kidney Pie

Serves 6
Cooking Time: 2–2½ hours

INGREDIENTS

puff pastry, made with: 1 cup flour, etc.
stewing beef, see cuts page 37: 1½ lb
veal or lambs' kidneys: ½ lb
onions (optional): 2–3 medium
flour: 2 tbsp
salt and pepper: to taste
fat: ¼ cup
beef stock: scant 2 cups
red wine: scant ⅔ cup
bouquet garni:
parsley: sprig
thyme: sprig
bay leaf: 1
to glaze:
egg: 1

6 Chop the olives and eggs, and blend with the meat mixture.

7 Sieve the flour and salt, rub in the butter or fat until the mixture looks like fine breadcrumbs, then add sufficient cold water to bind to a firm rolling consistency.

8 Roll out the pastry on a lightly floured board until about ¼ inch in thickness and cut out 8 large or 12 smaller rounds; make 'leaves' from any small pieces of pastry left, as in the picture on page 130.

9 Put half the pastry rounds onto a lightly greased baking sheet.

10 Spoon the filling into the centre of these rounds.

11 Moisten the edges of the bottom pastry; cover with the remainder of the pastry rounds and seal the edges firmly.

12 Press the leaves in position: beat the egg and brush over the pastry, to give a good shine to the small pies.

13 Bake in the centre of a moderately hot oven, 400°F, for approximately 12–15 minutes, or until the pastry begins to become golden, then reduce the heat to very moderate, 325°F, for a further 10 minutes.

To serve: Hot with salad.

To freeze: Not suitable for freezing.

This pie – deliciously 'feather-light' pastry over a savoury beef filling – is worthy of any gourmet's attention.

Although many people cook both meat and pastry together, I find that the following method gives a better result.

1 Make the pastry, page 134.

2 Cut the steak and kidney into small cubes: peel and dice the onions, if using these.

3 Blend the flour with the salt and pepper; coat the meat.

4 Heat the fat in a saucepan, fry the steak, kidney, and onions until pale golden, and stir well.

5 Add the stock, wine, and herbs, bring the liquid to the boil, and stir until thickened. Cover and simmer for 1½ hours or until the meat is *nearly* tender; do not over-cook.

6 Spoon the meat or meat and onions into a 10×1¾ inch pie dish and add only enough gravy to cover; save the remainder. If the pie dish is not well filled, put a pie support in the centre, so that the pastry will not drop during baking.

7 Roll out the pastry thinly, cut a long strip to fit the rim of the pie dish, damp the rim, and put the strip in position.

8 Support the rest of the pastry over the rolling pin and place over the filling.

9 Press the edges of the pastry to the pastry rim, *then* cut away any surplus. Make a slit in the pastry to allow steam to escape.

10 'Flake', then flute, the edges.

11 Make 'leaves' and a tassel, page 130, and put in position, making sure that the slit is not covered. Beat the egg and brush the pastry well with this.

12 Stand the pie on a baking tray and bake in the centre of a very hot oven, 450°F, for 15–20 minutes to allow the pastry to rise, then lower the heat and cook for a further 25–30 minutes at a moderate heat, 375°F.

To serve: Hot with vegetables and the gravy, from stage 6, as a sauce.

To freeze: This freezes well for up to 3 months.

To vary:
(i) Add diced mixed vegetables to the saucepan towards the end of stage 5.
(ii) *Steak, Kidney and Oyster Pie:* Include 6–8 sliced large oysters in the mixture.
(iii) Include about ½ lb button mushrooms in the mixture.

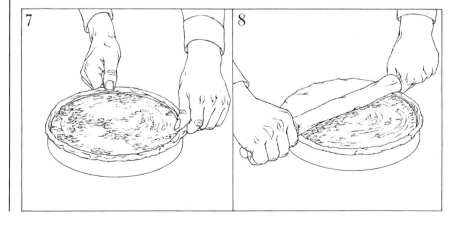

Puff Pastry

Servings depend upon recipe
Cooking Time: Depends upon recipe

INGREDIENTS

flour: 1 cup
salt: pinch
water: to mix
lemon juice: $\frac{1}{2}$ tbsp
butter: $\frac{1}{2}$ lb (2 sticks)

1 Sieve the flour and salt together.

2 Mix to a rolling consistency with the water and lemon juice. Make sure it is elastic and not too dry.

3 Roll out to an oblong shape.

4 Place the block or sticks of butter in the centre of the pastry dough, bring up first the bottom third of the dough, then bring down the top third to cover the butter completely.

5 Turn the pastry at right angles, seal both the top and bottom open ends with the rolling pin, then 'rib' the pastry carefully and regularly.

6 Roll out again until an oblong shape and fold the dough into an envelope shape, as in stage 4.

7 Repeat this 5 times, so making 7 rollings and 7 foldings.

8 Roll the pastry out thinly, for it should rise to 5 times its original thickness.

9 Cut into desired shapes, or shape and bake as the particular recipe.

To freeze: The uncooked pastry freezes well for up to 3 months. Defrost sufficiently to handle before trying to roll out the dough. Storage time for cooked dishes using puff pastry will vary with the filling.

To vary:
Modern opinion suggests using all high gluten flour (the type used for bread making) for this flaky pastry.

Suet Crust Pastry

Serves 4–6
Cooking Time: Depends upon recipe

INGREDIENTS

finely shredded or chopped suet: $\frac{1}{4}$ lb
flour: 1 cup
salt: pinch
baking powder (optional), see method: 2 teaspoons
water: to mix

1 If buying butcher's suet, remove the skin and gristle, and chop the suet on a floured board. Packet suet keeps for a considerable time in a cool place as it has flour added.

2 Sieve the flour, salt, and baking powder into a mixing bowl. The baking powder can be omitted if you want a very thin crust that does not rise.

3 Add the suet, mix to a *soft* rolling consistency with cold water, or to a slightly softer mixture if making the dumplings on page 56.

4 Use as the particular recipe.

To freeze: This pastry freezes well before or after cooking. Use the uncooked pastry within 3 months.

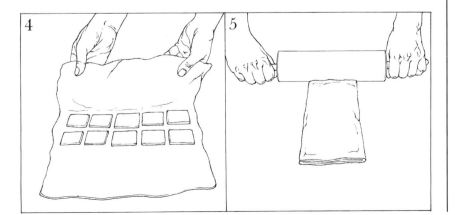

HOT-WEATHER FARE

'The appetite may sicken, and so die'.

It may seem disrespectful to quote a line from a famous Shakespearean soliloquy here, but it seemed to me to be singularly apt in describing what can happen to the appetite in hot weather.

The heat makes many of us long for a different kind of food. It is no problem to plan delicious desserts, but, all too often, I have heard people complain that they find salads and cold meat dishes monotonous. That should not be the case. It may surprise many of my readers to learn that our modern salads are dull and unimaginative compared with those 'salats' served in medieval times. The cooks of that time had no inhibitions about blending a variety of meats, salad greens, and fruits to create a dish that appealed to the eye as well as to the most fickle appetite. An example of this is Salmagundy, to be found in this section. As you will see from the description in the recipe, if the completed dish seemed to lack colour, then flower blossoms were

added. The salads in this chapter come from various countries and will, I hope, inspire you to create your own delicious dishes for hot weather.

I hope that the fact that I have included my recipe for a Galantine de Bœuf does not make those cooks who like to follow the traditions of classic cookery to the letter too unhappy. Many books point out uncompromisingly that this dish is made only with poultry. I believe that cookery, like every art, needs to develop and change with the times and that, while appreciating and respecting the works of bygone chefs, cooks, and gourmets, we all must help to create a superb modern cuisine.

I have enjoyed many happy visits to Scandinavia and always return full of praise and admiration for the artistic way in which the cooks of these countries present their dishes, especially their own open sandwiches, which are included in this chapter.

1 The classic galantine of France is made with poultry or game filled with a forcemeat, but that method is unsuitable for meat, so this is an adaption of the classic recipe.

2 Dice the beef and pork or bacon and grind coarsely.

3 Cut the ham into small dice.

4 Blend the meats with the sausage meat and sage.

5 Skin the nuts, dice the truffles, and stir these into the mixture, together with the eggs, and salt and pepper to taste.

6 Add enough brandy or consommé to make a mixture that is pleasantly soft in consistency but sufficiently stiff to form into a shape.

7 Brush a large piece of foil with the oil.

8 Press the galantine mixture into a neat roll, place on the foil and wrap this round the meat, as in the picture. Seal the ends firmly.

9 If preferred, oil a loaf-type pan and put in the mixture with the meat in the middle, then cover with oiled foil.

10 Place the roll or covered pan in a large steamer over a pan of boiling water; cover and allow the water under the steamer to boil gently for 1¾ hours.

11 It may be more convenient to bake the mixture in the oven, in which case use the loaf pan for the galantine. Stand this in a 'bain-marie' of cold water, as in the picture.

Galantine de Bœuf

Beef Galantine
Serves 6
Cooking Time: 1¾ hours

INGREDIENTS

top round of beef: 1½ lb
fatback or bacon: ¼ lb
cooked ham: ¼ lb
pork sausage-meat: ¼ lb
chopped sage: ½ teaspoon
pistachio nuts: 1 oz
truffles: 1 oz
eggs: 2
salt and pepper: to taste
brandy or consommé: to moisten
oil: 1–2 teaspoons
to coat and garnish:
aspic jelly, as page 142: 1¼ cups
truffle: 1
gherkin: 1

Bake in the centre of a slow oven, 300°F, for 1¾ hours. Check that the water in the 'bain-marie' does not evaporate, for this keeps the galantine moist during baking.

12 Allow the galantine in the foil or pan to cool. If using the loaf pan you could put a very light weight on top to give a closer texture to the meat and to make it easier to slice. Do not use a heavy weight, for that presses out the moisture and produces a dry galantine.

13 Meanwhile, make the aspic jelly, see the recipe on page 142, allow it to become cold and to begin to stiffen slightly.

14 Unwrap the galantine or turn it out of the pan.

15 Cut the truffle and gherkin into small pieces.

16 Brush the galantine with a thin layer of the aspic jelly.

17 Arrange the pieces of truffle and gherkin on this, allow to set, then brush the galantine with a second layer of aspic jelly.

To serve: Arrange the galantine on a serving dish with salad to garnish. If you have any aspic jelly left, allow this to set, chop finely, and spoon it round the meat roll.

To freeze: The galantine freezes well. Preferably, it should be frozen before coating with the jelly. Use within 3 months.

To vary:
(i) The proportions of bacon, ham, and sausage-meat can be varied to personal taste, as long as the sum total is similar.
(ii) Add a little diced cooked tongue as well as the ham.
(iii) If omitting the nuts and truffles, you could add a finely chopped fried onion and 6–8 diced uncooked mushrooms to the mixture.

Using Truffles
Truffles are an expensive but very delicious ingredient in cooking. The truffle is a fungus and varies between an almost black colour, which is better for garnishes since it is more obvious, and a white. The finest black truffles come from the Périgord area in France, and white truffles come from northern Italy.
To prepare a truffle:

1 Peel the truffle and halve, if desired.

2 Place in boiling water with a little salt and pepper; cook steadily for 8 minutes.

3 Remove from the liquid, cool, and cut into the desired shapes.

To freeze: When the truffles are soft, wrap and freeze; use within 3 months for the best flavour.

To vary:
Canned truffles are often easier to obtain than the fresh variety.

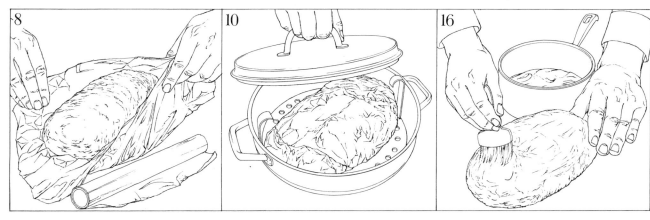

Fleischsalat

Beef Salad with Apples
Serves 4–6
No cooking

INGREDIENTS

cooked potatoes, preferably new: ½ lb
cooked beef: ½ lb
Gruyère cheese: ¼ lb
dessert apples: 3
celery stalks: 3
tomatoes: 4 medium
young carrots: 3–4 medium
gherkins: 4–6
Mayonnaise, see page 139: to bind
to garnish:
parsley: to taste

1 Dice the potatoes, beef, cheese, cored but not peeled apples, and the celery.

2 Cut the tomatoes into thin wedges.

3 Scrape and grate the carrots and chop the gherkins.

4 Blend all the ingredients and bind with some of the mayonnaise.

To serve: Spoon into a pyramid shape and garnish with chopped parsley; serve fairly soon after making.

To vary:
Bohemian Salad: This is another, but more unusual, German salad which blends apples with cooked meat.

Cut approximately ¼ lb cooked ham and chicken and veal into thin strips. Although beef is not the traditional meat in this salad, it may be used in place of one of the meats.

Blend the meats with approximately 12 diced small new potatoes, a finely grated small onion, 2–3 chopped hard-boiled eggs, several chopped canned anchovy fillets, and a chopped Bismarck herring.

Next, dice 2–3 peeled sharp cooking apples and add to the mixture with enough Vinaigrette Dressing, page 139, to bind.

To serve: Spoon onto a bed of lettuce and garnish with diced beets and sprigs of watercress.

Salmagundy

Beef and Chicken Salad with Herrings

This is the name given to a salad which was very popular in the eighteenth century. It consisted of a considerable variety of ingredients. The secret of a good Salmagundy was to have an artistic arrangement of the foods, and, to add to the 'eye-appeal', the dish was often decorated with flowers.

My favourite recipe is one I have adapted from one given by a good cook of the eighteenth century – a Mrs Glasse. It serves up to 8 people.

1 Bone and dice 2–3 pickled herrings. Hard-boil 4 eggs and shell and chop the whites and yolks separately.

2 Dice enough cooked chicken or game to give approximately 1 lb; dice the same amount of lean ham, or ham and veal, and 1 lb lean beef.

3 Chop several small cucumbers and dessert apples and keep them separate; sprinkle with Vinaigrette Dressing, see page 139.

4 Make a bed of shredded lettuce on a large dish, arrange the meats and herrings in rings, with chopped parsley, pickled red cabbage, egg white and yolk, to give a pleasing contrast to each food.

To serve: Garnish with lemon; add more Vinaigrette Dressing. Adorn the rim of the dish with nasturtium flowers.

To freeze: Not suitable for freezing.

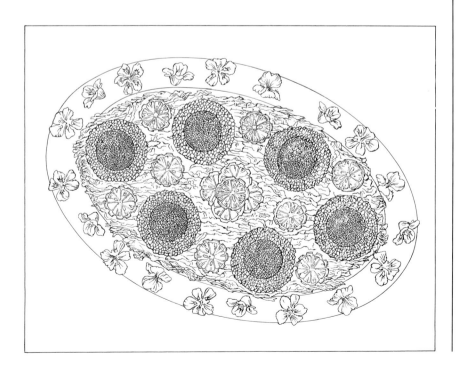

Beef Mould

Serves 4–6
Cooking Time: 2–3 minutes

INGREDIENTS

gelatine: 1 tbsp
dry sherry: 2 tbsp
beef consommé: scant ⅔ cup
eggs: 2
ground cooked beef: 1 lb
heavy whipping cream: scant ⅔ cup
salt and pepper: to taste
Worcestershire sauce: few drops
horseradish cream: 2 teaspoons
Tabasco sauce: few drops
to garnish:
lettuce: 1
pickled red cabbage: to taste
button mushrooms: ¼ lb
Vinaigrette Dressing, see page 139: to taste
Russian Salad, see page 139: to taste

This mould gives beef a more delicate taste than usual, for the meat is blended with cream and eggs.

That does not mean that the dish is bland and flavourless; the consommé and variety of flavours added at stage 7 give a piquant taste. No flavour should predominate, so taste the mixture critically at stage 7.

1 Soften the gelatine in the sherry.

2 Heat the consommé and dissolve the gelatine in this.

3 Whisk the eggs until thick and creamy, then gradually whisk the hot gelatine mixture into the eggs.

4 Add the minced beef and blend with the egg and gelatine mixture while it is warm; this softens the meat, which absorbs the flavour of the other ingredients.

5 Allow the meat mixture to cool and just begin to stiffen.

6 Whip the cream until it just holds its shape and fold into the jellied meat.

7 Add the salt and pepper and the other flavourings.

8 Brush the inside of a mould capable of holding more than a quart with a little oil and spoon in the mixture.

9 Allow to set, then unmould onto a serving dish.

To serve: Garnish the mould with lettuce, spoonfuls of red cabbage, and mushrooms tossed in a little Vinaigrette Dressing, and Russian Salad.

Spiced Moulded Salad
The American moulded salads can turn a small amount of cooked meat into a gourmet's delight.

While one may choose a sweeter flavour to the gelatine mixture, this

Mayonnaise

tomato-based jelly blends well with beef. This dish serves 4–6.

1 Soften 1 tbsp gelatine in 2 tbsp dry sherry, blended with a pinch each of garlic salt, celery salt, and grated nutmeg.

2 Add the softened gelatine to scant 2 cups heated tomato juice, stir until dissolved, then add 2–3 drops of Tabasco sauce.

3 Allow the gelatine mixture to cool and just begin to thicken slightly, then blend with 1 small diced sweet green pepper (discard the core and seeds), generous 2 cups grated raw carrots, generous 2 cups finely chopped celery, and 6 sliced stuffed olives.

4 Spoon the mixture into a rinsed ring mould and allow to set.

5 Blend approximately 1 lb diced cooked beef with enough Sauce Rémoulade, on the right, to moisten, and chopped chives.

To serve: Invert the mould onto a dish; garnish with green salad and fill the centre of the ring with the beef.

Russian Salad

Russian Salad is the name now given to diced cooked vegetables, such as carrots, rutabagas, potatoes, beans, and peas, which are then blended with Mayonnaise or a Vinaigrette Dressing.

The true Russian Salad, however, was more ambitious and interesting, for diced cooked tongue and hard-boiled eggs were included and the salad given a sharper flavour with the addition of a little pickled cabbage.

Whichever version you prefer, this makes an interesting garnish to the Beef Mould on the left.

One of the secrets of a good mayonnaise is the quality of the oil; this must be first-class. Some people vow that the only oil to use is olive oil, but in these days when people are reducing their intake of high-cholesterol foods, you may prefer to use a lighter vegetable oil such as corn oil.

Make sure both egg yolks and oil are at room temperature when they are blended together.

In most cases French mustard is better for mayonnaise, but I like the more definite flavour of English mustard with beef salads.

1 Put 2 egg yolks into a mixing bowl, add ½–1 teaspoon homemade English mustard, the same amount of salt, and a shake white pepper, then ½–1 tbsp vinegar or lemon juice. The vinegar can be white wine, white malt, or tarragon; use the smaller quantity first and add more, if required, at stage 3.

2 Add ⅔–1¼ cup oil very slowly, indeed drop by drop at first, blending with a wooden spoon; as the sauce begins to thicken you can increase the flow of oil very slightly. The amount used depends upon personal taste, the more oil used (up to the maximum given) the thicker the mayonnaise.

3 Gradually add 1 tbsp boiling water; this is not essential but tends to give a lighter texture. Finally, taste the sauce and add more seasoning and vinegar or lemon juice if desired.

To serve: With salads.

To freeze: Do not freeze.

To vary:
(i) It is possible to flavour the mayonnaise with more lemon juice, a little curry powder, and tomato purée — when it is known as Sauce Andalouse. All these flavours blend well with salads served with beef.
(ii) *Sauce Rémoulade* (Mustard Mayonnaise): Sieve the yolks of 2 hard-boiled eggs into a basin, blend with 1 uncooked egg yolk, salt and pepper, vinegar or lemon juice, as in Mayonnaise, ½–1 tbsp Dijon mustard. Gradually blend in the oil as above. Taste and adjust the seasonings and vinegar or lemon juice.
(iii) *Blender Mayonnaise:* Modern blenders and food processors enable one to make this mayonnaise in a fraction of the time taken by hand.

Put the egg yolks, seasonings and vinegar or lemon juice into the blender container, cover, switch on, and emulsify for a few seconds, then add the oil steadily, while the motor is running, through the gap in the lid or feed tube, until the desired consistency. Finally, add the boiling water, taste the sauce, and adjust the seasonings and vinegar or lemon juice.

Vinaigrette Dressing

1 Take ½–1 teaspoon English mustard or one of the many French mustards, all of which vary slightly in taste, and blend with a good shake of white or black pepper and salt.

2 Gradually blend in 6 tbsp olive or salad oil and approximately half this amount of white or red wine vinegar. This should give enough dressing for 4–6 people, but tastes vary so much that it is difficult to be definite. You can then add crushed garlic, chopped chives, chervil, parsley, and tarragon, or, if desired, other herbs that blend with the particular dish.

Very often, this is referred to as French Dressing or Sauce Ravigote; purists maintain that it is only Vinaigrette Dressing if the herbs *are* included.

To vary:
Blend all the ingredients in the blender or food processor.

Potato Salad

There is a saying, 'Mix a potato salad when hot and eat when cold', and this is very true, for the hot potato absorbs the dressing and other flavours; you never have such a good result if the potatoes are cold when you mix the salad.

1 Boil about 1 lb potatoes in their skins (to make sure that they keep firm), then skin, dice, and blend with some Mayonnaise, see the recipe on this page.

2 Add a little vinegar or Vinaigrette Dressing to sharpen the flavour, finely chopped or grated onion, and chopped parsley to taste. When serving the salad with beef, I like to add a very little extra mustard.

To serve: Chill well and garnish with watercress or chopped parsley.

To freeze: Dishes containing a fair percentage of Mayonnaise do not freeze well; this must be freshly prepared.

To vary:
(i) *Salad de pommes de terre à la Parisienne* (Potato Salad in Wine): When the potatoes are diced, marinate them in a little white wine, then blend them with Vinaigrette Dressing, not Mayonnaise, just before serving.
(ii) *Salad de pommes de terre Niçoise* (Potato Salad Nice Style): Cook and skin, then dice, enough new potatoes to give 1½ cup. Cook and dice the same amount of French or other green beans. Blend with the potatoes, 4–6 quartered tomatoes, 2 crushed cloves of garlic and Vinaigrette Dressing.

To serve: On shredded lettuce or endive; garnish with capers, black olives, and anchovy fillets, which blend surprisingly well with beef.

Beef Salads

There is something very impressive about a splendid roast of beef served cold with salad. I would like to stress the importance of careful cooking when the beef is to be served as a cold dish. On this page you have suggestions for combining the cooked beef with a variety of ingredients to produce interesting and unusual salads.

Sometimes, it is best to blend the beef with the particular dressing or selection of ingredients and allow it to marinate for several hours, so it can absorb the flavours and become more moist and tender. The recipes state when this is an advantage. In other cases, it is better to mix the ingredients and serve without delay, so ensuring a crisp salad in which the other foods contrast with the cooked beef.

These salads provide satisfying portions for 6 people and generous ones for 4.

Gazpacho Salad
(Spanish Beef Salad)
This may seem a strange title for a salad, since the word is generally associated with the chilled Spanish soup, for which you will find a recipe on page 152.

It seems that this word, in the past, was used to describe a selection of ingredients, and, as you will see, the basic foods used in this salad are similar to those in the soup. This salad blends well with cold beef, and particularly with the mould on page 138.

1 Prepare about 1–1⅓ cup coarse crumbs and fry these in a little butter or oil until crisp, then allow to cool.

2 Prepare Vinaigrette Dressing, see page 139.

3 Thinly slice approximately 1 lb firm tomatoes and a medium cucumber.

4 Peel and finely chop 2 medium onions and dice 1 or 2 green peppers, discarding the core and seeds.

To serve: Arrange the tomatoes and cucumber in layers, sprinkling each layer with the onion and pepper, and moistening with the dressing. Chill well. Sprinkle with the crumbs and chopped parsley just before serving.

New England Salad
The best beef to use in this salad is corned beef, see page 50.

1 First prepare a Vinaigrette Dressing, see page 139, but be very sparing with, or omit, the salt and slightly increase the mustard.

2 Dice about 1 lb of the beef and put into the dressing. Leave for an hour.

3 Hard-boil 3 eggs and allow to cool.

4 Add 3–4 diced cooked potatoes, 3 skinned diced beets, 2 chopped stalks of celery, and a few tablespoons chopped scallions to the beef, together with the coarsely chopped hard-boiled egg yolks.

5 Spoon onto a bed of crisp lettuce, top with the coarsely chopped egg whites and finely chopped parsley and chives.

To serve: As soon as possible after stage 5, so that the beets do not spoil the colour of the other ingredients.

Beef Coleslaw
Use roasted beef for this dish if possible, although boiled corned beef makes a good alternative.

1 Blend scant ⅔ cup sour cream with a few tablespoons of Mayonnaise (there is a recipe on page 139), a little horseradish cream or grated fresh horseradish, homemade English mustard to taste, and 2–3 sliced gherkins.

2 Wash, dry, and shred very finely the heart of a small green or white cabbage.

3 Cut the cooked beef into narrow strips, you need approximately ¾ lb.

4 Mix all the ingredients together.

To serve: Fairly soon after preparing.

To vary:
Blend a little pickled red cabbage with the other ingredients in stage 1.

Celery Root Rémoulade
(Celery Root in Mustard Mayonnaise)
This is not only a delicious hors d'œuvre, but a very good accompaniment to cold beef dishes.

1 Make a Sauce Rémoulade, see page 139.

2 Peel and grate or shred a large celery root into the sauce and blend well.

Aspic de Bœuf
Beef Aspic

1 Make deep slits in a roasting piece of fillet and spread with pâté see page 66.

2 Tie the meat and roast, see pages 35 and 36; make sure the meat is not over-cooked. Allow to cool.

3 Prepare the aspic jelly as on this page; the quantity required depends upon the size of the roast.

4 Allow the jelly to cool to the consistency of a thick syrup.

5 Stand the meat on a wire tray or oven rack with a dish underneath to catch any surplus aspic.

6 Brush or spread a layer of aspic all over the roast. Garnish with pieces of cooked carrot, asparagus tips, and truffle; leave to set.

7 Brush a second layer of aspic over the roast, always allowing one layer to set before adding the next. This means keeping the extra aspic from becoming too firm.

To serve: Arrange on a bed of green salad; garnish with artichoke bottoms, asparagus tips, and halved hard-boiled eggs, topped with piped pâté and chopped aspic jelly.

Aspic Jelly
As it is quite a lengthy business to prepare your own aspic jelly, many people prefer to buy a packet of aspic-jelly powder. This is very much improved if dissolved in a good stock, but since the powder is fairly salt in flavour, the stock must not be over-seasoned.

1 To make your own aspic jelly, place a diced carrot, onion, and piece of celery in 1½ quart stock. When dealing with beef, one uses a *good beef stock*, but obviously, the stock should be made from fish for fish dishes, and a white stock should be made for dishes based upon poultry. It is essential that the stock is as well flavoured as the consommé on page 145.

2 Add the juice and thinly skinned peel from a small lemon (be very careful not to use any bitter white pith), as well as a bay leaf, and salt and pepper to taste.

3 Simmer for 10–15 minutes, then add 2 stiffly whisked egg whites, and the shells from the eggs, and simmer for a further 10 minutes. This helps to clarify the liquid.

4 Strain through fine muslin or a jelly bag.

5 Measure the liquid; you should have a generous 3¾ cups.

6 Add 3 tbsp brown malt vinegar and 2 tbsp tarragon or red wine vinegar.

7 Finally, add sherry to make 5 cups liquid.

8 Put sufficient gelatine to set this quantity of clear liquid in a mixing bowl. With most makes it will be 1 oz but always check carefully.

9 Soften the gelatine by blending this with a little of the liquid, then stand over a pan of very hot water until thoroughly dissolved and clear; add to the remainder of the liquid.

10 The aspic jelly is now ready to be used.

To freeze: As this produces a fairly large amount (a small quantity does not seem worth making), freeze the strained stock from stage 4 and use as desired. The stock keeps well for 3 months.

Smørrebrød
Open Sandwiches

In every Scandinavian country you will be offered these open sandwiches, which, when served with drinks, may be tiny, but which may also be made large enough for a really substantial main meal.

I well remember my first introduction to Smørrebrød. It was in a Copenhagen restaurant where there was an almost unbelievable variety of toppings to choose from, and where the food could be eaten within sight of the 'Little Mermaid', made famous by Hans Christian Andersen.

Good-quality cooked beef is one of the popular toppings for these sandwiches, and below you will find some suggestions for combining the meat with other ingredients for a good blend of colour, texture, and flavour.

1 Butter generously fairly thin slices of fresh white, brown, wholewheat, or rye bread.

2 Put a little crisp lettuce on the buttered bread, then arrange the ingredients on this. The beef should be thinly sliced and arranged with a slight 'curl', thus giving height to the sandwich.

3 Keep the toppings moist by keeping them covered with waxed paper, foil, or damp muslin.

Here are some flavours to blend with the cooked beef slices:

Beef with pâté, see page 66, a 'fan' of gherkin, a little Horseradish Sauce, see page 56, and chopped parsley.

Beef with cold Béarnaise Sauce, see page 64, a few wafer-thin onion rings, and diced beets.

Beef with Russian and Potato Salads, topped with chopped chives; page 139 gives the salad recipes.

Beef with Celery Root Rémoulade, page 140, 1–2 cooked and well-drained prunes, and/or a crisp bacon slice.

Beef with mustard pickles and Potato Salad, see page 139.

Steak Tartare, see page 59, is one of the best toppings for an open sandwich.

WISE ECONOMY

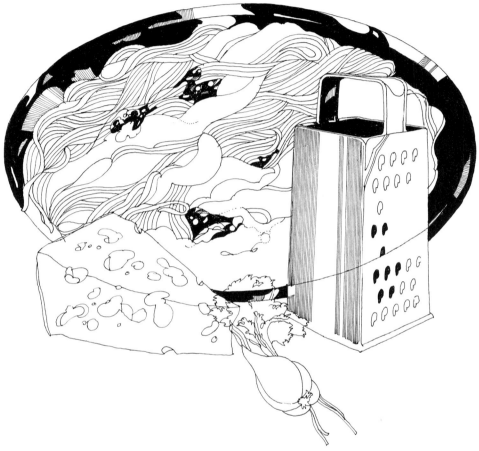

'Economy is going without something you do not want in case you should, some day, want something you probably won't want.'

Anthony Hope

Those words can be very true, for, often, we disdain the pleasures of today to save for something we *think* we may need. 'Economy' can also mean that we disregard the fact that an item which seems expensive is often, in the long run, an economical buy.

Beef, while being one of the more expensive foods, can be used economically to make a number of excellent dishes. Wise economy can produce a wide range of dishes, from the inexpensive but interesting recipes in this section to the frankly luxurious steaks and roasts elsewhere in the book.

From bones of beef we can obtain beef stock, the basis for soups, stews, casseroles, and even some sauces. Never waste beef bones or the stock they produce.

If you are fortunate enough to obtain beef marrow bones ('moelle de bœuf'), then you not only have the means of making particularly good stock, but you have the marrow, too. This, when poached in salted water until tender, is a classic garnish for steak dishes, but it can also be used on canapés, which, alas, are little known today (slice the poached marrow and serve on small squares of buttered toast or croûtons of fried bread).

Lastly, you can obtain drippings from beef. In this busy world we often feel that there is no time to bother about extra jobs like clarifying beef fat for drippings, and instead, we purchase the more easily obtainable fat. What a difference in flavour, though!

Beef has such a pronounced flavour that relatively small amounts give interest to other ingredients. Beef makes a splendid basis for the stuffing in a variety of vegetables, and for a superb meat sauce to serve with pasta and so many other dishes.

Beef – a wise economy indeed.

Kaalikääryleet

Finnish Stuffed Cabbage Leaves
Serves 4–6
Cooking Time: 1 hour 10 minutes

INGREDIENTS

medium cabbage: 1
salt and pepper: to taste
for the stuffing:
onions: 2 medium
butter or margarine: 2 tbsp ($\frac{1}{4}$ stick)
ground beef: 1 lb
fine breadcrumbs: $\frac{1}{4}$–$\frac{1}{3}$ cup
cooked rice (weight when cooked): 3 oz
allspice: $\frac{1}{2}$ teaspoon
heavy whipping cream: 3 tbsp
golden syrup or dark molasses: 2 tbsp
beef stock or water: to cover

1 Wash the cabbage well. Save the heart of the cabbage for another occasion or use it in the Kuminakaali recipe on this page. Remove 8–12 outer leaves without breaking them. Cook in boiling water with a little salt and pepper for about 3 minutes or until they are soft and pliable.

2 Drain the softened cabbage leaves and place on a flat surface.

3 Peel and chop the onions; heat the butter or margarine and fry the onions until just softened.

4 Add to the other ingredients for the stuffing.

5 Mix thoroughly, add salt and pepper to taste, then divide into 8–12 portions.

6 Place some stuffing in the centre of each leaf and fold in the edges, so that the stuffing does not come out during cooking.

7 Roll the cabbage leaves firmly; if they are large and are tightly rolled, they should not need securing with string or a wooden cocktail pick.

8 Place the cabbage rolls in a large shallow casserole, so that they form just a single layer.

9 Blend the syrup or molasses with an equal amount of beef stock or water and pour over the rolls, making sure they are evenly moistened.

10 Now add sufficient extra stock or water to cover the rolls.

11 Put a lid on the casserole and cook for approximately 1 hour in the centre of a moderate oven, 350°F.

12 The lid of the casserole can be removed for the last 20 minutes to allow the liquid to evaporate a little.

To serve: With mixed vegetables, including the Kuminakaali below.

To freeze: This dish freezes well for up to 6 weeks.

Kuminakaali
(Finnish-style Cabbage)

1 Shred a young cabbage or a cabbage heart finely, wash in cold water, then drain very well; peel and chop a medium onion.

2 Chop 3–4 medium tomatoes; if you want to skin them, see page 96.

3 Heat $\frac{1}{4}$ cup ($\frac{1}{2}$ stick) butter in a heavy saucepan and fry the cabbage and onion very gently, stirring frequently. Continue cooking until soft, but do not allow to brown.

4 Add the chopped tomatoes, together with scant $\frac{2}{3}$ cup water, a little salt, a good pinch of sugar (or more if desired), and $\frac{1}{2}$–1 tbsp caraway seeds.

5 Cover the pan and cook steadily for 25 minutes.

6 Taste the vegetables and add a little extra seasoning, sugar, or caraway seeds, if desired.

To serve: With main dishes. This is particularly good with pork.

To freeze: Although better when freshly cooked, this dish can be frozen for up to a month.

Consommé

Serves 8
Cooking Time: 2–3 hours

INGREDIENTS

beef stock, see method, stage 1: 10 cups
shin or shank of beef: 1½ lb
salt and pepper: to taste
onion (optional): 1
carrot (optional): 1
bay leaf: 1
egg whites and shells: 3
dark cream sherry: scant ⅔ cup

A *good* beef consommé is the basis for many clear soups, a selection of which is given on this page. Consommé contains practically no calories or carbohydrates, and so is an ideal soup for slimmers; it makes a light, but appetising, start to a meal, and it is equally good hot or cold. It uses the cheapest cuts of beef to give flavour, and the stock comes from beef bones.

1 Make a really good beef stock by simmering beef bones in water for several hours or for a shorter period in a microwave oven or pressure cooker (follow the manufacturer's directions carefully).

2 Cut the meat into small pieces or mince coarsely; put into a saucepan with the stock.

3 Bring just to boiling point, then taste and add salt and pepper. If the beef stock was well flavoured with vegetables, the vegetables and the bay leaf may be omitted.

4 Put in the egg shells and the lightly whisked whites halfway through cooking.

5 Simmer gently for about 1 hour, then strain through several layers of muslin.

6 Reheat, adding the sherry.

7 If the consommé is not sufficiently dark – it should be a deep glowing amber colour – then add a very small amount of beef extract or a portion of a beef bouillon cube.

8 If using less egg whites, it is advisable to make the consommé, strain this, then return the liquid to the pan with 1 whisked egg white and shell and simmer for about 20 minutes only.

9 Re-strain the consommé and add the sherry; the soup is now ready to heat and garnish or to chill, see below.

To freeze: The consommé freezes well for 3 months.

To vary:
Consommé Froid (Cold Consommé): The clear soup can be put into the freezer for a short time until lightly iced. Dip the edges of the soup cups in cold water, then in finely chopped parsley for a decorative edging. Serve the soup with wedges of lemon.

The following soups are made with the consommé on the left, the servings are similar to the basic recipe.

Klare Rindsuppe: (Austrian Beef Consommé with Liver Dumplings): Prepare the consommé, as on this page, and the mixture for the liver dumplings, as on page 56. Poach the dumplings in the soup for 5–6 minutes. Top the soup with chopped parsley.

Gulasch-Suppe (Paprika Soup): You could use any left-over Gulyás, see page 103; sieve this, and blend with consommé to make a thinner consistency, or follow this recipe.
Prepare the consommé; mean-while, fry a very finely chopped onion in 2 tbsp fat, together with ¼ lb ground beef, 1 tbsp paprika. Add the strained consommé, together with 1 tbsp tomato purée. Simmer for 30 minutes, stirring once or twice. Peel 2 medium potatoes, cut into tiny dice, add to the soup and continue cooking for approximately 10 minutes, or until the potatoes are tender. Taste and adjust the seasoning. A few caraway seeds may be added with the potatoes.

Consommé en Gelée (Jellied Consommé): If the consommé is very concentrated, it may form a jelly by itself, but if this does not happen, use a little gelatine. To each 2½ cups allow 1½ teaspoons gelatine. Soften the gelatine in a little cold consommé, then dissolve this over a pan of hot water and add to the remainder of the consommé. Prepare the soup cups as for *Consommé Froid*, left, then dice the jellied soup and pile into the cups.

Garnishes for Consommé
There are many garnishes for consommé; these are some of the best known:

Consommé Celestine (Consommé with Pancake Garnish): Make a pancake as on page 148, cut into tiny strips, add to the consommé.

Consommé Julienne (Consommé with Vegetable Garnish): Cut a selection of vegetables into matchstick shapes, cook in boiling salted water until tender, strain, and add to the hot soup.

Consommé Jardinière: This is similar to the soup above, but the vegetables should be cut into small dice.

Spaghetti alla Bolognese

Spaghetti with Meat Sauce
Serves 4
Cooking Time: 1 hour

INGREDIENTS

onion: 1 medium
garlic clove: 1
carrot: 1 medium
mushrooms: 2 oz
tomatoes, preferably plum type: 2 medium
butter: 1 oz
olive oil: 1 tbsp
ground raw beef: $\frac{1}{4}$–$\frac{2}{3}$ lb
tomato purée: 1 tbsp
salt and pepper: to taste
beef stock: $1\frac{1}{4}$ cup
red wine: $1\frac{1}{4}$ cup

spaghetti: $\frac{1}{2}$ lb
butter: 1 tbsp
Parmesan cheese, grated: to taste

1 Peel and chop the onion, garlic, and carrot; slice the mushrooms; skin and chop the tomatoes. These can be de-seeded, if desired.

2 Heat the butter and oil in a heavy saucepan, then gently fry the vegetables for 5 minutes.

3 Tip the meat into the pan, blend with the vegetables, and cook for 5–6 minutes, stirring all the time.

4 Add the rest of the ingredients for the sauce, simmer for 40–45 minutes.

5 A Bolognese sauce thickens by gradual evaporation, so it is advisable to leave the pan uncovered, but this means you must stir from time to time.

6 About 20 minutes before the sauce is cooked, place the spaghetti into at least $2\frac{1}{2}$ quarts boiling salted water, boil steadily until 'al dente', i.e., it yields a little when pressed with a fork against the side of the pan; never over-cook.

7 Strain the spaghetti and blend with the butter, then tip onto a hot serving dish.

To serve: Top with the Bolognese sauce and serve with the cheese.

To freeze: The sauce freezes well for up to 3 months, but spaghetti is inclined to lose texture and taste when frozen.

To vary:
Spaghetti alla Ghiotta (Spaghetti Gourmet Style): Cook the Bolognese sauce and spaghetti as the basic recipe; add a little diced prosciutto (smoked Parma ham) and 2 tbsp brandy to the sauce. Top the dish with grated Parmesan cheese, and slices of Mozzarella cheese, together with narrow strips of fried eggplant.

Lasagne Verdi al Forno

Lasagna with Meat and Cheese Sauces
Serves 4–6
Cooking Time: $1\frac{1}{2}$ hours

INGREDIENTS

Bolognese sauce: see left
green lasagna: $\frac{1}{2}$ lb
salt and pepper: to taste
for the cheese sauce:
butter: 3 tbsp
flour: 1 tbsp
milk: generous $1\frac{2}{3}$ cup
Mozzarella cheese, grated: $\frac{1}{4}$ lb
Parmesan cheese, grated: 3 oz

1 Cook the Bolognese sauce, as the recipe on the left.

2 Put the lasagna into salted water, which must be boiling, cook until just soft, drain, and allow the ribbon pasta to dry over a large sieve; this gives a better taste to the cooked dish.

3 Make the cheese sauce; heat the butter in a saucepan, stir in the flour, cook for 2–3 minutes, then blend in the milk.

4 Bring the sauce to the boil and stir over a low heat until thickened.

5 Add salt, pepper, the Mozzarella cheese, and half the Parmesan cheese.

6 Arrange layers of lasagna and the two sauces in an oven-proof dish; end with the cheese sauce.

7 Top with the remainder of the Parmesan cheese and cook in the centre of a moderate oven, 375°F, for 30 minutes.

To serve: With mixed or green salad.

To freeze: It is possible to freeze the dish without cooking the lasagna. Arrange layers of the pasta and sauces as the recipe, then freeze. This method prevents the pasta becoming over-soft in freezing.

To vary:
(i) Omit the cheese sauce and arrange the lasagna, which can be the plain type, or the green (spinach-flavoured) lasagna used in the recipe on this page, in layers with sliced Mozzarella, grated Parmesan, and soft creamy Ricotta cheese. End with grated Parmesan cheese and cook as the basic recipe. This version cannot be frozen without cooking the lasagna first.
(ii) Cannelloni, the large tube-type pasta, can be cooked and filled with the sauce mixture, but allow this to become a little thicker in consistency than the recipe on this page. Put the filled cannelloni into an oven-proof dish, top with the cheese sauce, made as per the recipe on this page, and grated Parmesan cheese. Heat in the oven, as for Lasagna, stage 7.

Potted Beef

This old-fashioned way of preparing beef has been used for centuries and is a forerunner of today's sophisticated pâtés.

You can take any really inexpensive cut of beef, even shin can be used, but obviously, the better the flavour of the beef, the better the potted meat will be.

Potted meat is used as a sandwich filling or served as an hors d'œuvre instead of a pâté.

1 Simmer the meat in a minimum of liquid until tender, adding salt and pepper to taste. The cooking time naturally depends upon the cut of meat you have chosen.

2 Grind the cooked meat once or twice until very fine, then put into a mixing bowl, add ¼ cup (½ stick) melted butter to each 1 lb cooked meat, a pinch of powdered mace, 1 tbsp brandy or dry sherry, and any extra salt and pepper to taste.

3 Pound firmly; the old-fashioned pestle and mortar is ideal for this purpose.

4 Spoon into several small containers and top with a layer of melted butter.

To serve: With lemon and hot toast, or with a salad garnish.

To freeze: This freezes well for up to one month.

To vary:
Meat from a roast may be used, but it should not be the outer parts which have become slightly firm and maybe a little crisp.

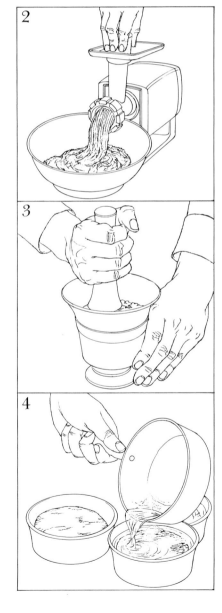

Bobotie

South African Beef and Vegetable Casserole
Serves 4–6
Cooking Time: 1 hour 40 minutes

INGREDIENTS

onions: 2 medium
butter: ¼ cup (½ stick)
white bread: ¼ lb
milk: 1 cup
cooking apple: 1 small
blanched almonds: 12
ground beef: 1½ lb
sweet chutney: 2 tbsp
sugar: 1 tbsp
curry powder: 1–2 tbsp
turmeric: ½–1 teaspoon
white or red wine or malt vinegar: 1 tbsp
seedless raisins: ¼ cup
salt and pepper: to taste
lemon or fresh bay leaves: 4
eggs: 2

In the past, when modern refrigeration was not so readily available, South African cooks made this from ready cooked mutton, but nowadays, freshly ground meat is used.

Mutton is still the prime favourite, but I have found that the dish, with its combination of curry and savoury custard, is equally good when prepared with freshly ground beef.

1 Peel and chop the onions; heat the butter and fry the onions gently until just golden in colour.

2 Put the bread into a basin, add half the milk, leave for 10 minutes, then mash with a fork until smooth.

3 Peel, core, and dice the apple; quarter the almonds.

4 Mix the meat with all the ingredients, except the remainder of the milk, the leaves, and the eggs.

5 Stir well to give a light texture.

6 Spoon the mixture into a greased casserole.

7 Roll the leaves and insert at intervals in the meat mixture.

8 Cover the casserole and bake for an hour in the centre of a moderate oven, 350°F, then remove the lid of the casserole.

9 Beat the eggs with the remaining milk and add a little salt and pepper.

10 Pour over the meat mixture and return to the oven for a further 25–30 minutes.

To serve: With rice and chutney.

To freeze: This dish freezes well; use within 2 months.

Rissoles

Serves 4
Cooking Time: 15–20 minutes

INGREDIENTS

onion: 1 medium
tomatoes: 2 medium
butter or beef drippings: $\frac{1}{4}$ cup ($\frac{1}{2}$ stick)
flour: 2 tbsp
beef stock: scant $\frac{2}{3}$ cup
cooked ground beef: $\frac{3}{4}$ lb
fine breadcrumbs: $\frac{1}{2}$–$\frac{2}{3}$ cup
dried mixed herbs: pinch
chopped parsley: 1 tbsp
salt and pepper: to taste
for the coating:
flour: 1 tbsp
egg: 1
crisp or toasted breadcrumbs: $\frac{1}{2}$–$\frac{2}{3}$ cup
for frying:
fat or drippings: $\frac{1}{4}$ cup

1 Peel and chop the onion; skin and chop the tomatoes.

2 Heat the butter or drippings and fry the vegetables until soft.

3 Blend in the flour, then the stock; bring to the boil and stir over a low heat until the mixture becomes a thick panada (binding sauce).

4 Add the beef, breadcrumbs, herbs, with salt and pepper to taste.

5 Allow the mixture to cool sufficiently to handle and form into 8 round cakes or cutlet shapes; chill them to make them firmer and easier to coat.

6 Blend the flour for coating the rissoles with a little salt and pepper and sprinkle over the meat mixture.

7 Beat the egg and brush the rissoles with this, then coat with the crisp breadcrumbs; page 63 illustrates how this is done.

8 Heat the fat or drippings in a large frying pan and fry them on either side until crisp and golden brown.

To serve: Drain the rissoles on absorbent paper and serve hot with Brown or Tomato sauces, see pages 85 and 96, and mixed vegetables, or serve cold with salads.

To freeze: Open-freeze the cooked rissoles, then wrap. Rissoles can be kept in the freezer for 3 months.

To vary:
(i) *Durham Cutlets:* Form the beef mixture into cutlet shapes, at stage 5; coat as stages 6 and 7 but put a small piece of elbow-length macaroni into the base of the cutlet shape to look like a cutlet bone. Fry and serve as for Rissoles.
(ii) *Beef and Rice Croquettes:* Omit the breadcrumbs in the basic recipe but add the same amount of well-drained cooked rice. Form into finger shapes, coat as stages 6 and 7, then fry in a good depth of hot oil or fat, see page 86. Drain on absorbent paper and serve.

Crêpes en Bœuf

Beef Pancakes
Serves 4–6
Cooking Time: 30 minutes

INGREDIENTS

for the filling:
onions: 2 medium
cooked beef: $\frac{3}{4}$ lb
butter: $\frac{1}{4}$ cup ($\frac{1}{2}$ stick)
flour: 3 tbsp
milk: $1\frac{1}{4}$ cup
salt and pepper: to taste
for the pancakes:
flour: $\frac{1}{2}$ cup
salt: pinch
eggs: 2
milk: scant 1 cup
butter: $\frac{1}{4}$ cup ($\frac{1}{2}$ stick)
for frying:
oil: as required

1 Peel and chop the onions; grind or dice the beef.

2 Heat the butter in a saucepan, fry the onions until soft, then blend in the flour, cook gently for 2–3 minutes, gradually add the milk, bring to the boil, and stir over a low heat until the sauce becomes thick; add the beef and a little salt and pepper. Put on one side while making the pancakes; reheat before filling the pancakes

3 Sieve the flour and salt into a mixing bowl, add the eggs and milk, beat to make a smooth pancake batter.

4 Melt the butter and add to the batter mixture just before cooking.

5 Heat enough oil to give a thin film over the bottom of the frying pan or pancake pan.

6 Pour in enough batter to give a paper-thin coating, fry steadily on one side until pale golden, then toss or turn, and cook on the second side.

7 Lift onto a heated dish, keep hot over a pan of boiling water.

8 Continue as stages 5 and 6 until all the pancakes are cooked.

9 Fill each pancake with a little of the hot beef mixture, roll and put into a flame-proof dish, then top with grated cheese.

10 Place under the broiler for a few minutes until the cheese has melted.

To serve: With mixed vegetables.

To freeze: The pancakes freeze well; use within 2 months.

To vary:
Fill the pancakes with the Bolognese sauce on page 146.

STEAK AND BEEF
MAKE THE MEAL

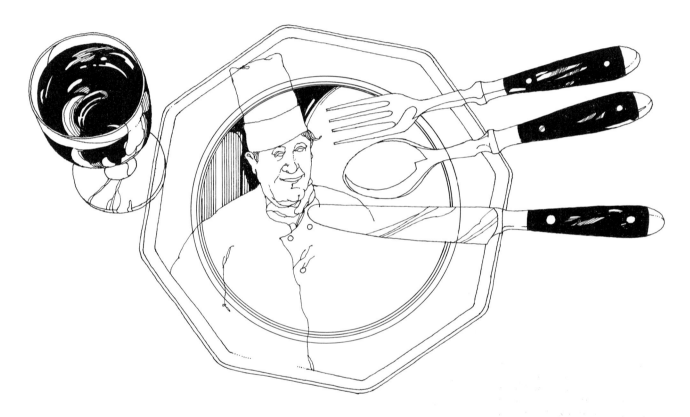

When considering the introduction to this chapter, I was browsing through various books, reading menus of the past. I found myself agreeing with Shakespeare that, when one thinks about a meal, it can

Cloy the hungry edge of appetite,
By bare imagination of a feast.

Before the beginning of the nineteenth century, formal menus were scarcely known, the list of dishes being a 'working order' only.

In a fifteenth-century type of menu, though, is given among the many dishes 'a side of beef'.

The menu that really highlights the importance of beef, and its versatility, is one arranged by the Duc de Richelieu in the eighteenth century. This was not to entertain invited guests, as one might suppose, but instead, princes, princesses, and their suites, who had been taken prisoner during the Hanoverian wars. Due to the privations of warfare, there was no other meat in the larder but a carcass of beef

and a selection of vegetables. Yet the Duc, who insisted on dictating the menu himself to his slightly worried secretary, compiled a menu of about twenty interesting and varied dishes, based upon beef.

This, of course, was an exceptional occasion, but throughout the centuries, steak and beef have held pride of place on menus.

Our modern menus are completely different from the long, elaborate, and leisurely meals of the past. Are they then a poor substitute?

It is reassuring to learn from Brillat-Savarin, the great French culinary expert and author of the work, *The Philosopher in the Kitchen* – often considered the gourmet's bible – that, in his august opinion, among the requirements for a perfect gourmet meal, one should 'let the dishes be few in number, but exquisitely choice, and the wines of the first quality, each in its class. ... Let the coffee be piping hot!'

Very practical and up-to-date advice from a man born in 1755!

Choosing a Menu

Well-planned menus are not exactly the same as a well-cooked meal. Obviously, no menu can be exciting if the cooking is less than first class, but a good menu means that each course must complement the next; no part of the meal should be so overpowering that it predominates, and spoils your palate for what follows.

Every course should have a slightly different character. A meal where everything is very bland or very highly spiced is not planned well, for it becomes monotonous.

Dishes based upon steak and beef give the cook enormous scope, for there is a great variety in the methods of presentation.

These menus are short, as befits our way of life today. If you want to make them longer and more elaborate, that would not be difficult, just follow a fish hors d'œuvre with a soup, or, where soup is the first course, add an interesting appetizer.

Now to practicalities. Make quite certain that cold dishes are really well chilled; keep them in the refrigerator until the last minute, covering the food so that it does not become dry.

If serving steak as the main dish, there will be last-minute cooking, but as you, your family, and your guests will appreciate, a steak must be enjoyed when freshly prepared. This means it is advisable to select those accompaniments which may be cooked a little earlier and kept hot, so that you can give your undivided attention to the meat. The modern habit of eating salads, even with hot dishes, is an excellent one. Obviously, you will not follow this routine on every occasion, and brief suggestions for suitable vegetable accompaniments are given with every main dish.

If you have an electric hotplate or similar appliance for keeping food hot before a meal, you have no problems. If one is not available, toss vegetables in a generous amount of butter, put into the serving dish, cover tightly with foil, then put on the lid and keep hot over pans of simmering water or in the oven with the heat turned very low.

Sauces and gravy should be covered with damp grease-proof paper to prevent a skin forming.

If your guests are delayed, cover roasted meats and turn the heat very low, so that the meat keeps hot without over-cooking.

Stews and casserole dishes, of course, pose no problems; that is why they are a wise choice when timing is uncertain.

Most of the desserts and some hors d'œuvre can be prepared ahead to chill or freeze, so making preparations for the meal relatively simple. Doubtless, there will be occasions when you will prefer to offer seasonal fruits instead of the dessert.

All that remains is to wish you 'Bon Appetit'.

Choosing Wine

Suggesting appropriate wines for food and choosing those wines worldwide is a never-ending delight and only two facts need emphasis; the 'folklore' about food and wine is the accumulated wisdom of many nations, so do not ignore it, but try to remember and record those combinations that you find agreeable. When you pass it on, you may be adding to, or changing, the folklore a little.

The wines suggested here reflect my personal enjoyment and you should find that some of your ideas are contrary to mine. The French wines from Alsace are amongst my favourites and the estate-bottled wines from northern Spain offer excellent value throughout the world. Californian wines now claim well-deserved attention and much more Australian wine is becoming appreciated.

I rarely decant wine, I object to excess chilling of whites, and I am quite encouraged by tartrate crystals, but you have your views on such things and there are no tips set out here. What I do find really encouraging, however, for all of us who enjoy wine, are the improvements taking place in viticulture and vinification, particularly in the warmer climates, because these will give us an even greater choice and increased enjoyment in the last part of this century.

Let us drink a toast to that.
Andrew Henderson

Choosing Cheese

A good cheese board is a very important part of a gourmet menu.

The cheese must provide a pleasing contrast to the dishes that precede or follow it.

You will notice that in each menu in this section I have highlighted several cheeses. This does not mean that you cannot have a larger selection on your cheese board, but that I felt that the particular varieties mentioned should be included. They have characteristics that make them ideal in that menu, and I give my reasons for the choice.

As you will observe, in some menus I have placed the cheese course before the dessert, French style. In other menus I have suggested that follow the dessert.

It has always seemed to me rather odd that 'rules' have been made for positioning the cheese in a meal, for sometimes it is better to eat the cheese after the main course and before the dessert, for it acts as a 'bridge' between the strong flavour of the meat and the sweet or fruit taste of the dessert.

On other occasions, the dessert follows quite happily after the main dish and cheese 'rounds off' an enjoyable meal.

Menu 1
Serves 4

Smoked Trout with Herb Mayonnaise

Chateaubriand with Madeira Sauce

Cheeses:
Gorgonzola
Lancashire
Neufchâtel

Pineapple Cheese Cake

The Herb Mayonnaise makes a pleasant change from the more familiar Horseradish Sauce served with the smoked trout. You will notice, however, that there is just a little horseradish added to provide an additional 'bite' to the well-flavoured mayonnaise.

Zucchini and/or really firm Brussels sprouts and a green salad containing the crisp texture of diced green pepper are excellent with the Chateaubriand and sauce; these recipes are on pages 78 and 85.

As a Chateaubriand is usually for 2 people only, you will need 2 portions of fillet steak.

The Pineapple Cheese Cake has a refreshing flavour, so is an ideal ending to the meal. It freezes well, so although the quantity would give up to 8 servings, the extra could be placed in the freezer.

Suggested Cheeses
It may seem strange to include cheese as well as a cheese cake in this menu, but it indicates the wide range of flavours and textures provided by cheese.

Although Neufchâtel is a soft cheese, it has a sharp bite. These three cheeses, although quite different from each other, are strong in taste; they bear no resemblance to the delicate cheese cake.

Suggested Wines
An Alsatian Gewürztraminer is ideal with the trout; or you may prefer an Australian Traminer or a Pinot Chardonnay.

The Châteaubriand demands the finest red you can obtain. Try an Australian Cabernet or maybe a Hermitage from the Rhône, or from South Africa a Nedeburg Cabernet.

This particular cheese cake could make an Asti Spumante or other sweet sparkling wine a fun combination for you.

Smoked Trout with Herb Mayonnaise

1 Arrange 4 smoked trout on the dish with lettuce, slices of lemon, and cucumber as garnish.

2 Prepare scant ⅔ cup mayonnaise, see page 139.

3 Add 2 teaspoons of chopped parsley and chives, and 1 teaspoon chopped dill or fennel.

4 Blend in ½–1 tbsp finely grated horseradish or enough prepared horseradish cream to give a delicate flavour. Serve with the trout.

To freeze: Smoked trout freezes well for up to 2 months.

Pineapple Cheese Cake

1 Crush ¼ lb graham crackers.

2 Cream ¼ cup (½ stick) butter, blend with 2 tbsp superfine sugar and the cracker crumbs.

3 Grease a 8–9-inch cake pan (preferably one with a loose base). Press the crumb mixture to the sides and bottom of the tin.

4 Cream ½ cup (1 stick) butter with ½ cup superfine sugar and the finely grated peel of 1 lemon.

5 Separate the whites and yolks of 3 eggs.

6 Beat the yolks into the butter mixture, add 1 tbsp cornstarch, 1 tbsp lemon juice, and 4 tbsp finely chopped fresh or *well-drained* canned pineapple.

7 Stir 1 lb cream cheese into the other ingredients, together with 3 tbsp unwhipped double cream.

8 Whisk the egg whites until they just hold their shape and fold these into the cheese mixture.

9 Spoon into the cracker-crumb lined pan and bake for 1¼ hours, or until firm to the touch, in the centre of a cool oven, 300°F. It is an advantage if the cheese cake is allowed to cool in the oven with the oven door just ajar and the heat turned off; this prevents any possibility of it wrinkling as it cools.

To serve: Top with rings of fresh pineapple and whipped cream or with sieved icing sugar.

To freeze: Freeze, then wrap. Use within 3 months.

Menu 2
Serves 4–6

Asparagus with Hollandaise Sauce

Bœuf en Croûte

Cheeses:
Double Gloucester
Gruyère
Roquefort

Rødgrød med fløde

Bœuf en Croûte is not only an impressive dish, but a sustaining one too. The other courses of the meal, therefore, should be kept fairly light. Although the recipe on page 130 suggests the dish is suitable for 4–6 people, it is possible to serve up to 8 portions if the whole beef fillet is used and the dish garnished with a good variety of seasonal vegetables.

Suggested Cheeses
The dessert is simple, light and refreshing; the menu will be better balanced, therefore, with sustaining cheeses. Both the superb Roquefort and Gruyère are famous cheeses. Many people do not appreciate that Double Gloucester cheese has been in existence for a thousand years. It is a cheese that never becomes sharp but is both rich and mellow in flavour.

Suggested Wines
Serve asparagus with the dry sherry; or, a dry white wine with flavour, like Chardonnay. I also enjoy a rosé, particularly in summertime.

With this impressive main course, a full red wine, and if Châteauneuf du Pape seems too big, try Cornas. Either of these wines would also be ideal with the strong firm cheeses. When you introduce a Roquefort cheese, then a really cold sweet Sauternes is interesting, and this could run on to finish the meal.

Asparagus with Hollandaise Sauce

1 Allow enough asparagus for 4 to 6 servings; trim the surplus from the base of the asparagus stalks and scrape the remaining ends. Handle the stalks lightly so that you do not break the delicate tips; wash in cold water.

2 Stand the asparagus upright and place in an asparagus pan or deep saucepan of boiling salted water; cook steadily until just tender. If you have no asparagus boiler, it is wise to tie the asparagus in bundles so that it does not fall during cooking. A cooking time of 15–30 minutes, depending upon the thickness of the stalks, makes them tender.

3 To make the sauce, put the yolks of 3 large eggs into a mixing bowl, or the top of a double boiler, add a pinch of cayenne pepper, salt and white pepper, together with 3 tbsp lemon juice or white wine vinegar.

4 Soften, but do not melt, ½–¾ cup (1–1½ sticks) butter and keep on one side.

5 Whisk the egg mixture over hot, but not boiling, water until it is thick and creamy, then *gradually* whisk in the softened butter; do this slowly and carefully so that the sauce does not separate.

To serve: Drain the asparagus and serve on hot plates with the sauce at the side of the plates, so that the tips may be dipped into this.

To freeze: Cooked frozen asparagus may be used.

To vary:
Cook the asparagus; allow to cool, and serve with Vinaigrette Dressing, see page 139, or with cold Mousseline Sauce. To make this sauce, follow the directions in stages 3–5 above but use only ¼ cup (½ stick) butter. Allow the sauce to cool, then add several spoons of whipped cream and a little grated nutmeg.

Rødgrød med Fløde
(Danish Red Fruit Fool)

1 Put 1 lb raspberries and 1 lb redcurrants, or the same quantity of other seasonal fruit, into a saucepan with just enough water to cover. Simmer gently until the fruit is soft, then rub through a sieve to give a smooth purée.

2 Allow a 1 tbsp cornstarch or arrowroot to each 1¼ cup purée; blend this with a little cold water, add to the fruit, return to the saucepan, and stir over a low heat until thickened and clear; add sugar to taste.

To serve: Cool slightly, then pour into a shallow serving dish, top with chopped almonds. Chill thoroughly and serve with cream.

To freeze: It is better to freeze the purée before adding the cornstarch or arrowroot. Use within 6 months.

To vary:
Thicken with potato flour instead of cornstarch or arrowroot.

Menu 3
Serves 4

Clam Chowder

Filet Cordon Bleu

Linzertorte

Cheeses:
Camembert
Roquefort
Wensleydale

Filet Cordon Bleu is a most delicious way of serving steak; as it is a fairly rich dish and it follows a sustaining fish chowder, complement the main course by cooking simple vegetables, such as broccoli, okra, zucchini or Brussels sprouts, with tiny new potatoes or young carrots. The recipe for cooking the steak is on page 61.

The quantities given in the recipe for Linzertorte provide generous portions, but if any of this dessert is left, it will freeze very well.

Suggested Cheeses
I felt that cheese should 'round off' this particular menu. Many people feel that nothing can surpass a rich creamy mature Camembert, well known in every country. Personally, I would choose a Roquefort after these fairly rich dishes.

Originally, Wensleydale was a veined blue cheese somewhat similar in flavour to Roquefort; nowadays, the blue variety is difficult to obtain, the white Wensleydale being readily available. This still retains the creamy texture and relatively mild flavour of the original cheese.

With the soup, try any Australian Riesling that has flavour.

With this beef dish, find a lighter or younger red, or an estate-bottled Valpolicella.

With the spiced and chocolate Linzertorte, it is difficult to recommend a wine, but whatever you try, do not select a really good white or anything too delicate or fragrant; it would almost be better to wait for the port wine with the cheese.

Clam Chowder

1 Prepare a fish stock by simmering the bones and skin of white fish with water to cover; add a little salt, pepper, and lemon juice to flavour. After 15–20 minutes' cooking, strain and retain $2\frac{1}{2}$ cups of the stock.

2 Cut 3–4 strips of fairly fat bacon into matchstick pieces; peel and finely chop a medium onion and a medium potato (keep the potato in water so that it does not discolour, dry well before adding to the pan).

3 Place the bacon in a saucepan and heat gently until the fat begins to run; add the onion and potato, continue frying for 2 minutes, then stir in 2 tbsp flour and cook for 1–2 minutes, stirring all the time, so that the flour and vegetables do not discolour.

4 Blend in the fish stock, prepared at stage 1, together with $7/8$ cup milk or light cream. Bring to the boil, stir until slightly thickened, simmer for 10 minutes, then add about a cup prepared or canned clams.

5 Add any extra salt and pepper required.

To serve: Serve with crisp croûtons of toasted or fried bread.

To freeze: This soup is better freshly made.

Linzertorte

1 Cream $\frac{3}{4}$ cup ($1\frac{1}{2}$ stick) butter or margarine with $\frac{1}{4}$ cup sugar and the finely grated peel of 1 lemon, then beat in 1 egg.

2 Blend together $\frac{1}{4}$ cup ground almonds, $7/8$ cup (14 tbsp) all-purpose flour, 2 tbsp chocolate powder, $\frac{1}{2}$–1 teaspoon ground cinnamon.

3 Stir these dry ingredients into the butter mixture and mix well.

4 Turn the soft dough onto a lightly floured pastry board and knead until smooth.

5 Place a 8-inch fluted flan ring on an upturned baking tray and brush with a very little oil or melted butter.

6 Take two-thirds of the dough and press into the prepared flan ring; chill for 30 minutes.

7 Roll out the remaining pastry and cut into narrow strips about $\frac{1}{4}$ inch in width and just over 8 inches in length.

8 Spread a thick layer of raspberry jam or *well-drained* sweetened cooked, frozen, or canned raspberries over the base of the torte; arrange the strips on top in a lattice design.

9 Bake for approximately 35 minutes in the centre of a moderate oven, 350°F; meanwhile, melt 3 tbsp redcurrant jelly; brush over the fruit and allow the torte to cool.
torte to cool.

10 Dust with a thick layer of sieved powdered sugar.

To serve: With cream or ice cream.

To freeze: This freezes well for up to 3 months; serve immediately it has defrosted.

To vary:
Omit the chocolate powder and use 1 cup flour.

Menu 4
Serves 10–12

Gazpacho

Bœuf Fondue Bourguignonne

Cheeses:
Danbo
Gorgonzola
Lancashire

Vareniki

This menu is planned to give a new kind of buffet party, for the guests can cook the beef themselves for the Bœuf Fondue Bourguignonne, the recipe for which is on page 68, and the Vareniki. This means having table heaters available, unless you can plan a less formal meal in the kitchen.

All the preliminary preparations can be made ahead, for the Gazpacho is a cold soup, which looks most inviting with its colourful garnishes.

The sauces to serve with the fondue can be pre-cooked and served cold or reheated; the recipes for these are on page 69. Quantities of beef and sauces will need to be increased to serve up to 12 people.

Suggested Cheeses
The sauces served with the Bœuf Fondue Bourguignonne will dictate your particular choice of cheese, but as most of these sauces have very definite flavours, I would choose either the blue-veined Gorgonzola or the highly flavoured crumbly Lancashire cheese.

If these are too strong, then select the milder Danish Danbo cheese. I would prefer the kind to which caraway seeds have been added.

Suggested Wines
Gazpacho and a chilled fino sherry, or a Manzanilla, are a classical combination.

An estate-bottled Panades or Rioja red could accompany both the Bœuf Fondue and the cheese. It is very interesting here to make the comparison between two areas, so try a wine from Rioja and finish with a Panades wine.

Gazpacho
(Cold Spanish Vegetable Soup)

1 Put a jug containing approximately a quart water into the refrigerator to become quite cold.

2 Skin or peel and finely chop 3 lb *ripe* tomatoes, 1 large cucumber, 2–3 large onions or the equivalent in scallions, 4 cloves garlic, and a large green and a large red sweet pepper (discard the cores and seeds).

3 Rub all these vegetables through a sieve or put through a blender until a smooth purée. The blender does not remove all the tomato pips, so sieving is better in this recipe.

4 Gradually add several spoons of olive oil (the amount depends upon personal taste), salt, pepper, and enough cold water to give a flowing consistency. Add lemon juice or white wine vinegar to flavour. Chill very well.

To serve: Pour the soup into a large tureen or bowl and arrange dishes of finely diced cucumber, onion, pepper, and coarse soft breadcrumbs around, so everyone can help themselves to the garnish.

To freeze: Some of the texture of the soup is lost in freezing, but you can freeze the tomato purée for up to 6 months and add the other ingredients when making the soup.

Vareniki
(Cherry Dumplings)

1 Pit about $1\frac{1}{2}$ lb black or Morello cherries, sprinkle with a little sugar; allow to stand for an hour, then drain away all the surplus liquid; use this as a sauce.

2 Blend 1 lb cream cheese with the yolk of an egg and 2 tbsp sugar.

3 Sieve together 3 cups all purpose plain flour and a pinch of salt, then blend with 4 eggs and enough milk to give a rolling consistency.

4 Knead the pastry dough until perfectly smooth, roll out until almost paper-thin, and cut into 2-inch rounds; put a little of the cream cheese in the centre of each piece of pastry, top with 1 or 2 cherries.

5 Moisten the edges of each pastry round with water and gather these together to cover the filling; roll gently and make a small ball.

6 When ready to cook, drop a few at a time into steadily boiling water and cook for a few minutes until they rise to the top of the water.

To serve: Top with the cherry juice, sour or fresh cream, and a little sugar; eat while hot.

To freeze: These are better freshly cooked.

Menu 5
Serves 4

Vichyssoise

Tournedos Béarnaise
with green salad

Cheeses:
Bleu de Bresse
Roquefort
Tomme de Marc de Raisin

Crème Renversée
with Milles Feuilles

No cold soup is more delicious than a well-made Vichyssoise, and this would be an ideal choice before the richness of the steak with Béarnaise sauce. Serve baby carrots and peas round the meat to provide an interesting colour contrast as well as a good flavour. The recipe for the main dish is on page 64.

Although Crème Renversée is such a well-known dessert, it is always popular.

This would be a practical menu for busy people, as both the hors d'œuvre and dessert can be prepared ahead.

Suggested Cheeses
Although each course has its own individual flavour, there is a gentle creaminess about all of the flavours. This can be emphasized by selecting the Tomme de Marc cheese with its coating of crushed grapes.

However, if you would prefer a more robust cheese course, select the classic blue-veined Roquefort or the fresh-flavoured Bleu de Bresse.

Suggested Wines
Choose a light Tokay d'Alsace to start the meal; it is not too rich or too full-bodied.

With the Tournedos Béarnaise, select your favourite from the Côte-du-Nuits in Burgundy, a Saint-Emilion in Bordeaux, or a big Beaujolais like Moulin-à-Vent. (Do not go for a really majestic or old wine because of this sauce).

And to finish, stay in France with a Sauternes or sweet white wine which you have found that you enjoy, or a semi-sweet Champagne.

Vichyssoise
(Iced Potato and Leek Soup)

1 Cut the tops from 6 medium leeks, leaving only a little of the green leaves, and chop; peel and dice 2 small to medium old potatoes.

2 Heat ¼ cup (½ stick) butter in a saucepan, turn the vegetables in this but do not allow to colour; add 3¾ cups well-clarified chicken stock, 1 tbsp chopped parsley, and 1 tbsp chopped chives, together with salt and pepper to taste.

3 Simmer for 25 minutes or until the leeks are tender; do not overcook, as this spoils the colour of the soup.

4 Rub through a fine sieve or liquidize until a smooth purée, then allow this to cool.

5 Add scant ⅔ cup heavy whipping cream and any more salt and pepper required.

To serve: Chill thoroughly and top with chopped chives.

To freeze: Although this mixture can be frozen, it tends to separate during storage and needs sieving or liquidizing again. Use within 2 months.

To vary:
(i) Use only half the stock at stage 2 and add dry white wine at stage 5 to give the desired consistency.
(ii) A peeled chopped onion can be added to the leeks at stage 2.

Crème Renversée
(Caramel Custard)

1 Put 6 tbsp sugar into a small heavy saucepan with 3 tbsp water, stir over a low heat until the sugar has dissolved, then allow to boil steadily, without stirring, until a golden-brown caramel; do not allow the caramel to become too dark, as it continues cooking with the heat of the pan.

2 Add another spoonful of water to give a slightly less thick caramel, pour this into one large or 4 smaller cooking containers immediately, but cool slightly before adding to ovenproof china or glass containers.

3 Allow the caramel to become quite cold before topping with the custard.

4 Whisk 2 whole eggs and the yolks of 3 eggs with 2 tbsp sugar, add a few drops of vanilla essence or 1–2 tbsp brandy, and 2½ cups warm milk.

5 Strain into the container(s) and stand in a 'bain-marie' (pan of cold water); bake for approximately 2–2½ hours, if using a large mould, or 1¼–1½ hours with smaller moulds, in the coolest part of a slow oven, 275°F, Gas Mark 1. Test and remove as soon as firm, as cooking for too long a period, as well as at too great a heat, causes the custard to curdle.

To serve: Allow to become nearly, but not quite, cold, then invert on the serving dish or dishes.

To freeze: Do not freeze.

Milles Feuilles
(Pastry Gâteau)

1 Make puff pastry according to the recipe on page 134, but as the pastry slices are just an accompaniment to the dessert, you need only ½ cup flour and the same amount of butter. If buying ready-prepared frozen puff pastry, purchase ½ lb.

2 Roll out the pastry until wafer-thin and cut into narrow fingers; make these all the same size. Put onto an ungreased baking tray and chill for at least 1 hour, then bake just above the centre of a very hot oven, 450°F, for about 8 minutes or until the pastry is well risen.

3 Lower the heat to moderate, 350°F, and cook for a further 5–6 minutes, or until golden-coloured and crisp; allow to cool. Trim the edges if the slices have not remained exactly the same size during baking.

4 Whip a small quantity of heavy whipping cream; add a little sugar and vanilla essence, then sandwich the pastry slices together in pairs.

To serve: Top with a liberal coating of sieved icing sugar and arrange on a dish. The crisp pastry makes a pleasing contrast and accompaniment to the softness of the custard dessert but must not be put onto the same serving dish, otherwise it will lose its firm texture.

To freeze: It is better not to freeze the completed Milles Feuilles, for the cream softens the pastry as this defrosts; see the comments on freezing under the recipe for puff pastry, given on page 134.

Menu 6

Serves 4

Terrine au Poivre Vert

Roast Beef with Yorkshire Pudding

Cheeses:
Camembert
Chevret
Port-Salut

Lemon Syllabub

Two classic British dishes, the main course and dessert, combine with a French terrine. The colour and flavour imparted by green pepper give an added interest to this dish.

Full information on roasting beef is found on pages 35 and 36, and information on the combination of beef and Yorkshire Pudding on page 91.

Roast potatoes are one of the accepted vegetables to serve with this dish, see page 86, and you could select other vegetables in season.

Suggested Cheeses
The Lemon Syllabub with its high wine and lemon content seems to me to be a perfect ending to a meal, so I feel that in this menu the cheese certainly should precede the dessert. One might imagine that a typical British dish should be followed by cheeses from that country. That would be a pity, for the choice of the more varied flavours of creamy yet full-flavoured Camembert, soft Chevret made from goats' milk, and the firmer yet milder Port-Salut is more suitable.

Suggested Wines
This menu gives you an admirable opportunity to choose some really good claret, starting with a lesser-known growth and moving on with the Roast Beef to the very finest that you can obtain, and, if not one of the top growths, like Lafite, from a classified growth that you particularly like. My choice would be Ch. Palmer 62.

Whilst I might enjoy the Syllabub on its own, it would be a pleasant finish to the meal to drink the wine used in the dish or to enjoy English wine such as Chilford Hundred or, perhaps, Lamberhurst Priory.

Terrine au Poivre Vert
(Pâté of Pheasant and Green Peppers)

The word 'terrine' really refers to the type of dish in which the food is cooked, the traditional lidded dishes being made of china or earthenware. The term 'terrine' is also used to describe the type of pâté in which one finds solid pieces of food; sometimes, the savoury mixture is baked in a pastry casing, but this is too substantial for an hors d'œuvre.

Poultry, meat, or game can be used to make a terrine. The recipe below is made from pheasant. It would provide adequate servings for 6–8 people as an hors d'œuvre, but any left freezes well.

1 Cut all the flesh from a young pheasant, keep the breast meat on one side.

2 Put the flesh from the legs and back through a fine grinder, together with $\frac{1}{2}$ lb fat bacon, the pheasant liver, and $\frac{1}{4}$ lb calves' liver.

3 Flavour with salt, pepper, a pinch of allspice, and a good pinch of finely chopped or dried thyme.

4 Put 1 large or 2 medium sweet green peppers into a fairly hot oven for a few minutes, until the skin breaks; pull this away from the flesh.

5 Dice the flesh neatly, discard the core and seeds, blend with the minced pheasant mixture, and moisten with an egg and a small wineglass of brandy.

6 Line the dish in which the terrine is to be cooked with fat strips of bacon.

7 Put about a third of the minced mixture into the bottom of the dish, over the bacon.

8 Cut the breast meat into neat slices, add half to the dish, then half the remaining minced mixture, the rest of the breast meat, and finally the rest of the minced pheasant mixture.

9 Cover with more bacon; put on the lid or cover the dish with foil.

10 Stand the terrine in a pan half filled with cold water, cook in a slow oven, 300°F, for 2 hours. Fill up the pan with cold water from time to time, to prevent the terrine mixture from becoming dry on the sides.

11 Remove the lid, place a plate with a light weight on top, allow to cool, remove any surplus fat.

To serve: With hot toast and butter, garnished with lemon.

To freeze: This freezes well for a period of 1 month.

Lemon Syllabub
The old traditional recipes for syllabub suggested taking the bowl to the cow, milking the fresh milk into this, and then blending it with wine. The following, however, is a more practicable recipe and gives a very soft-textured syllabub.

1 Blend 4 tbsp sugar with the finely grated outer peel of 1 lemon.

2 Blend with 1 tbsp lemon juice until the sugar is dissolved.

3 Whip scant 2 cups heavy whipping cream until it just holds its shape; fold into the sugar mixture.

4 Gradually beat in 4 tbsp brandy, 2 tbsp sweet sherry, and another 1 tbsp lemon juice.

5 Chill well.

To serve: In tall glasses; decorate with crystallized violet or rose petals or leaves of angelica.

To freeze: Do not freeze.

Menu 7

Serves 8–10

Smoked Salmon Pâté

Glazed Brisket of Beef
with Cumberland Sauce
and salads

Pêche Melba

Cheeses:
Munster
Pont l'Evèque
Stilton

This menu would be equally suitable for an informal buffet indoors or in the garden. The pâté is a practical way of extending expensive smoked salmon.

Cumberland Sauce, with its combination of flavours, is an old traditional recipe and is ideal with salted beef, for which you will find the recipe on page 53.

If a Pêche Melba sounds rather uninspiring, it may well be because you have not tried the classic methods of making the delicious sauce or a home-made ice cream; both these recipes are given.

Suggested Cheeses
The dessert, in spite of the high fruit content, is very sweet, and it is probably wiser to end this meal with cheese. Munster has a distinct 'tangy' flavour, Pont l'Evèque a flavour and texture like a very good Camembert (it looks different as it is a square cheese). The British Stilton is one of the great veined cheeses and, as its flavour is more mellow than most other veined blue cheeses, it would not be too great a contrast to the dessert.

Suggested Wines
With the pâté, try estate bottled Alsace Gewürztraminer, such as Hugel; the flavour and bouquet will be a match. A Beaujolais Nouveau of a good year (chilled if you so choose), or an Italian Veronese red, like Valpolicella, will be very enjoyable with the beef.

Something sweet, such as a Barsac, if you enjoy wine with the Melba. Serve a Madeira with the cheese; Verdelho, which has a pleasantly 'nutty' flavour, or Bual, a sweeter wine.

Smoked Salmon Pâté

1 Put 1 lb smoked salmon through a fine grinder.

2 Peel and crush 1–2 cloves of garlic; squeeze out enough lemon juice to give 4 tbsp.

3 Blend the salmon with the garlic, ⅔ cup light cream, a good shake of pepper, and the lemon juice. Taste the pâté as you add the last of the lemon juice to check the flavour; it should have a delicately sharp taste.

4 Stir briskly so that the mixture stiffens, the light cream thickens slightly; heavy whipping cream is inclined to make the pâté over-rich and solid.

5 Spoon the mixture into one large or 8–10 individual dishes, cover with a little melted butter; chill.

To serve: Turn out onto lettuce, garnish with lemon, and serve with hot toast and butter.

To freeze: This freezes well for a month.

To vary:
(i) Blend all the ingredients in a blender.
(ii) Save a little smoked salmon, chop this finely, then add to the soft pâté; this gives an interesting change of texture.
(iii) Use smoked cod's roe, smoked trout, or smoked mackerel instead of smoked salmon.

Pêche Melba

1 Prepare the ice cream and Melba Sauce as the recipes that follow.

2 Skin, halve and pit 8–10 fresh peaches.

To serve: Arrange portions of ice cream in 8–10 sundae glasses, top with the halvthe halved peaches, Melba sauce, and a little whipped cream.

To freeze: The completed dessert does not freeze, but see under Ice Cream and Melba Sauce.

Ice Cream

1 Separate the whites from the

---

yolks of 5 eggs; whip the egg yolks with ½ teaspoon vanilla essence and ⅔ cup sieved powdered sugar until light and fluffy.

2 Whisk 2½ cup heavy whipping cream until it holds its shape, then gradually whip in 1¼ cup light single cream.

3 Blend the cream and egg yolk mixture together.

4 Whisk the 5 egg whites until very stiff, blend with the cream and egg yolk mixture.

To freeze: In the freezing compartment of a refrigerator or a freezer. Use within 6 days if stored in the freezing compartment of a refrigerator or 6 weeks in a freezer.

Melba Sauce

1 Put 1 lb raspberries into a saucepan with 2 tbsp brandy and ¾–1 cup redcurrant jelly; stir over a low heat until the jelly has melted.

2 Blend 3 *level* teaspoons arrowroot or cornstarch with ½ cup water, pour into the raspberry mixture, and stir over a low heat until the mixture is clear; add sugar as desired.

3 Sieve to make a smooth sauce and allow to cool.

To freeze: This sauce freezes well for up to 4 months.

Menu 8
Serves 6–8

Œufs en Cocotte Bénédictine

Carpet Bag Steak

Pavlova

Cheeses:
Cheshire
Limburger
Tilsiter

Although this menu serves up to 8 people, it can be adjusted by reducing the quantity of the steak and stuffing as well as of the hors d'œuvre and dessert.

The filling for the Carpet Bag Steak can be prepared earlier and placed into the meat. Keep this well refrigerated as the shell fish deteriorate quickly. Serve a green salad and tiny new potatoes with the steak. If cooking the steak in the oven (details of this method are given on page 82), the potatoes could be baked or roasted in their skins.

Do not fill the Pavlova until just before the meal.

Suggested Cheeses
Unless you are very fond of sweet flavours, you will prefer to end this meal with cheese.

Cheshire, while not known worldwide, as is Cheddar, is a fascinating cheese. It is believed to be one of the oldest of all British cheeses, and it can be obtained as a white, orange-red, or blue-veined cheese which rivals Stilton in taste. The white and orange-red Cheshire cheeses have a nutty and faintly salty taste.

Limburger is another full-flavoured cheese, but Tilsiter (or Tilsit) would appeal to those of you who prefer a milder taste.

Suggested Wines
A simple medium dry wine or a good Amontillado sherry to start the meal would be very enjoyable.

Let the wine find the oyster, so choose a Chablis or a Riesling, and preferably an Alsace wine.

Pavlova needs a sweet well-chilled white, and you might try a Hungarian Tokay, or a sweet sparkling wine could be fun.

Œufs en Cocotte Bénédictine
(Baked Eggs Bénédictine)

1 Butter 6–8 small ramekin or other individual oven-proof dishes.

2 Break an egg into each dish and top with a little salt, pepper, and 1 teaspoon melted butter.

3 Add a layer of finely chopped cooked mushrooms or truffles; peel a clove of garlic, crush this finely, and blend with ⅔ cup heavy whipping cream.

4 Spoon the garlic-flavoured cream over the eggs and bake for 8–10 minutes towards the top of a moder-

---

ately hot oven, 400°F, or until the eggs are just set.

To serve: With a teaspoon and fingers of crisp toast and butter.

To freeze: Do not freeze.

Pavlova
This famous dessert was named after the renowned ballet dancer, who enjoyed it greatly. The meringue case can be made well ahead and stored in an airtight tin. It gives 6–8 portions, depending upon the filling.

1 Whisk the whites of 4 eggs until they stand in peaks; do not over-beat until very dry and crumbly.

2 Use either 1 cup superfine sugar or equal quantities of superfine and sieved powdered sugar. Blend ½ teaspoon cornstarch with the sugar(s).

3 Gradually whisk half the sugar mixture into the egg whites, then fold in the remainder, together with ¼–½ teaspoon vanilla essence or to your personal taste, and ½ teaspoon white or brown malt vinegar. The cornstarch helps to give a firm crisp outside to the meringue and the vinegar produces a slightly soft centre.

4 Prepare the baking pan by oiling lightly or by using a lining of oiled grease-proof paper or the special silicone paper that does not need oiling.

5 Spread or pipe part of the meringue mixture onto the prepared pan to give a round or square shape. Use the remainder of the meringue mixture to produce the sides of the Pavlova; it should be shaped like a flan.

6 The way in which the Pavlova is baked depends on a) how soft you like the centre and b) whether you intend storing it for any length of time.

7 To give a Pavlova that will be served the day it is baked, with a soft, almost marshmallow-like centre, place it in a moderately hot oven, 400°F, then *immediately* reduce the heat to the lowest setting, as below, and dry out for 1½–2 hours. If storing a Pavlova, it is better to use the

lowest setting from the beginning of the cooking period; this varies but can be from 150°F. Cook for 2–3 hours until firm. Cool, remove from the tin.

8 One of the most delicious fillings is made by blending the pulp of grenadillas (passion fruit) with an equal amount of whipped cream and a little sugar, but the meringue case can be filled with any kind of fruit or fruit purée and cream or ice cream. Decorate with whipped cream.

To freeze: See under the Vacherin, page 157.

Menu 9
Serves 6–8

Salmon Walewska

Bœuf à la Mode

Gâteau de Marrons

Cheeses:
Cheddar
Limburger
Stilton

The Bœuf à la Mode is a dish that can be allowed to cook gently so that you can devote your attention to the very special hors dœuvre.

Since the beef has a selection of vegetables added, as you will see from the recipe on page 41, the only accompaniments needed are potatoes or noodles and a green salad.

Prepare the gâteau some time ahead so that the moist filling penetrates through the sponge.

Suggested Cheeses
Buy a really mature Cheddar, for cheeses with a pronounced flavour would be an ideal choice at this stage of the meal. The Cheddar would be in good company with pungent Limburger and the incomparable taste of a ripe Stilton.

Suggested Wines:
I would start the meal with a Sauvignon Blanc or a Pouilly-Fumé, for the flavour blends well with the luxurious salmon in lobster sauce.

There is an almost limitless choice of red wines to serve with the classic Bœuf à la Mode, but a Cabernet, Châteuneuf-du-Pape, Margaux, or Italian Montepulciano would be equally good with the cheese.

If you are serving wine with the gâteau, a pleasant choice would be a Madeira, such as Bual or the less sweet Sercial.

Salmon Walewska

1 Take the flesh from the body and claws of a small to medium lobster, dice this neatly and put in a cool place; simmer the shell with a little water to give 3 tbsp very concentrated lobster stock; strain this carefully. Save the small lobster claws for garnish. You may use defrosted frozen lobster.

2 Make Hollandaise Sauce, see page 151, but add the lobster stock, made as stage 1, before incorporating the butter and continue whisking until the sauce thickens again.

3 Meanwhile, poach or grill 6–8 small salmon steaks (frozen, if no fresh is available).

4 Add the lobster meat to the sauce and heat gently for a few minutes.

To serve: Arrange the salmon on a serving dish. Top each portion with the sauce and garnish with the small lobster claws, wedges of lemon, and parsley.

To freeze: Do not freeze.

To vary:
(i) Use white fish in place of salmon.
(ii) Use canned lobster meat and the liquid from the can in place of fresh lobster and the lobster stock.

Gâteau de Marrons
(Chestnut Gâteau)

1 Make or buy a plain sponge cake measuring 7–8 inches in diameter and cut into three layers.

2 Blend 1 cup (8 oz) canned unsweetened chestnut purée with 2 tbsp Kirsch and ¼ cup sieved powdered sugar.

3 Place the first round of sponge

on the serving dish, moisten with Kirsch, and spread with half the chestnut mixture.

4 Cover with the second round of sponge, moisten this with Kirsch, and spread with the remaining chestnut mixture; top with the third round of sponge and moisten this with Kirsch.

5 Leave for several hours, then cover the top and sides of the cake with whipped cream, to which should be added a little sugar and Kirsch.

6 Decorate with marrons glacé or grated chocolate.

To freeze: This cake freezes well for up to 2 months; wrap *after* freezing.

Menu 10
Serves 4–6

Crab and Salmon Soup

Carbonades de Bœuf

Cheeses:
Brie
Boursin
Camembert

Mango Vacherin

The combination of fresh crab and salmon in the soup is both interesting and unusual, and as this dish has a light texture, it is not too sustaining a course before the beef.

Pickled red cabbage gives an interesting flavour to the Carbonades, the recipe for which is on page 108, and green beans and boiled potatoes would be the ideal vegetables to serve with this.

Do not fill the Vacherin until just before the meal, otherwise the crisp texture of the meringue is lost.

Suggested Cheeses
The cheeses in this menu are all somewhat familiar but would, I feel, be a good choice after the very sustaining main course. Creamy Brie and Camembert are often considered so similar that you select one *or* the other; that is not really the

case. Try some of each at the same meal and enjoy the subtle differences; remember Brie can vary from a mild creamy cheese to one that is very strong in taste. Boursin enables you to introduce a 'fine' cheese with a diversity of flavourings.

Suggested Wines
Try a white wine with character, such as Sicilian Corvo, to accompany the soup, although you may prefer to wait and have two reds on the table.

A good Italian Chianti Classico will match the Carbonades, or a full Californian or Australian wine will be enjoyable. I would serve a Californian Cabernet.

Any sweet German wine, but for preference a Mosel wine, could accompany the dessert.

Crab and Salmon Soup

1 Take all the white meat from the body and large claws of a medium-sized cooked crab and put on one side. Remove the dark meat and save this for the topping on the canapés or for another dish.

2 Remove any skin and bone from a salmon steak, weighing about ½ lb. Dice the uncooked fish.

3 Put the crab shell, small crab claws, and salmon skin and bone into a saucepan with 2½ cups water, 1 tbsp lemon juice, and a little salt and pepper; simmer for about 15 minutes or until the liquid is reduced to scant 2 cups; strain and return the fish stock to the saucepan.

4 Add the salmon and simmer for 10 minutes. Blend with the white crabmeat, then sieve or use a blender to give a smooth purée.

5 Reheat with 1¼ cup light cream.

To serve: Top with finely chopped fennel. Top narrow fingers of toast with the dark crabmeat and serve with the soup.

To freeze: The soup is better freshly made.

Mango Vacherin

A vacherin is a meringue case, similar to the Pavlova, but the classic French recipes omit both the cornstarch and the vinegar. Bake in the same way as for the Pavlova. A vacherin for 4–6 servings can be made with 3 egg whites and ¾ cup sugar.

1 To make the mango filling, skin 2 good-sized ripe mangoes and spoon the pulp away from the centre stone.

2 Mash the pulp with a little sugar and a squeeze of lemon juice; whip 1¼ cup heavy whipping cream and fold half into the mango pulp.

3 Spoon the pulp into the cold meringue case and decorate with the remaining whipped cream and finely chopped almonds or other nuts.

To serve: Soon after filling, so that the soft mixture does not spoil the crispness of the meringue.

To freeze: Meringues can be put in the freezer; they do not lose their crisp texture, but the very high percentage of sugar prevents their becoming frozen. As meringue cases keep well in an airtight container, it is a little pointless to freeze them, but if you freeze filled meringues of any kind, they must be eaten as soon as the filling is defrosted.

Menu 11

Serves 6

Barquettes de Poisson

Madras Tournedos with Lemon Pickle

Cheeses:
Cottage Cheese
Feta
Smoked Cheese

Soufflé au Grand Marnier

Do not fill the pastry cases with the fish mixture until just before serving, otherwise the crisp pastry will be softened.
To make Madras Tournedos, prepare Curry Sauce, see page 85; broil or fry the tournedos to personal taste, top with the hot sauce and serve in a border of cooked rice. In addition to the Lemon Pickle, see page 101, you can serve fried Poppadums. These can be obtained ready for frying in hot butter.
The Soufflé can be prepared before the meal and then placed in the oven when serving the hors d'œuvre, see note on page 159.

Suggested Cheeses
The definite flavour of curry, however mild, makes it important to refresh your palate before eating a dessert. All these cheeses are mild in flavour and not too substantial in texture, so they would be a good introduction to the liqueur-flavoured hot soufflé.

Suggested Wines
This is a good opportunity to begin with an excellent Champagne, or to try a top-rank white Burgundy such as a Chablis.
The main dish's flavour is not too hot, but even so, a really cold full-bodied white wine is the obvious choice. I would drink Italian Orvieto or maybe a Chenin Blanc or a young Lindeman White. Very cold medium white wines are always an acceptable combination with a curry.
The final course needs a sweet wine that is not too delicate. A German Rhine wine would be interesting.

Barquettes de Poisson
(Patties filled with Caviar and Smoked Trout Mousse)

1 Make a rich short crust pastry by sieving ¾ cup flour with a pinch salt, a shake cayenne pepper, and a pinch dry mustard powder; rub in a generous ½ cup (1 stick) butter and bind with an egg yolk and a little ice-cold water. If the pastry is rather soft, chill before handling again.

2 Roll out the pastry and line 12 medium or 18 very small boat-shaped tartlet pans and prick the bases; chill well before baking.

3 Stand the tartlet pans on a baking tray and bake for approximately 10 minutes just above the centre of a moderate to moderately hot oven, 375–400°F, then allow to cool.

4 Skin 2 small or 1 large smoked trout, remove the flesh and pound until very fine, blend with ⅔ cup light cream, 2 teaspoons horseradish cream, 1 tbsp lemon juice, and continue beating until quite light in texture.

5 Hard-boil 1 or 2 eggs, separate the white(s) from the yolk(s).

To serve: Fill the cold pastry cases with the trout mixture; spoon a little caviar at either end, garnish with a line of sieved egg yolk and a line of finely chopped white. Serve 2–3 per person and garnish with lettuce and lemon wedges.

To freeze: The pastry cases may be baked and frozen for up to 3 months. The trout mixture can be frozen for up to a month.

To vary:
Fold a stiffly whisked egg white into the trout mixture at the end of stage 4.

Soufflé au Grand Marnier

1 Brush the inside of an 7-inch diameter soufflé dish with a little melted butter; sprinkle with sugar.

2 Blend 4½ teaspoons cornstarch with ⅔ cup milk.

3 Pour into a saucepan; add 2 tbsp (¼ stick) butter and ¼ cup sugar.

4 Stir over a low heat until a very thick mixture.

5 Remove from the heat; gradually stir in 2 tbsp heavy whipping cream and the same amount of Grand Marnier.

6 Gradually beat in 4 egg yolks; whisk 6 egg whites and fold into the sauce.

7 Spoon into the soufflé dish, smooth flat on top, bake in the centre of a moderate oven, 375°F, for 30–35 minutes.

8 Sprinkle the top with sieved icing sugar and serve at once. Top each portion with a little more Grand Marnier.

To freeze: This cannot be frozen.

Zabaglione

1 Separate the yolks from the whites of 4 large eggs. The whites could be used for the Pavlova on page 155.

2 Put the yolks into a good-sized bowl or the top of a double saucepan. Add ¼ cup superfine sugar.

3 Stand the container over a pan of hot, but not boiling, water and whisk until light and fluffy in texture. Gradually whisk in 4 tbsp Marsala and continue beating until fluffy again.

4 While this dessert can be served by itself, it is particularly delicious over skinned and sliced fresh peaches or pineapple, or pitted black cherries which may be raw or poached in a little sugar and water flavoured with cherry brandy. This dessert gives 4 good portions if served without fruit, but 6 portions if spooned over fruit. It is always served warm.

To freeze: Better freshly prepared.

Menu 12

Serves 4

Lobster Thermidor

T-bone Steak Niçoise

Zabaglione

Cheeses:
Esrom
Gorgonzola
Sage Derby

Lobster Thermidor combines lobster meat with an interesting sauce and makes a good prelude to the main dish.
The Niçoise garnishes, given on page 65, to serve with tournedos, are all suitable for the less delicate T-bone steaks, but I would choose the second variation; serve tiny new potatoes and green beans with the meat.
After the fairly sustaining hors d'œuvre and main dish, the light fluffy texture of Zabaglione would be very suitable.

Suggested Cheeses

These cheeses enable you to change the flavour of the meal in various ways. Esrom is a full-cream relatively mild cheese, so would echo the creamy taste of Zabaglione, whereas the bite of the famous Gorgonzola blue-veined cheese would make a pleasing contrast. Sage Derby is a less well-known cheese; it has a similar flavour to Cheddar but is highly flavoured with sage.

If you serve fruit with the Zabaglione, you may prefer to end on its refreshing flavour and have the cheese before the dessert.

Suggested Wines

Lobster Thermidor would take me straight to Champagne, but for those less keen on sparkling wine, I suggest a Chardonnay or an excellent Graves like Laville-Haut-Brion.

The T-bone demands a big red; if you are having the Graves, great care must be taken in choosing a red which could follow it, so make it Ch. La Mission-Haut-Brion. If you made a different choice, then try a Hermitage or a classic Brunello di Montalcino.

I do not think that there is a real alternative to a golden Marsala from Italy with the Zabaglione.

Lobster Thermidor

1 Purchase 2 freshly cooked small to medium lobsters; split the bodies lengthways. Remove the intestinal vein and discard this; pull off the small claws (these can be kept for garnish), but discard the grey fingers which are at the end of the claws.

2 Remove the lobster meat from the body and large claws; dice this and put on one side.

3 Clean the shells, for the filling is generally served in the shells.

4 Heat ¼ cup (½ stick) butter in a pan, stir in ½ cup flour, and cook gently for several minutes; then gradually blend in scant ⅔ cup fish stock and 1¼ cup light cream. Bring to the boil and cook until thickened, then add a chopped shallot, a small sprig of fresh tarragon, a small bunch of chervil, salt and pepper to taste, up to 1 tbsp French or English

mustard and scant ⅔ cup dry white wine.

5 Simmer the sauce, *without boiling*, for 10 minutes, then strain and blend with the lobster meat, reheat gently, spoon into the shells, top with a little grated Parmesan cheese and brown under the broiler.

To serve: Garnish with lemon wedges, lettuce, and the small lobster claws.

To freeze: Do not freeze the cooked dish.

Menu 13
Serves 4–6

Moules à la Provençale

Bœuf à la Bourguignonne

Lemon Sorbet

Soufflé au Fromage

This menu is an admirable choice for a special occasion, because all the dishes can be pre-prepared, and then heated when desired. The note on allowing uncooked soufflés to stand for a limited period, page 159, may be helpful, since there is a belief that soufflés must be cooked immediately after combining the ingredients.

Serve the Bœuf à la Bourguignonne, see page 96, with boiled potatoes or Pommes Duchesse, page 107, or Jerusalem artichokes and a green vegetable such as French beans or broccoli.

Suggested Wines

Mussels call for one of those crisp clean wines for which the Loire is famous, and a Muscadet or Sancerre would lead on to a big Burgundy from the Côte-de-Nuits or, for preference, a fine Côtes-du-Rhône with the beef.

And to finish on a really fine note, you should take a dry Champagne or a fine white Burgundy such as Puligny-Montrachet, with the soufflé.

Moules à la Provençale
(*Mussels Provence Style*)

1 You will need 1½–2 quarts (about 5 dozen) fresh mussels. Scrub them well in cold water; discard any that will not close when sharply tapped, as this will indicate that the mussel is no longer alive.

2 Place the mussels into a large saucepan; this ensures the minimum depth and the shortest possible cooking time.

3 Add 1¼ cup of a dry white wine, or use half water and half wine, a small bunch of parsley, and a little salt and pepper.

4 Heat steadily only until the mussels open; do not continue cooking them.

5 Strain the liquid, to use in stage 6; in this particular recipe the mussels are removed from both shells. If any mussel shells have not opened, discard them.

6 Peel and chop 2 cloves of garlic and 2 medium onions, skin and slice 4–6 large tomatoes.

7 Heat 2 tbsp oil in a pan, add the vegetables; cook gently for 5 minutes, then add the wine and continue cooking for another 5–10 minutes or until the vegetables are soft; they should, however, retain a certain texture and not become a complete purée.

8 Add 1–2 tbsp tomato purée, a little salt and pepper to taste, 1 tbsp chopped parsley, and the mussels.

To serve: Heat thoroughly, but do not continue cooking; spoon into individual dishes and top with more chopped parsley. The mussels are eaten most easily with a spoon and fork.

To freeze: This dish can be frozen for 2–3 weeks.

Lemon Sorbet

Sorbet is a 'relic' from nineteenth-century banquets, when it was presented between two of the main courses to refresh the somewhat over-fed diners. In these modern times, when more modest menus are

the order of the day, sorbet has become a very popular dessert.

1 The sorbet mixture serves 6 portions, so save 6 good-sized lemons. You need to cut a slice from the top of each lemon and to scoop out all the pulp and seeds; strain, and keep the juice. Check that the inside of the lemon skin is quite free from pulp.

2 Measure out 6 tbsp juice for this dessert.

3 Pare the yellow peel from 1 large lemon; do not use any white pith.

4 Put 1¼ cup water and 6 tbsp sugar into a saucepan, stir until the sugar has dissolved, add the lemon peel, and simmer for 10 minutes.

5 Blend 1 teaspoon gelatine with 1 tbsp of the lemon juice, add to the syrup, and stir until dissolved.

6 Strain, and add the rest of the lemon juice. Pour into a freezing tray and freeze very lightly until the mixture is slightly stiffened.

7 Whisk 2 or 3 egg whites until stiff, fold into the lemon mixture. Taste and add a little more sugar if desired.

8 Spoon into the lemon skins, piling the mixture high, and freeze. If you have lemon or orange leaves, place them on the lemon mixture to decorate.

To freeze: This freezes well for 3 months.

To vary:
(i) Although a sorbet is not generally made with egg yolks, this particular recipe is especially good if the liquid is strained over 2–3 whisked egg yolks at stage 6.
(ii) Other fruit juices or purées could be used.

Soufflé au Fromage
(*Cheese Soufflé*)

1 Brush the inside of an 7-inch diameter soufflé dish with a little melted butter.

2 Heat 3 tbsp (scant ⅓ stick) butter in a saucepan; stir in 6 tbsp flour and cook for 2–3 minutes.

3 Gradually blend in very scant cup (7½ fl oz) milk and stir as the sauce comes to the boil; add salt, pepper, and a little prepared mustard to taste.

4 Blend in 2 tbsp heavy whipping cream.

5 Gradually beat in the yolks of 4 eggs and ¼ lb grated Gruyère cheese.

6 Whisk the whites of 4–6 eggs until stiff, fold into the cheese sauce.

7 Spoon into the soufflé dish, smooth flat on top, bake in the centre of a moderate oven, 375°F, for 30–35 minutes until just set. Serve at once.

To freeze: This cannot be frozen.

To vary:
A little grated Parmesan cheese can be added at stage 5 to give a stronger flavour.

To prepare soufflés ahead of cooking:

1 Follow the soufflé recipe to the end of stage 6. Spoon into the soufflé dish.

2 Place a large bowl over the soufflé dish. The mixture can stand for up to 1 hour before cooking, provided that all the air is excluded.

Menu 14
Serves 4

Coquilles de Crabes

Medallions de Bœuf du Barry

Lemon Chiffon Pie

Devils on Horseback

Canned or frozen crabmeat may be used when the fresh variety is not available. The dish may be prepared ahead of time and heated when required.

The Medallions, see page 75, are garnished with cauliflower, so a green salad and new potatoes are the only accompaniments to prepare.

Suggested Wines
With the starter choose an Alsace estate-bottled Riesling or a good dry white from your favourite country.

The Medallions lead me to a Cabernet Sauvignon and whether from California or a simple, but sound, Bordeaux from Côtes de Bourg, depends on the occasion. Try an Australian red as another alternative.

Coquilles de Crabes
(*Scalloped Crab*)

1 Remove all the meat from the body and claws of a cooked medium-sized crab.

2 Wash the shell and put this into a saucepan with water to cover, a sprig of dill or fennel, and a little salt and pepper.

3 Simmer until the liquid is reduced to ⅔ cup, strain this, and use for the sauce.

4 Wash and slice ½ cup mushrooms and fry in 2 tbsp (¼ stick) butter.

5 Heat 2 tbsp (¼ stick) butter in a saucepan, stir in ¼ cup flour, and cook for several minutes.

6 Add the crab stock with ⅔ cup light cream and bring to the boil, stir until a smooth sauce, then simmer gently for about 10 minutes.

7 Add the crabmeat and mushrooms, together with a little salt and pepper; spoon into 4 scallop shells or individual oven- or flame-proof dishes.

8 Top with a layer of soft breadcrumbs and a little melted butter.

To serve: Heat in the oven or under a hot broiler, when *flame*-proof dishes must be selected.

To freeze: These freeze well for up to 2 months.

Lemon Chiffon Pie

1 Make sweet short-crust pastry. Bake an 8-inch flan case 'blind', i.e., without a filling. Allow this to cool.

2 Meanwhile, prepare the filling. Soften 2 teaspoons gelatine in 3 tbsp water, then dissolve over hot water.

3 Separate the yolks from the whites of 2 large or 3 smaller eggs and whisk the yolks with 6 tbsp sugar until thick. Whisk the hot gelatine mixture into the egg yolks; add 1 teaspoon very finely grated lemon peel and 3 tbsp lemon juice.

4 Allow this mixture to become quite cold and to stiffen until the consistency of a syrup.

5 Whip ⅔ cup heavy whipping cream; add to the mixture.

6 Leave for a short time to become a little firmer.

7 Finally, whisk the egg whites until stiff and fold into the lemon cream.

8 Spoon the fluffy mixture into the flan case and leave until quite firm. Do not fill the pastry case too soon before the meal, as the filling will soften this.

To freeze: It is better to freeze the pastry case and filling separately. Defrost and combine just before serving.

Devils on Horseback

1 Cut off the rinds and halve 2 long strips of bacon; stretch the bacon as described on page 121.

2 Roll each piece of bacon round 2 cooked and pitted prunes.

3 Cook under a hot broiler until the bacon is crisp.

4 Meanwhile, toast and butter 4 small slices of bread.

To serve: Put the bacon and prunes on the hot toast, garnish with parsley and a shake of cayenne pepper or paprika.

To freeze: Not suitable for freezing.

To vary:
Fill the prunes with a little pâté.

Menu 15
Serves 4–6

Solyanka

Beef Stroganoff

Iced Cranberries

Cheeses:
Camembert
Carré de Saint-Cyr
Dolcelatte

As the Beef Stroganoff should be freshly cooked, I would suggest that everything else is prepared in advance, so that you can give your undivided attention to this delicious meat dish, the recipe for which is on page 84, together with suggested accompaniments.

Remove the container of cranberries from the freezer a short time before serving, so that they are not too iced and hard.

Suggested Cheeses
A creamy Camembert would be excellent after the iced fruit, but if you can obtain the lesser known Carré de Saint-Cyr, you will enjoy its gentle bite. Dolcelatte is one of my favourite veined cheeses: soft and creamy in texture, yet full of flavour.

Suggested Wines
The only problem with soups of any kind with wine is the combined liquid intake, and with Beef Stroganoff to follow maybe we ought to wait for the wine and enjoy a dry sherry with the soup.

A full wine, typical of a hot climate (Australian, Italian, South African, or Spanish), would be a good choice with the beef. Try a Cabernet from South Africa or a Spanish Rioja.

The iced cranberries are better without a wine, and the cheese can be served with a port.

Solyanka
(*Meat and Vegetable Soup*)

1 Prepare 3¾ cups good beef stock, see the recipe on page 37.

2 Peel 2 medium onions, 1 medium carrot, and chop these into small neat dice; wash and slice ⅛–¼ lb mushrooms.

3 Heat 2 tbsp oil in a saucepan, fry the vegetables for 5 minutes, add 1

159

tbsp tomato purée, the stock, and 1 bay leaf; bring the liquid to the boil, lower the heat, cover the pan, and simmer for 5 minutes only.

4 Dice approximately ¼ lb cooked meat; this can be ham, beef, sausages, or other meat. Slice enough pickled cucumbers or gherkins to give 2–3 tbsp; chop about 8 pitted olives and enough parsley to give 1 tbsp.

5 Add the meat, cucumbers or gherkins, olives, and parsley to the stock, together with 2 teaspoons capers, 1–2 teaspoons lemon juice or white wine vinegar, and salt and pepper to taste; the soup should have a distinctly sharp flavour.

To serve: Top each portion of soup with 1 or 2 spoonfuls of sour cream or yoghourt and a little chopped parsley.

Iced Cranberries

1 Make a syrup by heating 6 tbsp sugar with ⅔ cup water, add the juice of 2 large oranges and 1 small lemon, together with 1 lb cranberries.

2 Simmer gently until the cranberries are just soft; lift out about one-third with a perforated spoon and put on one side.

3 Liquidize the remaining fruit in a blender with the liquid or rub through a sieve, cool, and then pour into a freezing tray and freeze until only just beginning to stiffen.

4 Whisk 2 egg whites until stiff, fold in 2 tbsp sugar, then blend with the frozen mixture and the whole cranberries; return to the freezer until firm.

To serve: Spoon into glasses and top with whipped cream and fresh orange segments.

To freeze: The cranberry mixture can be kept for up to 3 months in the freezer.

Menu 16

Serves 4–6

Quiche aux Epinards

Filete Vascongado

Cheeses:
Bleu d'Auvergne
Limburger

Iced Fruit Pudding

This menu would be an ideal choice if you want to prepare part of the meal ahead, for the Quiche can be baked earlier and then reheated gently or served cold, and the dessert is a frozen one.

Beef is roasted with sausage, mushrooms, and onions, as pages 88–89 show. The ideal accompaniments would be Jerusalem artichokes and a green vegetable. The quantity in the recipe on pages 88–89 is a generous one for 4–6, so you could buy slightly less meat.

The Iced Pudding blends pineapple and Maraschino cherries in a creamy mixture.

Suggested Cheeses
As a small amount of cheese has been included in the quiche recipe, I have given just two outstanding cheeses in this menu.

Bleu d'Auvergne is highly esteemed in France for both its gentle flavour and inviting odour. It is a cheese that is believed to stimulate the appetite as well as to be easy to digest.

If your taste is for stronger cheeses, then the Limburger will please you.

Suggested Wines
You could always take an aperitif dry white wine and continue to drink it with the Quiche. In Europe the obvious choice would be from Alsace, and I would have a Muscat. With the mouth-watering fillet of beef try to find a full red of character with bottle age, such as a Hermitage Private Bin, a Rhône wine, a Chianti Classico, or a red from Panades.

The Iced Fruit Pudding calls for a well-chilled white wine; you could finish any of the white wine left over from the beginning of the meal.

Quiche aux Epinards
(Spinach Tart)
The following proportions will give a 9-inch flan, which is sufficient for generous portions as an hors d'œuvre.

1 Make short-crust pastry as per the method on page 134, but using 2 cups flour, pinch salt, generous ½ cup (1 stick) butter, and an egg yolk and cold water to bind.

2 Roll out and line a 9-inch fairly deep flan tin or dish, or a flan ring on an upturned baking tray.

3 Bake 'blind' (without a filling) for 15–20 minutes in the centre of a moderate to moderately hot oven, 375–400°F, until golden only and set.

4 Meanwhile, cook, strain, and sieve or finely chop enough fresh or frozen spinach to give 1 cup cooked purée.

5 Beat 3 egg yolks, add 1¼ cup light cream (or cream and milk), 2 tbsp finely grated Gruyère cheese, the spinach, a pinch of grated nutmeg, and salt and pepper to taste.

6 Spoon into the flan case, return to the oven, lowering the heat to very moderate, 325°F, for 40 minutes or until the filling is set.

To serve: Hot or cold. For a more interesting topping, add a lattice of narrow strips of smoked salmon.

To freeze: This freezes excellently; use within 3 months.

To vary:
(i) Use fried diced bacon plus ¼ lb grated cheese instead of spinach.
(ii) Use shelled prawns instead of spinach.

Iced Fruit Pudding
Although the creamy fruit mixture is served on rings of fresh pineapple, I have found canned pineapple combines better with the mixture to be frozen.

1 Put 4 tbsp milk into a saucepan with ¼ lb marshmallows.

2 Heat *gently* only until the marshmallows have melted and then cool.

---

3 Drain a small can of pineapple rings and dice the fruit.

4 Chop enough Maraschino cherries to give 4 tbsp.

5 Whip 2 cups heavy whipping cream until it holds its shape.

6 Add the marshmallow mixture, chopped pineapple and cherries, 1 tbsp Maraschino liqueur, and ¼ cup sieved powdered sugar.

To freeze: Keeps for up to 6 days in the freezing compartment of a refrigerator or for up to 6 weeks in a freezer.

To serve: Arrange thin rings of fresh pineapple in a serving dish and top with the iced fruit mixture.

Menu 17

Serves 6–8

Les Crudités

Tortilla

Estofado de Vaca à la Catalana

Cheeses:
Boursin
Livarot
Ricotta

Stuffed Apples and Kulfi Malai Wali

A colourful dish of crisp fresh vegetables would be a pleasing preface to the soft delicate texture of a perfect Spanish omelette and the well-flavoured main dish, in which the beef is stewed with sausage and vegetables. The recipe for this interesting method of cooking beef is on page 105. The ideal accompaniments would be rice and green beans. You will need to increase the quantities in the recipe by fifty per cent to serve 6–8 people.

The dessert combines a refreshing baked apple with a nut filling that blends perfectly with an Oriental version of ice cream.

Suggested Cheeses
Soft creamy Boursin provides great variety; you can have a crushed peppercorn coating on it, or it can be

herb-flavoured; either would be a good choice after the substantial main course.

If there is too much taste in these cheeses, then try the gentle, creamy, Italian Ricotto or the refreshing French Livarot.

Suggested Wines
The Tortilla does not demand a wine, but there is a wide choice for the Catalan stew. One of the pedigree Catalan wines would be ideal; start with a younger Coronas and move on to an older Gran Reserva wine.

Stuffed Apples do not really need a wine, but a Catalan Malvasia, or very sweet cold wine, such as a Sauternes, could be tried.

Les Crudités
(Raw Vegetables)
Arrange prepared radishes, florets of cauliflower, baby carrots, strips of cucumber and celery, spring onions, quartered firm tomatoes, and any other fresh seasonal vegetables on a platter with dishes of mayonnaise and French dressing.

Keep a length of stalk on the radishes and spring onions so that they are easy to handle.

Tortilla
(Spanish Omelette)
While a 'true' Spanish omelette is flavoured with onions and potatoes, there are endless varieties that can be created, and the following is an excellent hors d'œuvre or light first course. As this menu is for 6–8, it is better to make two omelettes rather than one.

1 Dice 2 sweet red peppers and discard the cores and seeds; peel and finely chop 2 small onions; chop enough parsley to give 2 tbsp.

2 Simmer the peppers and onions in 4 tbsp white stock for 10 minutes.

3 Beat 12 eggs with a little salt and pepper, add the peppers, onion, and parsley together with ½ lb shelled prawns, and several diced anchovy fillets.

4 Heat ¼ cup (½ stick) butter in each of two 9–10-inch omelette or frying pans:

5 Pour in the egg mixture and cook for several minutes until just set. This type of omelette is not folded but served flat.

6 Top each omelette with a little finely grated cheese and hot asparagus tips; cut into the desired number of portions.

To serve: As soon as cooked.

To freeze: This dish cannot be frozen.

Stuffed Apples

1 Separate the yolks and whites of 2 eggs.

2 Blend scant ½ cup sieved powdered sugar with ½ cup ground almonds, 1 tbsp brandy, and 2 egg yolks.

3 Core 6–8 medium-sized cooking apples and split the skin round the centre of each apple.

4 Put into a baking dish and bake for about 30 minutes in the coolest part of the oven set at 375°F.

5 Remove the apples from the oven and spoon the soft almond mixture into the holes in the apples.

6 Return to the oven for a further 20–25 minutes or until cooked.

7 Remove the skin from the top of the apples; it is rather difficult to remove the bottom skin without breaking the apples.

8 Whisk the 2 egg whites until stiff, fold in ¼ cup superfine sugar.

9 Spoon the meringue over the top of each apple; decorate with a few blanched and split almonds.

10 Heat for about 30 minutes in a very cool oven, 275°F.

To serve: Hot with cream or the ice cream on page 155.

To freeze: Do not freeze this dish.

Kulfi Malai Wali
(Oriental Ice Cream)

1 Make the ice cream recipe as given under Pêche Melba on page 155,

using the same proportions; begin to freeze the mixture.

2 While the mixture is freezing, skin and chop about ¼ lb (1 cup) mixed nuts (use almonds, pistachios, walnuts or pecans, and Brazils) and dice about ¼ lb (½ cup) glacé cherries, pineapple, and angelica, together with 4 tbsp preserved ginger.

3 When the ice cream is half frozen, stir in the nuts, fruits, and ginger and continue freezing.

To freeze: See the comments on page 155.

To serve: As a separate dessert or with Stuffed Apples.

To vary:
A lighter texture can be given to the ice cream if the light cream is omitted and *full cream* yoghourt is used instead.

Menu 18
Serves 6

Herb Baked Trout

New Zealand Savoury Roast

Caramelled Oranges

Cheeses:
Gouda
Neufchâtel
Saint-Paulin

The combination of herbs gives fresh trout a subtle flavour. The recipe suggests either a hot or a cold version of this simple hors d'œuvre.

As the traditional accompaniments for the Savoury Roast, the recipe for which is on page 90, include a vegetable and fruit, a salad or green vegetable such as Brussels sprouts would provide a good contrast of texture and flavour.

Do not prepare the dessert more than 12 hours ahead, as the oranges lose their flavour.

Suggested Cheeses
Although a relatively simple menu to prepare, each course has a highly individual flavour, and the cheeses must echo this.

After the combination of the sweet plus sharp orange dessert, I felt one would enjoy a cheese with a fairly mild taste, which you will find in Saint-Paulin, Dutch Gouda, or the slightly sour-tasting Neufchâtel.

Suggested Wines
Herb Baked Trout will need a white wine; an Australian Traminer, or Pinot Chardonnay would be excellent with the trout.

For the Savoury Roast Beef, select a good full wine; a Cabernet Sauvignon, an estate-bottled southern European vineyard like Panadés or Rioja in Spain, or a red Corvo from Sicily.

This dessert needs a sweet white, maybe a sparkling Asti Spumante, if not too much of a luxury.

Herb Baked Trout

1 Wash then split 6 small to medium fresh trout; carefully remove the backbones but leave the heads on the fish.

2 If serving the fish hot, melt then blend ¼ cup (½ stick) butter with the finely grated peel and juice of 1 medium lemon, ½ teaspoon of each of the following chopped herbs: parsley, fennel, dill, tarragon, and chives, together with a little salt and pepper.

If serving the fish cold, use olive oil in place of butter; this gives a more pleasing appearance to the cold fish.

3 Place the fish in a buttered or oiled oven-proof dish, top with the butter or oil mixture, and cover the dish with foil.

4 Bake for 25–30 minutes in the centre of a moderately hot oven, 400°F.

To serve: Top the hot fish with any butter mixture left in the dish and a purée of cooked fresh tomatoes. Top cold fish with sliced tomatoes and sliced cucumber.

To freeze: Frozen fresh trout could be used for this dish; if freezing the cooked dish, use within one month.

161

Caramelled Oranges

1 Choose 6 very large or 12 medium oranges, of the seedless variety if possible, and cut away the outer skin and pith but leave the oranges whole.

2 Take the peel of 2–3 oranges and cut the orange part only into very thin matchstick-shaped pieces. Soak this peel for about 30 minutes in 1¼ cup water, then simmer gently in the same water in a covered pan for 15–20 minutes. Save both the peel and the liquid.

3 Put 6 tbsp sugar into a heavy saucepan with 3 tbsp of the liquid used to soften the peel. Stir until the sugar has dissolved, then boil without stirring, until a pale golden caramel. The caramel should not darken too much for this particular recipe.

4 Add the peel and the remaining liquid to the caramel and simmer for a few minutes.

5 Cut the oranges into horizontal slices, then replace to form the complete orange shape again; secure with cocktail sticks and decorate the sticks with Maraschino or glacé cherries.

6 Arrange the oranges in a dish and spoon the peel and sauce over the fruit.

To serve: With cream or ice cream.

To freeze: Do not freeze.

Menu 19

Serves 6

Seafood Cocktail

Galantine de Bœuf
with salads

Cheeses:
Bleu de Bresse
Cheddar
Neufchâtel

Crêpes Suzette

This menu is ideal when you lack time for last-minute preparations, as so much is done beforehand.

The ingredients for the fish cocktails and the salads to serve with the Galantine de Bœuf can all be ready, so that they just need blending together. Naturally, the galantine, for which the recipe is on page 136, must be cooked and garnished beforehand. Have dishes of Potato, Russian, and green salads to serve with the galantine; recipes for salads are on pages 138–140.

The pancakes can be ready filled and the sauce made, so that all you need to do is heat the completed pancakes in the sauce.

Suggested Cheeses
Bleu de Bresse is a small blue-veined cheese which could be compared to Gorgonzola, except that its flavour is milder. Do not underestimate the good taste of a well-matured Cheddar, just because it is such a familiar cheese. The slight salt taste of white Neufchâtel would be a pleasing contrast to the fairly bland main course and the richness of the dessert.

Suggested Wines
Seafood Cocktail calls for a clean dry white wine such as abound along the Loire, or if from a warmer climate, one that has not aged in wood.

With the Galantine de Bœuf, a Cabernet from North America or indeed South America, or – provided it is dry, as usually found – a Zinfandel. With this summery dish, you have an enormous choice, maybe you would prefer a Beaujolais crus or a claret, both of which would be ideal with the cheese.

With Crêpes Suzette, nothing but a sweet sparkling wine, made by the champagne method. Drink a 'sec' Champagne rather than a 'brut'.

Seafood Cocktail
The whole secret of any fish cocktail is to prepare a superb sauce.

1 Make the mayonnaise on page 139 or use top-quality commercial mayonnaise, then give this your own individual touch.

2 Add a little fresh tomato purée, made by sieving ripe tomatoes, then give a sharper taste with lemon juice, sherry, or brandy; finally, incorporate a little cream and extra flavouring with 1 or 2 drops of Tabasco, Worcestershire, or soy sauce.

3 Shred lettuce finely, put into the glasses, then top with a selection of shell fish or shell fish mixed with diced cooked white fish and/or salmon, all blended with the cocktail sauce.

4 You can add extra interest with finely diced celery, sweet red or green peppers (discard the cores and seeds), or matchsticks of cucumber. If you enjoy an unusual blending of flavours, include a little diced avocado, or ripe dessert pear or apple. Garnish with lemon.

To serve: Well chilled, preferably on a bed of ice.

To freeze: Do not freeze.

Crêpes Suzette

1 Make a pancake batter by mixing 1 cup flour, a pinch salt, 2 eggs, and 1¼ cup milk.

2 Add 2 teaspoons melted butter or oil to the batter just before cooking the pancakes.

3 Heat a little oil in a pancake pan, spoon enough batter into the pan to give a paper-thin covering. Cook for 1–2 minutes on each side until firm. Keep the pancakes a very pale colour for this recipe. The mixture gives 8–12 small pancakes.

4 To make the filling: if you are using cube sugar, you require 16–20

lumps; rub these over the outside of 2 large oranges or 3–4 tangerines to absorb the oil and flavour from the skin, then crush and blend with the butter. If using superfine sugar, cream 6 tbsp with 6 tbsp (¾ stick) butter and the *finely* grated peel of the oranges or tangerines. Blend with 1–2 tbsp Curaçao or brandy.

5 Spread a little of this mixture over the pancakes and fold each pancake into quarters, so enclosing the filling.

6 Poach the pancakes in the sauce, made as follows.

7 Put 4–6 tbsp white sugar into a frying pan. Add 2 tbsp butter. Stir over a very low heat until the butter and sugar melt.

8 Allow this mixture to heat for a few minutes until pale golden caramel. Add ⅔ cup orange or tangerine juice, boil for several minutes until the mixture forms a fairly thick syrup.

9 Place the pancakes in the syrup and heat for 2–3 minutes, turning over once. Add 2–3 tbsp Curaçao or brandy, warm for a minute, then ignite and serve.

To freeze: The filled pancakes freeze well for up to 2 months.

To vary:
The pancakes could be filled with redcurrant jelly instead of the more traditional orange or tangerine mixture.

Serves 6

Lofoten Caviar

Entrecôtas con Acciughe e Olive

Cheeses:
Brie
Danish Blue
Port Salut

Cassata Sicilienne

As both the caviar and the accompaniments to the steak have a distinctly salt flavour, a mixed or green salad and/or green peas and zucchini would be suitable accompaniments to the beef. The recipe for this particular method of cooking entrecôte steak is on page 67, but you would need to increase the quantities of the meat and flavourings to serve 6 people.

The Cassata gives considerable scope in flavourings, as the recipe indicates; the quantity given in the recipe is generous for 6 people, but it is easier to form the layers of ice cream with this amount of the mixture; any left can be stored successfully in the freezer or freezing compartment of the refrigerator.

Suggested Cheeses
Both the hors d'œuvre and main course will have left a slightly salt taste in the mouth, so it is wise to have the cheese before the dessert. The three cheeses suggested give a good balance between the very strong flavours already enjoyed and the mild sweetness of the dessert.

Suggested Wines
The Lofoten Caviar is a good excuse for Champagne, and the best suggestion is to open the bottle as an aperitif and continue through the first course.

This meal centres around the entrecôte steak, when we can enjoy a full red: try an Italian Gattinara or Barbera, but for me the choice would be Barolo. Decanting would help, and it must have at least six or seven years' bottle age.

Lofoten Caviar

This relatively economical pâté is an excellent hors d'œuvre.

1 Put 1 lb fresh cod's roe into $\frac{2}{3}$ cup cold water; add a generous pinch of salt, a shake of pepper, and 1 teaspoon sugar.

2 Leave for 2 hours.

3 Boil steadily for 15–20 minutes until the roe turns white; strain away any surplus liquid.

4 Skin the roe, dice, then mash and gradually blend in 4 tbsp olive or salad oil, 2 tbsp lemon juice, and a little garlic salt.

5 Chill thoroughly.

6 Hard-boil 2 eggs.

7 Chop the yolks and whites separately.

8 Spoon the 'caviar' into small individual containers, top with finely chopped yolk and white, and garnish with wedges of lemon.

To serve: With hot toast and butter.

To freeze: This freezes well for up to 4 weeks.

To vary:
i Use rather less oil and blend the roe with several spoons of double cream.
ii Add a little finely chopped dill, parsley, or chives to the mixture.
iii Use hard herring's roe in place of cod's roe.

Cassata Sicilienne

1 Prepare the ice-cream mixture as the recipe under Pêche Melba on page 155, stages 1–3, but use only 4 egg whites and $3\frac{3}{4}$ cups heavy whipping cream and no light cream. Omit the vanilla essence at stage 1.

2 Divide the mixture into 3 portions and put each into a bowl.
First portion: Add 1 cup thick strawberry or raspberry or other fruit purée, blended with 2–4 tbsp extra sugar. Do not be too generous with the sugar as it hinders freezing.
Second portion: Add $\frac{1}{3}$–$\frac{1}{2}$ cup melted and cooled plain chocolate blended with 2 tbsp brandy, Curaçao, or Tia Maria, $\frac{1}{3}$ cup seedless raisins, and $\frac{1}{4}$ cup chopped blanched almonds; then fold in 2 stiffly whisked egg whites.
Third portion: Stir in $\frac{1}{4}$ cup chopped Maraschino cherries, 3 tbsp finely chopped candied orange peel, and 3 tbsp finely chopped angelica, together with 1 tbsp dry sherry or Curaçao. Finally, fold in 2 stiffly whisked egg whites.

3 Freeze each portion separately until it just begins to stiffen. Take the first portion and spread round the inside of a basin or mould and allow to freeze firmly, then spread the second portion over this and freeze again. Finally, fill the centre with the third portion and complete the freezing.

To serve: Dip a table napkin or cloth in hot water, wring out, then wrap around the outside of the basin or mould for a few seconds; invert the container over the serving dish. Decorate the cassata with whipped cream.

To freeze: See Pêche Melba on page 155.

To vary:
(i) Use other flavourings, liqueurs, or fruits in each portion.
(ii) Another way of freezing the cassata is to freeze the third portion in a small basin, then turn the ice cream out into the centre of the large mould, spread the second portion round this and freeze, then finally, add the third portion. The secret of success is to have each portion the consistency of a *thick* whipped cream.

Serves 4

Seafood Pancakes au Gratin

Tefteli

Black Forest Gâteau

Cheeses:
Caerphilly
Gorgonzola Bianca
Livarot

In this menu you have a mixture of the luxurious – in the hors d'œuvre and the dessert – and of the economic – in the main dish.

The meatballs given on page 113 provide just the right flavour after the creamy fish dish, especially if they are served with rice and a good mixture of seasonal vegetables.

There are many recipes for a Black Forest Gâteau; I have chosen the generally accepted one, in which the bite of cocoa gives a pleasing and very strong chocolate flavour. Some recipes suggest putting the chocolate gâteau on a shortbread base, and although the recipe for this is given under *To vary*, I feel it would provide too substantial an ending to this particular menu.

Suggested Cheeses
The white version of Gorgonzola is less readily available than the blue-green veined cheese, but it has a distinctively piquant and faintly bitter taste which is most enjoyable. Caerphilly, the crumbly Welsh cheese, is milder but never insipid. Livarot would be my choice after the very creamy dessert, for although the taste is relatively mild, it is an unusually refreshing cheese.

Suggested Wines
You might like to begin with schnapps or iced vodka, but I would use this hors d'œuvre as an excuse for a Russian dry sparkling wine, with its hint of apple. Another suggestion is Champagne or a sparkler from Spain.

Meatballs provide a good opportunity for the Russian red Mukuzani or Hungarian Bullsblood, but any of a variety of good reds, light or robust according to your preference, would be delicious.

The Black Forest Gâteau would be best just on its own.

It can be interesting to have an alternative red wine with cheese, so that you can compare the two wines drunk with the meal.

Seafood Pancakes au Gratin

Although the idea of pancakes as a first course is based on the Russian Blini, in which pancakes are generally made with buckwheat and yeast, I feel it is easier to produce a light pancake with ordinary flour.

1 Sieve together 1 cup flour and a pinch of salt.

2 Gradually beat in 2 eggs, then 1¼ cup milk or milk with a little water.

3 Gradually cook spoonfuls of the mixture in hot oil or fat to produce 8–12 small thin pancakes.

4 Make a sauce with 2 tbsp (¼ stick) butter, ¼ cup flour, ⅔ cup milk, and ⅔ cup light cream. Add salt and pepper to taste.

5 Blend flaked cooked lobster meat, prawns, diced cooked salmon, or other cooked fish with the sauce.

6 Fill the pancakes with this mixture, roll, and put into a flame-proof serving dish.

7 Make more sauce as stage 4, spoon over the pancakes, top with fine breadcrumbs, a little melted butter, and a sprinkling of finely grated cheese.

8 Heat in the oven or under the broiler until the pancakes are hot and the sauce on top is bubbling.

To serve: Hot, garnished with lemon.

To freeze: These freeze well for 2 months.

Black Forest Gâteau

1 Grease and flour two 9-inch diameter cake pans or line these with greased grease-proof paper.

2 Melt 6 tbsp (¾ stick) butter; allow it to cool.

3 Put 4 eggs and ⅝ cup superfine sugar into a large bowl.

4 Whisk until the mixture is sufficiently thick to show the trail of the whisk.

5 Sift together ¾ cup flour (see note under *To vary*) and 2 tbsp cocoa powder.

6 Fold into the egg mixture.

7 Finally, fold in the cool butter, melted at stage 2.

8 Divide the mixture between the pans and bake just above the centre of a moderate oven, 375°F, for about 12 minutes, or until firm to the touch.

9 Turn out carefully, remove the paper from the base of the cakes, if using this.

10 Put ¼ cup sugar with 2 tbsp water and the same amount of Kirsch into a saucepan; boil for 2–3 minutes until the sugar has melted.

11 Prick each chocolate sponge and moisten with the syrup.

12 Sandwich the gâteau with ripe black or red Kirsch-soaked cherries and whipped sweetened cream.

13 Top the gâteau with more whipped cream and cherries and curls of chocolate, made by shaving wafer-thin slices of chocolate from a block of chocolate with a very sharp small knife.

To serve: Well chilled.

To freeze: Freezes well for up to 3 months; do not wrap until frozen.

To vary:
(i) As so much air has been beaten into the eggs and sugar, baking powder is not really necessary in this recipe, but if preferred, sift 1 teaspoon baking powder with the flour at stage 5.
(ii) For a shortbread base, cream ¼ cup (½ stick) butter with 2 tbsp sugar, then gradually add ¾ cup flour, form into a 9-inch round, and place in an ungreased tin of this size. Bake in the centre of a moderate oven, see stage 8, for just 10 minutes. Cool, then spread with cherry jam and top with the gâteau.

Prosciutto e Melone
(Parma Ham and Melon)

Barbecued Steaks

Strawberry Shortcake

Cheeses:
Camembert
Cheddar
Romano

In order to make the Parma ham (prosciutto) and melon easier to serve in the open air, dice the melon flesh, or cut it into balls with a small scoop; form small rolls of the smoked ham and arrange round the fruit.

There are various suggestions for cooking the steaks over a barbecue in the chapter beginning on page 117. Serve jacket potatoes and various salads as an accompaniment.

The particular recipe for shortcake given here has a fairly firm texture, so that it is not too fragile to carry out of doors. It can be made to look more decorative by piping cream around the top edge of the shortcake.

Suggested Cheeses
Camembert is a good cheese to follow the semi-sweetness of the Barbecued Steak and the creamy dessert. Choose one that is really well matured. Most people are hungry when eating in the open air, and few cheeses are more satisfying than Cheddar. For the less hungry, a soft Romano would be pleasant to eat with, rather than after, the dessert.

Suggested Wines
Prosciutto is a nice opportunity for a good Italian medium white, such as Frascati or Verdicchio, but a Sylvaner would be very suitable.

Barbecued Steaks would go well with Zinfandel or Lambrusco, but a chilled young Beaujolais would be my choice. It is not usually recommended to chill red wines, but Lambrusco, Beaujolais Nouveau, or Vin de l'année, do benefit, particularly for summer drinking.

Choose a sweet light Muscat, maybe from the Californian vineyards, and chill well for the Strawberry Shortcake.

The Cheddar will be nice with port or a big strong red wine.

Strawberry Shortcake

1 Cream together ¾ cup (1½ stick) butter and 1 cup superfine sugar, gradually beat in 3 medium eggs.

2 Sieve 3 cups flour with only 2 level teaspoons baking powder, and gradually work this into the creamed butter mixture; do not add any liquid.

3 Grease and flour two 10-inch cake pans divide the mixture between these and press out flat with damp fingertips.

4 Bake for approximately 20 minutes near the centre of a moderate oven, 350°F, or until firm; cool for several minutes in the tins before turning out onto a wire cooling tray.

To serve: Sandwich the shortcakes together with whipped cream and sliced sweetened strawberries; serve soon after filling.

To freeze: The shortcakes freeze well for up to 3 months, but do not fill with fruit and cream until defrosted, otherwise the firm texture is spoiled.

To vary:
(i) For a more biscuit-like texture which produces a fragile shortcake, increase the butter to 1 cup (2 sticks) and use only 2 eggs. Bake this version at 325°F.
(ii) Top the shortcakes with whipped cream and whole fruit.

BIBLIOGRAPHY

The American Heritage Cookbook. New York, 1975.

Beard, James. *Delights and Prejudices.* New York, 1971.

Bessinger, Bernard N., ed. *Recipes of Old England*. Newton Abbot, 1973.

Fitzgibbon. Theodora. *A Taste of London*. London, 1973.

Gerrard, Frank, and Mallion, F.J. eds. *Complete Book of Meat*. Coulsdon, 1976.

Guérard, Michel. *Cuisine Minceur*. London, 1977.

Montagné, Prosper. *Larousse Gastronomique: The Encyclopedia of Food, Wine, & Cooking*. New York, 1961.

Pellaprat, Henri-Paul. *Great Book of the French Cuisine*. London, 1976.
———. *Modern French Culinary Art*. Coulsdon, 1972.

Soyer, Alexis. *The Pantrophon: A History of Food & Its Preparation in Ancient Times*. New York and London, 1977.

Tannahill, Reay. *Food in History*. New York, 1973.

White, Florence, ed. *Good Things in England*. London, 1932.

INDEX